Lexical Layers of Identity

Focusing on Slavic languages, Danko Šipka provides a systematic approach to lexical indicators of cultural identity. In contrast to existing research, which focuses heavily on syntactic and phonological approaches, Šipka's approach is novel, more systematic and encompassing, and postulates three lexical layers of cultural identity: deep, exchange, and surface. The deep layer pertains to culture-specific words, divisions, and features that are generally not subject to change and intervention. The exchange layer includes lexical markers of cultural influences resulting from lexical borrowing, which situates the speakers into various cultural circles. This layer is subject to gradual changes and some limited level of intervention from linguistic elites is possible. Finally, the surface layer encompasses the processes and consequences of lexical planning. It is subject to abrupt changes, and it is shaped in constant negotiation between linguistic elites and the general body of speakers.

DANKO ŠIPKA is Professor of Slavic Languages and Applied Linguistics at Arizona State University. His research interests include lexicography, lexicology, morphology, and computational linguistics. His publications encompass over 150 papers and reviews as well as thirty books including *Lexical Conflict* (Cambridge, 2015).

Lexical Layers of Identity

Words, Meaning, and Culture in the Slavic Languages

Danko Šipka

CAMBRIDGE
UNIVERSITY PRESS

CAMBRIDGE
UNIVERSITY PRESS

University Printing House, Cambridge CB2 8BS, United Kingdom

One Liberty Plaza, 20th Floor, New York, NY 10006, USA

477 Williamstown Road, Port Melbourne, VIC 3207, Australia

314–321, 3rd Floor, Plot 3, Splendor Forum, Jasola District Centre,
New Delhi – 110025, India

79 Anson Road, #06–04/06, Singapore 079906

Cambridge University Press is part of the University of Cambridge.

It furthers the University's mission by disseminating knowledge in the pursuit of
education, learning, and research at the highest international levels of excellence.

www.cambridge.org
Information on this title: www.cambridge.org/9781108492713
DOI: 10.1017/9781108685795

First published 2019

Printed and bound in Great Britain by Clays Ltd, Elcograf S.p.A.

A catalogue record for this publication is available from the British Library.

Library of Congress Cataloging-in-Publication Data
Names: Sipka, Danko, author.
Title: Lexical layers of identity : words, meaning, and culture in the Slavic
languages / Danko Sipka.
Description: New York, NY : Cambridge University Press, 2019.
Identifiers: LCCN 2018048005 | ISBN 9781108492713 (hardback)
Subjects: LCSH: Slavic languages – Lexicology. | Slavic languages – Foreign
words and phrases. | Slavic languages – Word formation. | Language and culture –
Europe, Eastern.
Classification: LCC PG319.5 .S54 2019 | DDC 491.8/042–dc23
LC record available at https://lccn.loc.gov/2018048005

ISBN 978-1-108-49271-3 Hardback

Contents

Figures

Tables

Preface

It is a truism in cross-cultural linguistic studies that the lexicon of any language or group of related languages represents a repository of cultural identity markers. The same holds true for the policies and the attitudes about these identity markers (e.g., inherited, i.e., "domestic" versus borrowed, i.e., "foreign" words). While there exists a rich literature about specific words and concepts from a linguistic anthropology viewpoint, borrowing and other contact-driven changes from a contact linguistic perspective, as well as a body of works on policies and attitudes toward lexical markers of cultural identity from a sociolinguistic point of view, these works remain enclosed in their particular fields and a big picture about lexical layers of cultural identity remains elusive.

The principal goal of this book is to bring the three fields together and provide a synthesis of the states and processes relating to the lexical markers of cultural identity. The aforementioned fields (lexical structure, lexical borrowing, and lexical planning) are relevant in answering the questions about what lexical elements culturally define speakers of various languages. Speakers of any language are culturally defined by how their lexicon carves out their field of thinking (e.g., if they have a separate word for *foot* and *leg, older brother* and *younger brother*, and so on). They are furthermore defined by belonging to a cultural circle and geographical or historical setting of some kind, the lexical expression of which are borrowings from various culturally, geographically, or historically relevant languages or their absence. Examples of this include Greco-Latin borrowings in various European languages and their absence in many other languages, borrowings from English in Japanese and their absence in Mandarin Chinese, where new words are coined for new concepts, Norman lexicon in English, etc. Finally, in standard languages, they are defined by the constant negotiation of lexical choices between linguistic elites and the general body of speakers (e.g., efforts to declare a word "incorrect," to replace one word with the other, to introduce a word for a new concept) and the attitudes of the body of speakers toward these activities of lexical planning.

It could not be emphasized enough that the present monograph represents a first step toward a systematic exploration of lexical markers of cultural identity. As such, it does not offer definite answers to any questions but rather points to the need for a comprehensive construal of these markers and proposes techniques for their exploration. In light of this, the material from Slavic languages is used primarily to illustrate the approach rather than to conduct its comprehensive analysis.

The present monograph uses materials from three major Slavic languages: Russian, Polish, and Serbo-Croatian[1] (with numerous references to other Slavic languages) to identify three lexical layers of cultural identity and explore relationships between them. These three languages are most widely spoken in their respective branches, and they represent various anthropological-linguistic, contact-linguistic, and sociolinguistic environments. The lexicons of these Slavic languages are explored in the following three layers rooted in the aforementioned phenomena that culturally define speakers and the three separate research traditions devoted to them. The following three layers concurrently represent the three main parts of the book, divided further into chapters.

a. The first component is the deep cultural layer, comprising culture-bound concepts, different carving of various conceptual spheres, etc. – the first previously mentioned lexical expression of cultural identity, studied in anthropological linguistics.

b. The second element of the present model encompasses the exchange layer, which pertains to the inbound lexical transfer from other languages in Slavic and the way the lexicons of Slavic languages are incorporated and perceived in other languages that culturally defines speakers, and is studied in the literature on linguistic contacts.

c. The final component is the surface layer, encompassing planned intervention in the lexicon and speakers' attitudes toward the lexicon and the interventions, i.e., the third lexical sphere that culturally defines the speakers, studied in lexicological sociolinguistics.

The analysis strives to provide the tools and initiate research that would eventually be a basis for answering the following questions. First: which cultural identity markers can be found in each of the three proposed layers? Second: what is the best way of exploring lexical markers of cultural identity in these layers? Third: which segments of the layers are stable, and which ones exhibit a higher susceptibility toward changes? Finally: how do the

---

[1] This language is also known as Bosnian/Croatian/Montenegrin/Serbian, i.e., under the names of its ethnic standards. The term Serbo-Croatian versus Bosnian/Croatian/Montenegrin/Serbian is hotly debated just like the issue of whether it is one polycentric standard language or whether each of its varieties represents a separate language (for more about these debates, see Kordić, 2010). These politicized debates are generally not of interest here. Changing the name or the approach to the language(s) is not going to change the findings of this research. The intricate sociolinguistic status of this language will be discussed further in Chapters 10–12. Some examples in this text will pertain to Serbo-Croatian in its entirety, and some to one of its ethnic variants, which will be clearly noted.

three layers interact? My goal here is to initiate the process of answering these questions, not to provide answers to them.

A key idea behind this project is that there is a kind of cultural identity that profiles each speaker of any standard language as a member of the group that shares that standard language. In other words, rather than assuming that standard languages (and in many cultures and increasingly so, the standard language is the principal linguistic form for most of the population) only encapsulate national or any other identity, I will make a claim that they create an identity on their own. The speakers are then culturally defined as users of their respective standard language, one of its ethnic or geographical variants, and of a group of related languages. Clearly, the cultural identity of speakers profiled by the language and language group is connected to all other identities and to many other intersecting cultures, but one can also legitimately talk about linguistic cultural identity. As noted, there are areas of stability and change in linguistic cultural identity and there are areas of cross-speaker, cross-region, cross-generational, cross-gender variation, but all speakers are profiled by the markers of this linguistic identity, if with nothing else, then by the potential to use or not use any of the relevant markers. It is of utmost importance to realize at the very outset that the phenomena discussed here represent only a part of the markers of cultural identity. Not only do they interact internally and exibit interpersonal and intergroup variance, but they also engage in exchange with various other markers of cultural identity, which moderate them in the final outcome.

The lexicon of a language is the primary repository of the aforementioned linguistic markers of cultural identity. Standard languages have a broader repertoire of those markers than other forms that a speaker may use (e.g., rural or urban dialects) given that the surface layer remains by and large their exclusive preserve. Other linguistic forms typically evolve without linguistics elites having any prominent role, as they may be present only marginally rather than systematically. Hence the decision to explore lexical layers of cultural identity in standard languages in the present monograph.

Focusing on the lexicon does not mean that no other markers of cultural identity exist. For example, any student of Slavic languages will be familiar with morphosyntactic frames such as Russian *мне не хочется* and Polish *nie chce mi się* 'I do not feel like, I do not want' (literally: It does not want itself to me), Serbo-Croatian *hladno mi je, dosadno mi je* 'I am cold, I am bored' (literally: cold to me it is, boring to me it is), and many others. One might argue that they may be related to some widespread beliefs, but it would be extraordinarily difficult to find consistent proof for such claims. Not only is the lexicon the principal repository of the markers of cultural identity, it also lends itself to consistent qualitative and quantitative analyses much better than other linguistic elements. And last but not least, large dictionary datasets of lexical elements are readily available, which is not the case with morphosyntactic structures.

The book addresses general linguistic states and processes in the lexicon using material from Slavic languages, which could be of interest to researchers and students at Slavic and linguistic departments. Sections devoted to the three explored layers should additionally attract the attention of students and professionals in the field of anthropology, psychology, history, sociology, and political science. Cultural anthropologists and intercultural psychologists will be interested in the analysis of the deep layer, as it discusses how the categories of cross-cultural anthropology (e.g., polychronism versus monochronism) find their expression in the lexicon. Historians may be attracted to the sections about the exchange layer, as these markers of cultural identity are a clear consequence of historical contact and interaction. Sociologists and political scientists may find the analysis of the surface layer interesting as it discusses the mechanisms of establishing authority in society and the reactions to these attempts. As is the case with any broadly conceived monographs in social and behavioral sciences, not all parts will be of interest to all readers. Each such project maintains a fine balance between accessibility and scholarly rigor. My goal was to make the introduction and the conclusion accessible to all potential readership constituencies and to make other segments of the text that had to maintain some level of technicality to keep them rigorous enough accessible to those who may take interest in them.

One should note that the nexus of language and culture features an extremely high level of complexity. The task at hand here is not to provide a definitive account of all factors at play but rather to establish the mechanisms that elucidate some relevant issues and provide a systematic account of this field in a broader context. To use a metaphor, the task here is to come up with basic ingredients for a GPS to facilitate moving through the lexical jungle of cultural linguistics rather than to catalog everything that dwells in that jungle.[2] To add a simile to a metaphor, the work here is akin to that of an astrobiologist – I am looking for the places where something that has not yet been proven may be sought and for the ways of proving it.

The book is organized into five parts, each with three chapters. Nesting between the introductory and concluding parts are the parts covering the three lexical layers of identity, the deep layer, the exchange layer, and the surface layer, that reflect the triad model proposed in the book. The segmentation into the five parts reflects the triad model proposed in the book. The parts about the deep, the exchange, and the surface layers are thus nested between an introduction and conclusion.

The first part of the present monograph comprises three chapters: "The Conceptual Map," "Relevant Research Traditions," and "Research

---

[2] I am grateful to Wayles Browne for pointing this out to me using a fine reference to Prutkov's (1854) aphorism: "Никто не обнимет необъятного" (Nobody can encompass the non-encompassable) (repeated as aphorism 3, 44, 67, and as a part of aphorism 160).

Methodology." Chapter 1 introduces three key concepts: *culture, identity,* and the *lexeme*. It also introduces the derived idea of Slavic cultural identity, which is an additional important concept given that the analysis is conducted using the example of Slavic languages. Additionally, important concepts of authority and ethnicity are discussed. With these concepts in mind, an introductory definition and an exemplification of the deep, exchange, and surface lexical layers of cultural identity are proposed. Chapter 2 discusses relevant intercultural research traditions, most notably Russian "linguoculturology," the Natural Semantic Metalanguage (NSM) theory, and cultural linguistics. Given the broader scope of the model proposed in this book, work from the fields of contact linguistics and sociolinguistic lexicology is also discussed. Chapter 3 proposes a methodological framework for the study of lexical markers of cultural identity based on the epistemological construct of the three layers. The framework is proposed with an eye to partially resolving the challenges of the research discussed in the previous chapter.

The second part discusses the deep layer. Chapter 4, "Lexeme-level Culture-bound Words, Divisions," explores how language-specific words and their features reflect the cultural identity of their speakers. Chapter 5, "Features, Lexicon-level Culture-bound Field Density," looks into how the depth and breadth of lexical fields express cultural characteristics. Finally, the last chapter in this part, Chapter 6, "Stability and Change," tells the story of stability and change in the lexical markers of cultural identity.

The third part of the book is devoted to the exchange layer. Chapter 7, "Cultural Influences," looks into the major sources that have shaped the cultural markers in the exchange lexical layer. Chapter 8, "Geographical Contact," explores the words from surrounding and substrate languages. Finally, Chapter 9, "Inbound and Outbound Exchange," addresses the different statuses of Slavic languages as a source or recipient of lexical transfer.

The fourth part of this monograph discusses the surface layer. Chapter 10, "Lexical Planning," offers a general overview of various paths of linguistic interventions. The next chapter, "Lexicographic Traditions," looks into the practice of enforcing lexical solutions in lexicography, the most direct manner of lexical engineering. Finally, Chapter 12, "Attitudes," analyzes the dynamic of accepting or rejecting lexical solutions by the speakers of Slavic languages.

The final part of this book first discusses, in Chapter 13, the interaction between the three layers before proceeding, in Chapter 14, to summing up the books main findings and providing, in Chapter 15, an account of the prospects for further research in this field.

Acknowledgments

I would like to express my gratitude to the Slavic-Eurasian Research Center of Hokkaido University for a trimestral fellowship that enabled a part of my research on this present monograph. Most notably, I am deeply indebted to the Center Professor Motoki Nomachi for his most generous support at all junctures of my stay in Sapporo, from providing most insightful and valuable comments on earlier versions of this manuscript, to helping with bibliographic references, to organizing my guest lectures in Tokyo and Sapporo. My profound gratitude is also due to Wayles Browne for his comments on the earlier drafts of the manuscript that led to its significant improvement. Similarly, I am most indebted to L'upčo Spasovski for his punctilious interventions in an earlier draft of this manuscript, which have improved the text enormously. I am furthermore grateful to Ilija Čašule for his most valuable comments on an earlier draft.

I am grateful to Olja Šipka for proofreading the manuscript.

I am most grateful to Helen Barton for her generous editorial support. I am also indebted to the two publisher's reviewers whose valuable comments have led to further improvements to previous versions of this text. I am also grateful to Jacqueline French for her excellent copy-editing and to Stephanie Taylor and Bethany Johnson for their help in the production process.

Robert Lew also helped by bringing some minor omissions to my attention.

I am grateful to the following colleagues, who responded to my survey about cross-linguistic anisomorphism between Japanese and Slavic languages: Tadashi Nakamura, Shinichi Yamazaki, Susumu Nonaka, Go Koshino, Yoko Kumanoya, Ikuo Onisi, Alma Okajima, and one informant who wished to remain anonymous.

The generous help that I received from these esteemed colleagues does not mean that they share my political or linguistic views. Furthermore, any shortcomings of the book are to be ascribed to me and to me only.

Parts of Chapter 4 have appeared as "Slavic Lexical Borrowings in English: Patterns of Lexical and Cultural Transfer," *Studia Slavica Hungarica* 49/3–4 (2004), pp. 353–364. Parts of Chapter 6 have appeared as "Semantic Change in the Slavic Inherited Lexicon: An Initial Analysis," *Wiener Slawisticher*

Almanach 79 (2017), pp. 1–24. Parts of Chapter 7 have appeared as "The Challenges of Contrasting Interactional Lexical Layers of Slavic Cultural Identities," *Mundo Eslavo* 16 (2017), pp. 441–452. Parts of Chapter 11 have appeared as "Sociolinguistic Factors in South Slavic Lexicographic Traditions," in Domínguez-Rodríguez, Mª Victoria et al. (eds.), *Words across History: Advances in Historical Lexicography and Lexicology,* Grand Canaria University Press, 2016, pp. 413–424, and "Exclusion Labels in Slavic Monolingual Dictionaries: Lexicographic Construal of Non-Standardness," *Colloquium* 1/1 (2016), pp. 1–17.

Part I

Introduction

1   A Conceptual Map

The topic of the present monograph rests on the concepts of culture, identity, and the lexicon. They will hence be addressed in turn. Given that the analysis is conducted on material from Slavic languages, Slavdom is an important additional concept that needs to be defined. This will be followed by a brisk discussion of two auxiliary concepts: authority and ethnicity, based on their importance in the surface layer of cultural identity.

The concept of culture clearly belongs among the so-called notational terms (see Lipka 1992:5), where definitions depend on the approach in which the term is defined. Spencer-Oatey (2012:2) illustrates a range of possible definitions for this term.

Culture ... is that complex whole which includes knowledge, belief, art, morals, law, custom, and any other capabilities and habits acquired by man as a member of society. (Tyler [British anthropologist], 1870:1; cited by Avruch, 1998:6)

Culture consists of patterns, explicit and implicit, of and for behaviour acquired and transmitted by symbols, constituting the distinctive achievements of human groups, including their embodiment in artifacts; the essential core of culture consists of traditional (i.e. historically derived and selected) ideas and especially their attached values; culture systems may, on the one hand, be considered as products of action, on the other, as conditional elements of future action. (Kroeber & Kluckhohn, 1952:181; cited by Adler, 1997:14)

Culture consists of the derivatives of experience, more or less organized, learned or created by the individuals of a population, including those images or encodements and their interpretations (meanings) transmitted from past generations, from contemporaries, or formed by individuals themselves. (Schwartz, 1992; cited by Avruch, 1998:17)

[Culture] is the collective programming of the mind which distinguishes the members of one group or category of people from another. (Hofstede, 1994:5)

[It is] the set of attitudes, values, beliefs, and behaviors shared by a group of people, but different for each individual, communicated from one generation to the next. (Matsumoto, 1996:16)

Culture is a fuzzy set of basic assumptions and values, orientations to life, beliefs, policies, procedures and behavioural conventions that are shared by a group of people,

3

and that influence (but do not determine) each member's behaviour and his/her interpretations of the "meaning" of other people's behaviour. (Spencer-Oatey, 2008:3)

One should note that even this range of definitions does not give justice to the
variations in the definition of culture. Thus Kymlicka (1995:18) uses
a completely different definition: "I am using 'a culture' as synonymous with
'a nation' or 'a people' – that is, as an integrational community, more or less
institutionally complete, occupying a given territory or homeland, sharing
a distinct language and history." Further variations of the definition of culture,
often far apart from one another, can be found in Eagleton (2016), who provides
a review of how the concept has changed historically, and Jenks (1993), who
offers a review of the concept of culture in philosophy and literary theory,
among many others. It seems that theories of culture (in which its definition is
part and parcel) constitute a scholarly discipline on their own based on the
elusiveness of the concept. One can see this from early reviews such as Keesing
(1974) and Moore (1980) to more recent ones like Jahoda (2012).

    In this monograph, realizing that the definition of the concept will ultimately
depend on its use, I am taking the aforementioned definition proposed by
Spencer-Oatey as the point of departure, inasmuch as it offers a realistic
assessment of the complexity of the concept and a broad scope, while it brings
the definition down to the level of individuals. The same complexity and
individual variation exist within linguistic features, which makes this definition
of culture highly operational in discussing the linguistic markers of cultural
characteristics.

    Let us dissect this definition and put it in the context of the lexical markers of
cultural identity to make it operational. I understand "fuzzy" to mean that there
is no one straightforward version of the assumptions, values, etc. but rather a set
of complex converging belief systems and practices with some degree of
individual variation. From all aforementioned elements that define a culture,
of particular interest here are basic assumptions, values, beliefs, and behavioral
conventions. In making basic assumptions, the speakers are defined by the way
their lexicons carve out the concepts within reality and by the way their meanings and words are interconnected. Higher and lower value is placed on
different lexical spheres, speakers share beliefs about the lexicon and changes
in it (e.g., believing that inherited lexicon is preferable to borrowed lexicon).
They also linguistically behave in a certain way in a given culture (e.g., being
defined by a stricter or looser adherence to the norms of linguistic authorities).
All this, as the author of the definition notes, influences but does not determine
each speaker's behavior and interpretation of others. To connect this discussion
to the aforementioned three layers, the central theme of this book, what
culturally defines the speakers in the deep layer is a set of basic assumptions
about reality, values, and beliefs that find their expression in the lexicon in

a coarser or finer division of the conceptual sphere, the way that meanings and words are interconnected, and the richness of words that are available in certain semantic fields. In the exchange layer, speakers are culturally defined by the values and beliefs about the civilizational circles to which they belong, and this is reflected in the lexical exchange of their respective language, most notably by the borrowings from certain language groups. Finally, in the surface layer, what defines the speakers is the set of values and beliefs about norms established by linguistic authorities and their behavior in following them either strictly or loosely, or opposing them. In the lexicon this is reflected in the groups of words that are "correct" or "incorrect," and therefore more or less desirable.

I will now address identity, the second key concept. One should keep in mind the following observation by Hofstede (2001:10):

Culture is not the same as *identity*. Identities consist of people's answers to the question: Where do I belong? They are based on mutual images and stereotypes and on emotions linked to the outer layers of the onion, but not to values. Populations that fight each other on the basis of their different "felt" identities may very well share the same values. Examples are the linguistic regions in Belgium, the religions in Northern Ireland, and tribal groups in Africa. A shared identity needs a shared Other: At home, I feel Dutch and very different from other Europeans, such as Belgians and Germans; in Asia or the United States, we all feel like Europeans.

The concept of identity is equally problematic as culture albeit for a different set of reasons. It is indisputable that social identity is the kind of identity relevant in this study. It is quite clear from the following two quotations that such a notion of identity relies on the existence of a collective, i.e., a group to which one belongs, which is identified and categorized in relation to other social groups.

A social identity is based on a person's identification with a social group ... A social group is a set of individuals who share the view that they are members of the same social category. Through a social comparison and categorization process, persons who are similar to the self are categorized with the self and are labeled the ingroup. Correspondingly, persons who differ from the self are categorized as the outgroup. (Burke et al. 2009:118)

Defining "us" involves defining a range of "them" also. When we say something about others, we are often also saying something about ourselves. In the human world, similarity and difference are always functions of a point of view: our similarity is their difference and vice versa. Similarity and difference reflect each other across a shared boundary. At the boundary, we discover what we are in what we are not, and vice versa. (Jenkins 2014:104–105)

This latter author also lists basic characteristics of social identity as understood in the presently dominant social psychological approaches (Jenkins 2014:

114–115). (1) There are fundamental differences between social and individual identity; (2) social identity gives sense to the members of the group; (3) it is a base for separating in- and out-groups; (4) the society is organized into categories; (5) social categories build identity; (6) stereotypes and other cognitive simplifications are formed around identity; (7) in-group uniqueness is a base for group comparison; (8) the group is distinct from other groups in order to maintain a positive image of themselves; (9) people and groups with negative self-perception strive for a positive self-perception; (10) in-group dynamics leads toward cohesion; (11) individuals are establishing collective existence using stereotypical categorization; and (12) individuals will determine themselves differently in different contexts.

All of the aforenamed characteristics will be present and even conspicuous in some types of social identity, e.g., in the ethnic identity of southern Slavs. Other types of social identity are not so clearly prototypically organized. Slavic group identity certainly falls into the latter category and so does the identity of a speaker of any given language. What is important is the realization that Slavic social identity (and the analysis here is based on Slavic languages and cultures) and the identity of speakers of any individual Slavic language or their ethnic variants does not fall under an ideal type of category – it is not the most prototypical type of social identity, the way many ethnic identities are. Thus, for example, the speakers are generally aware that somebody else may speak a similar or the same language (e.g., when communicating with speakers who share that broader identity), and these speakers may also be aware of the similarities in making judgments or handling matters, but that identity is generally not as mobilizing and dominant as ethnic identity. I am thus adopting a definition of Slavic identity and that of the speakers of individual Slavic languages as a rather loose social identity – a type of identity on the very edge of a prototypically organized concept of identity.

Obviously, just as with culture, a great degree of variation in defining identity exists between various authors, as evidenced by Preston (1997), Worchel et al. (1998), and Wearing (2011).

At this point, just as was done with the concept of culture itself, I will put the notion of identity in the context of the three layers and connect it to the previously adopted definition of culture. What is part and parcel of the present discussion is cultural identity. In defining this type of identity, I will start with the following definition, which emerges from a very careful review of relevant literature.

Cultural identity is a special case of social identity ... and is defined as the interface between the person and the cultural context ... Cultural identity refers to a sense of solidarity with the ideals of a given cultural group and to the attitudes, beliefs, and behaviors manifested toward one's own (and other) cultural groups as a result of this solidarity. (Schwartz et al., 2006:10)

The kind of cultural identity addressed here is certainly an interface between a person and his/her cultural context. However, rather than *solidarity*, which may be decisive in some spheres (e.g., with ethnic aspects of cultural identity) and rather inconspicuous in others (e.g., with being a speaker of a standard language, or being a Slav in this concrete case), I will use *belonging* in the operational definition of cultural identity deployed here. I will then consider cultural identity as a complex interface between a person (in this particular case a speaker of a standard language) and his/her cultural context. consisting of belongingness to overlapping cultural circles of the groups united around common linguistic, ethnic, or religious heritage resulting in basic assumptions, values, beliefs, and behavioral conventions that are widely distributed among the members of these groups. What is of particular interest here is that the speaker self-identifies but also gets identified by others. Identity is thus a two-way street and it can exist even without overt self-identification.

To finally come to the layers I am proposing, in the deep layer, speakers are following basic assumptions about reality, values, and beliefs that find their expression in the lexicon in coarser or finer division of the conceptual sphere, in the way the meanings and words are interconnected, and in the richness of words that are available in certain fields. In the exchange layer, speakers identify with the values and beliefs toward civilizational circles to which they belong, and this is reflected in the lexical exchange of their respective language, most notably by the borrowings from certain language groups (e.g., Greco-Latin borrowings are an important part of the cultural identity of speakers of European languages). Finally, in the surface layer, speakers identify with the set of values and beliefs about the norms established by linguistic authorities or with the strategies of their contestation. In the lexicon this is reflected in the groups of words that are "correct" or "incorrect," more or less desirable, and so on.

To conclude the review of the three key concepts used in this monograph, one should say that the notion of the lexeme (which is a technical term for what is known as "word" in common parlance) is equally elusive as those of culture and identity. I have shown, in Šipka (2005), that various criteria have been proposed to define a lexeme (independent use, pronunciation unity, ability to change information structure of utterances, ability to convey meanings, incommutability of its parts, separation in writing and pronunciation). Various authors, such as Eluerd (2000), Jackson (2000), Lehman and Martin-Bethet (1998), Lipka (1992, 2002), Niklas-Saliminen (1997), Picoche (1977), Polguère (2002), Rey (1980), Schwarze and Wunderlich (1985) in Western lexicology, and Dragićević (2010a), Filipec and Čermak (1985), Fomina (1978), Kalinin (1971), Kuznecova (1982), Miodunka (1989), Ondruš (1972), Šmelev (1977) in Slavic lexicology have ascribed varied degrees of importance to all those criteria. While they are all useful in differentiating lexemes from other linguistic elements, there is no single criterion, or their cluster that can unequivocally define a lexeme. This concept, then, remains a prototype with a core of typical lexemes and a periphery where lexemes and non-lexemes (sublexemic elements like affixes and supralexemic elements like phrases) overlap. One can assume various strategies in this field, but, for all practical purposes, I will consider lexemes those items one would normally look up in a dictionary: words, idioms, and lexical affixes (but not grammatical affixes, syntactic frames, collocations, etc.). These entities participate in all three layers of cultural identity to be discussed further in this text. In this regard, the distinction between a *lexical unit* and *lexeme*, introduced by Cruse (1986:49) may be helpful:

Lexical units are those form–meaning complexes with (relatively) stable and discrete semantic properties which stand in meaning relationships such as antonymy (e.g., *long : short*) and hyponymy (e.g., *dog : animal*) and which interact syntagmatically with the contexts in various ways ... Lexemes, on the other hand, are the items listed in the lexicon, or 'ideal dictionary' of a language.

The objects of our research here, as was the case in Cruse (1986) are lexical units rather than lexemes (given their embeddedness in the context). In addition, the fuzziness of the border between lexicon and grammar has long been identified in cognitive linguistics (e.g., Langacker 1987, 1991) and systemic-functional linguistics (see under "lexicogrammar" in Matthiessen et al. 2010).

One important standard lexicological distinction is that between open and closed lexical classes, nicely summarized in Lipka (1992:133):

We will start with a simplified summary of the treatment in Quirk et al. (1985:77ff.). The following categories of words can be distinguished in English:
(1) (a) **CLOSED CLASSES**: preposition, pronoun, determiner, conjunction, auxiliary verb
     (b) **OPEN CLASSES**: noun, adjective, verb, adverb
     (c) **LESSER CATEGORIES**: numeral, interjection

Category (a) is often referred to as function words, because of their grammatical function. Traditional lexicology, however, is almost exclusively concerned with category (b); but dictionaries normally include (a) and (c). Category (b) is often called "major word classes," content words (contentives), or lexical items.

This distinction is germane here given that open classes change with the ebbs and flows of historical events, social environment, and sometimes even ideological programs, which is not the case with closed classes. This makes open classes the primary subject of the surface layer. They are also much more readily borrowed, which makes them important in the exchange layer. Finally, they are somewhat more embedded into culture-specific elements of thinking (while closed classes typically relate to more broadly distributed cognitive categories), which makes them more important in the deep layer.

As previously noted, being aware of the ultimate elusiveness of the concept, I will use a very broad notion of a lexeme as a linguistic unit that can carry conceptual meaning or signal meaning of some kind, encompassing thus one-word and multiword lexemes and also affixoids (affixes that can carry lexical meaning, e.g., *ethno-* and *-logy* as found in the word *ethnology*). Just as in the case of the other two key concepts, culture and identity, the definition deployed here is one from the range of possibilities. This particular one is selected, as it gives clear focus on the elements that are readily accessible in lexicographic datasets. This certainly does not mean that a different approach would be impossible or inappropriate in another attempt at exploring the phenomena under discussion here.

Another distinction relevant to the study of the lexicon is that between local and global levels of analysis. Lexemes do not exist in isolation; they are a constituent part of the lexicon. When comparing and contrasting two different languages, we can establish links between a lexeme in one language with one or more lexemes in another. We can thus say that the Russian word *нога* [noga] corresponds to two English words: *foot* and *leg*. This is a local (or lexemic) level of analysis. If the number of such local differences forms a trend of some kind, we can notice global differences. For example, Slavic languages are less precise in forming concepts for body parts than English. As previously noted, they do not have to differentiate between *foot* and *leg*, but this difference is a part of the trend. Slavs also do not have to separate *hand* and *arm*, *finger* and *toe*, *ankle*, and *wrist*, *chin* and *beard*, *nipple*, and *wart*, and in some of them the speakers do not even have to distinguish between the *brain* and the *spinal cord*. The establishment of this trend belongs to the lexicon, or the global level of analysis.

I will now turn to the concept of Slavic cultural identity, which is pivotal to the concrete material on which the analysis will be conducted, and also for the secondary agenda item of this monograph – the question of whether Slavic linguistics is possible as opposed to linguistics using Slavic language data. While speakers of English will not have a problem in identifying someone as, for example, Russian or Polish, a general Slavic cultural identity is somewhat more elusive. The very word *Slavdom* (Slavic people collectively) is rather exotic in English even in professional circles.[1]

---

[1] According to www.merriam-webster.com/dictionary/Slavdom, it belongs to the bottom 10 percent of English words. One should say that the word is actually close to the bottom of that bottom 10 percent. Another source (www.forgottenbooks.com/worddata/slavdom), which covers fiction and non-fiction sources from 1869 to 1945 (i.e., in the period of efflorescence of Slavic studies), shows that the word *Slavdom* is found once in 45,454,545 words (the frequency of 0.000002%). According to Google Books (https://books.google.com/ngrams/), the peak use of this word was in 1918, the usage then fell and reached two short-lived minor increases in 1949 and 1963, and it continued falling to reach 0.0000014188% in 2008. On a side note, one should say that this

In sharp contrast to the obscurity of Slavdom in English, a vast majority of major research universities in English-speaking countries feature a department of Slavic languages and literatures or at least sections, chairs, etc. Similarly, major universities feature Slavic and Eurasian research centers. There are, furthermore, professional organizations.[2]

This brings us to the underlying dilemma of Slavic studies, the question that an established field of study may not have a well-established subject of study. Needless to say, the obscurity of a word that covers a subject does not necessarily mean that the subject itself remains obscured or non-existent. It seems that in non-Slavic countries, departments of Slavic languages around the world remain the only remnants of Slavdom-based philology. A thorough recent review about the development of the idea of Slavdom in the work of linguists in one particular narrow field of Slavic studies can be found in Krečmer (2015). A serious challenge to earlier understanding of Slavic ethnic identity was offered by Curta (2001:350), who showed that the idea of Slavic ethnicity was much younger and much less clear than previously believed: the first clear statement that 'we are Slavs' comes from the twelfth-century *Russian Primary Chronicle*. The idea of Slavdom is based on genetic and structural similarities of Slavic languages and, to a lesser extent, cultures. The range of this concept is not problematic – it extends to cover the speakers of all Slavic languages. The problematic question at hand is if linguistic similarities mean cultural similarities. The areas of Slavic languages feature a high degree of diversity. Geographically and climatically, they range from Mediterranean landscapes in the south to polar tundra in the north. Historical differences are no less important – Slavic peoples were a constitutive part of various European, Middle Eastern, and Central Asian empires, and they exhibited considerable differences as to the emergence and duration of their own statehood. Finally, among Slavic peoples we find Orthodox Christianity, Catholicism, Protestantism, Islam, and various less commonly practiced religious systems. The question is, then, if one can talk about Slavdom as a cultural category and a type of identity. Mere structural and genetic similarities of languages surely do not suffice to prove cultural similarity. One should note that in the course of human events one can find areas and periods of strong feelings of Slavic unity (in many areas in the context of the nineteenth-century national revivals of Slavic peoples and their resistance to Germanization or German geopolitical influences) but also ongoing conflicts between Slavic peoples (e.g., rebellions of the Poles against Russian rule). As for now, I will use Slavic cultural identity

source gives a considerably higher frequency to the Russian equivalent of *Slavdom*, i.e., славянство, ranging from its peak in the 1880s of 0.000250% to 0.0000702942% in 2008.

[2] Some examples include the American Association of Teachers of Slavic and East European Languages, British Association of Slavonic and East European Studies, Canadian Association of Slavists, Australia and New Zealand Slavists' Association, Slavic Linguistics Society.

to refer to the basic assumptions, values, beliefs, and behavioral practices that are widespread across Slavic cultures and that stem from their speakers' sense of belonging to the community of Slavs. At this point it is important to realize that the idea of Slavic cultural unity is highly convoluted and even controversial.

Two additional auxiliary concepts need to be addressed here given their pivotal role in the maneuvers in the surface level, namely, authority and ethnicity. These two concepts are what greatly defines the cultural context of Slavic speakers in the surface layer. Both concepts represent notational terms, which have as many definitions as there are definers. Given that they are of limited interest here, it would be unproductive to go through the variations of their defining. I will therefore concentrate on those characteristics that are germane to the present research.

Authority has been the focus of social sciences since the publication of Max Weber's ground-breaking essay (1992, 1919) established its three main types: traditional, charismatic, and rational-legal. In a recent book, Huemer (2013) reviews the notion of authority (primarily political) in various authors and intellectual traditions, most of them after the aforesaid Weber's seminal essay. The picture that emerges is that a multitude of justifications have been used and a variety of sources have been introduced. In the particular context of this monograph, it is important to realize that the establishment of normative linguistic authority can take various forms and resort to various justifications. Linguistic authority is the one form of authority often intertwined with the political kind. It is based on the fact that the source of authority (e.g., linguists, writers, journalists, educators) establishes a model that the general body of speakers is expected to follow (e.g., in a word being "correct" or "incorrect"). Obviously, normative linguists and other sources of authority will always make claims that the source of their authority is rational, but in reality their decisions may have various other motivating factors behind them. This particular idea of normative linguistic authority is widespread in all Slavic cultures, and it is considerably more prominent than in some other cultures, e.g., in English, where normative linguists have extremely limited impact, as demonstrated by Milroy and Milroy (2012), who explored the idea of authority in the English language.

When we talk about ethnicity here, the line of research is leading from Gellner (1983), who emphasized the constructivist nature of nationalism to Brubaker (2002, 2004, 2009), who understands ethnicity not as a state but rather as a process. The following quote is representative in that regard.

Ethnicity, race and nation should be conceptualized not as substances or things or entities or organisms or collective individuals – as the imagery of discrete, concrete, tangible, bounded and enduring "groups" encourages us to do – but rather in relational, processual, dynamic, eventful and disaggregated terms. This means thinking of ethnicity, race and nation not in terms of substantial groups or entities but in terms of *practical categories, cultural idioms, cognitive schemas, discursive frames, organizational routines, institutional forms, political projects* and *contingent events*. It means thinking of *ethnicization, racialization* and *nationalization* as political, social, cultural and psychological *processes*. (Brubaker, 2002:167)

It is exactly these processes of ethnicization and nationalization that play a pivotal role in numerous maneuvers across the Slavic world. In some regions the process is painfully conspicuous, in others, subtler.

Now that the key concepts are tentatively in the conceptual landscape of this study, I will turn to discussing the lexical layers of Slavic cultural identity. The following distinction proposed by Morkovkin and Morkovkina (1997:64) will be useful in that discussion: "Язык, в частности, можно описывать без учета и с учетом его присущности говорящему человеку. Первый подход мы называем лингвоцентрическим, а второй – антропоцентрическим" (Language in particular can be described by taking or not taking into account its belonging to a speaking human being. The former approach is called the linguocentric approach, the latter anthropocentric). Of course, the discussion about the lexical layers of Slavic cultural identity is only possible within a general anthropocentric approach.

Another important distinction is that of the level of analysis. Cross-cultural psychologists Triandis and Suh (2002:136) have rightly noted that "studies that use culture as the N can provide different results than studies that use individuals as the N."[3] In studying languages, the situation is even more intricate as we can talk about idiolects, at the level of individuals, sociolects, as the level of social groups, dialects at compact geographic areas, variants as a common norm of the standard language, languages, language groups, etc. Prominent Russian authors, who are developing an idea about the linguistic image of the world (to be discussed in detail in the next chapter), note the dynamics between the level of the individual and that of the language:

Необходимо понимать, что хотя язык навязывает носителю определенную картину мира, человек не является её рабом. Эксплицировав соответствующие представления в рамках метаязыковой рефлексии, говорящий имеет возможность подвергнуть их сомнению.

(It is necessary to understand that although the language imposes a specific image of the world to its speakers, the individual is not its slave. Externalizing particular conceptualizations within metalinguistic reflection, the speaker has the possibility to doubt them.) (Zaliznjak et al., 2005:9)

While this kind of dynamics certainly exists, there are a range of other factors that need to be accounted for. First, there exists a range of environmental

---

[3] N stands here for the sample that is being researched.

factors (geography, climate, etc.) in the Slavic world, from the vast cold plains of Russia to the warm jagged coastline of Croatia. These environmental factors can be attested inter- and intra-lingually. Needless to say, Slavic languages, and often the territories within the same language, are clearly diversified because of different historical development. Compare, for example, the five centuries of Ottoman Turkish rule in the Balkans versus a century and a half of the partition of the Polish language space between Prussia, Russia, and Austria-Hungary.

Furthermore, cross-cultural psychology has established a number of parameters, from Hall's classic patterns of polychronism versus monochronism and high versus low-context cultures (Hall, 1959, 1966) to Hofstede's cultural dimensions, originally about power distance, individualism/collectivism, masculinity/femininity, and uncertainty avoidance, with long-term orientation added later (see Hofstede and Hofstede, 1994), to a very elaborate network in Schwartz's Value Inventory: self-direction, stimulation, hedonism, achievement, power, security, conformity, tradition, benevolence, and universalism (Schwartz, 1992, 1994). All these parameters that are well established in cross-cultural psychology create a complex network of intercultural and intracultural differences in Slavic languages.

The next important factor is interlexical interaction in each particular language. Words do not exist in isolation, they participate in an intricate network of words and their features. Those other words and, more generally, the status of each word in the lexicon can profile the role a word plays in shaping lexical layers of Slavic cultural identity. For example, the fact that there are two words in Serbian for one's own country, i.e., *otadžbina* 'fatherland' and *domovina* 'homeland' along with the fact that their usage differentiation is such that the former is felt as somewhat archaic or belonging to a more nationalistic discourse mean that these two words are primarily percieved as a couple of archaic vs. neutral synonyms rather than cultural keywords. The relationship between the two words and their status trumps any cultural identity impact (the fact that one is related to father and the other to home). Similarly, it would be difficult to prove that the fact that standard Macedonian features three words for rainbow (*божилак, виножито, суница*) has something to do with a specific attitude of Macedonians toward this atmospheric phenomenon. This kind of dialectal variation is found in many languages and the decision to include all of them, rather than just one, in the standard was a maneuver in the surface layer. The three words are metaphors with a poetic touch to them, the first two visual ('God's arc' and 'wine-and-grain'), the third synesthetic ('the clinging thing'). That all of them have made it into the standard language might be due to the fact that the key codifying figure, Blaže Koneski, was a world-class poet with a sensitivity for such poetic pictures encapsulated in words.

A key question in the analysis of the differences in lexical resources of the present-day Slavic languages is that of what mechanisms caused the split of the initially one Proto-Slavic system into a number of different systems. It goes without saying that this question can be asked about any group of genetically related languages (e.g., Indo-European languages). However, Slavic languages represent a particularly interesting case given that the number of languages is limited, they are culturally diverse, and their split is relatively recent, particularly against a vast backdrop of diachronic linguistic and general historical development. Slavic material lends itself then to analysis much better than those of many other related language branches (e.g., those language groups that have many more languages or those where the split happened much earlier). The question about the separation of specific languages from the same source is concurrently a question about their unity. The factors that have influenced the lexical split of Slavic languages have also left some sectors of the lexicon unchanged and thus common to some or all Slavic languages. The latter sectors connect Slavic languages and often separate them from other language groups. My intention here is not to explain the mechanisms of change and emergence of identity but rather to explore the resulting elements of those changes as a small step toward the elucidation of change.

Let us take a look at the following three lexical differences in Slavic languages:

a. Russian[4] *синий* 'deep blue': *голубой* 'grayish blue' versus Serbo-Croatian *плав* 'blue';
b. Russian *подушка* 'pillow' versus Serbo-Croatian *јастук* 'pillow';
c. Polish *tłok* 'piston' versus Serbo-Croatian *klip* 'piston'.

The first example features a difference of a less or more precise differentiation of a conceptual field. It would be hard to imagine geopolitical or historical generators of this difference. Similarly, this difference is not a product of linguistic planning. The difference seems to have risen spontaneously, and it would be very difficult to trace its underlying mechanisms.

Obviously, one can trace the etymology of the words in both languages and the link to the same conceptual field reconstructed for Proto-Slavic, but that still does not explain what caused a more precise division in Russian than in Serbo-Croatian. On a side note, it is important to keep in mind the famous formulation by Jakobson (1959:236): "languages differ essentially in what they must convey and not in what they may convey." In this particular case, a speaker of Russian has to break up the concept of blue into two values, while a speaker of Serbo-Croatian does not.

In the second case the difference is a direct result of historical and geopolitical circumstances. In Russian (just as in Polish and some other Slavic

---

[4] When using a language name without any qualification, I am implying the modern standard variety of that language. Other varieties (e.g., regional dialects, sociolects) may or may not follow the modern standard variety in their lexical systems.

languages) the word for 'pillow' is inherited from the common Slavic lexical pool, while Serbo-Croatian features a Turkish loanword. Without intensive and direct cultural contact of the Serbo-Croatian speaking areas with the Turkish language and its culture, this difference would not exist. We can thus easily identify historical and geopolitical underlying mechanisms that have generated this difference. We can also see that this difference is not a result of planned intervention.

Finally, the third example shows a result of planned intervention. In establishing car mechanic terminology, the introduction of the new word for piston in Polish was based on what that part does in the internal combustion engine. The noun *tłok* 'piston' is derived from the verb *tłoczyć*, roughly: 'to compress'. We thus have a function-based word formation at play. In contrast to this, the new word in Serbo-Croatian is a metaphor based on visual similarity. The word *klip* means 'corncob, ear of corn' and it extended its meaning into 'piston'. The process was possibly influenced by the same metaphor in German *Kolben* 'corncob, piston'. As with the previous two examples, the difference in these two particular words is irrelevant, but if a pattern of differences of some kind in introducing new words emerges, then this may become relevant.

As noted before, speakers are culturally defined by how their lexicon carves out their field of thinking (e.g., by what seems to be a pattern of less precise division of body parts in Slavic languages than in English). They are further-more defined by belonging to a cultural circle and geographical or historical setting of some kind, the lexical expression of which is borrowing from various culturally, geographically, or historically relevant languages or their absence (e.g., Greco-Latin borrowings that separate Slavic languages from Mandarin Chinese). Finally, in standard languages, identities are defined by the constant negotiation of lexical choices among linguistic elites and the general body of speakers (e.g., efforts to declare a word "incorrect," to replace one word with the other, to introduce a word for a new concept, and the attitudes of the body of speakers toward these activities), which seems to be more prominent in Slavic language than in English.

The three aforementioned cases exemplify the three layers of lexical differences and similarities between Slavic languages (again, individual examples never exemplify relevant differences but rather the fields where patterns may form). If the differences form a pattern, then they build the cultural identity of Slavic languages, in the sense that the differences mark the identity of particular Slavic languages and their cultures while the similarities point to a common Slavic cultural identity. The following three layers where these patterns of differences and similarities emerge can be identified.

a. The deep layer – the lexical expression of cultural identity, which determines the speakers by giving them certain lexical choices and links between the words. It features the highest degree of stability, which does not seem to be directly influenced by historical developments or the political will of the community of speakers.

b. The exchange layer – the lexical expression of cultural identity that situates the speakers in the circles of various civilizations, which is a result of direct or indirect intercultural communication.

c. The surface layer – the lexical expression of cultural identity that determines speakers through their adherence (or lack thereof) to the lexical norms of the standard language. This type of identity is created by conscious negotiation between the interventions of linguistic elites and attitudes among the general population of speakers.

There is a certain degree of interaction between the three layers. For example, a conscious intervention (i.e., a maneuver in the surface layer may consist of replacing lexical items from the exchange layer, e.g., loanwords from another language in a terminology of some kind). Although the three layers can also be distinguished in any language or group of languages, Slavic languages constitute a particularly interesting case study, in that they feature intense interaction with other languages (which is not the case with many other languages, at least not to such a degree), and prominent lexical interventionism; again, in other linguistic cultures, normative activities may not be prominent even if they do exist. For these reasons, the epistemological construct of the three layers of identity seems particularly suited for the study of Slavic lexicons.

Now that the preliminary task of outlining the epistemological construct of the three lexical layers of cultural identity has been done (to be further elaborated upon in Chapter 3), in the next chapter I will review relevant literature to then lay out the research methodology for the study of Slavic lexicons, based on the aforementioned construct of the three layers of cultural identity and the state of the art in the research field.

2   Relevant Research Traditions

In the present review, I will first address relevant work in the field of the deep layer to then proceed with the exchange layer and conclude with the surface layer. Quite naturally, the review of the approaches to the deep layer will be most thorough – the deep layer is the primary field of cultural identity, and the other two layers, as will became clear throughout the text, are de facto operating on the given material of the deep layer (by adding to it, attaching values to it, and so on). Furthermore, the approaches to the deep layer relate to cultural identity directly, unlike the approaches in the other two layers that are more closely related to other aspects of linguistic and extra-linguistic functioning, such as international relations, politics, economics.

2.1   The Research Traditions of the Deep Layer

There exists a rich tradition of cross-cultural anthropocentric linguistics in the study of Slavic languages. Three approaches are of particular interest in the context of the deep lexical layer of cultural identity. The first is so-called linguistic culturology (Russian: лингвокультурология), as advocated in the last several decades by numerous Russian authors, along with some Polish and Serbian followers. The second is the Natural Semantic Metalanguage (NSM) theory, initially proposed by Anna Wierzbicka and further developed by Cliff Goddard. The third approach of interest here is cultural linguistics, whose main current proponent is Farzad Sharifian. Additionally, non-linguistic approaches of cross-cultural anthropology and psychology will be discussed, given their pertinence to the topic of the present book. In discussing these approaches, I will limit myself to the components of these approaches that are relevant to the research questions addressed in this monograph. What follows is in no way an exhaustive review of these approaches.

One cannot emphasize enough that the approach that I am advocating does not rely on or follow any of these three aforementioned approaches. As is common in any field of scholarship, some ideas in each of these approaches may be relevant building blocks for the present project. Each approach will therefore be reviewed with an eye to the cognitions that may be incorporated into the present analysis, and those that could be modified and improved to better serve the purposes of the present book project. That certainly does not mean that I am agreeing or, what is more, that I am following the main tenets of these approaches. The points of criticism will be inserted in appropriate places in this chapter, and differentiating features of the present approach will be addressed at the beginning of Chapter 3. I will also discuss the major principles of cross-cultural psychology, in an attempt to build a more functional epistemological construct for the study of the deep layer of cultural identity in Slavic languages.

Russian linguistic culturology can best be described through the following key concepts advanced by proponents of the theory: the linguistic image of the world, national linguistic mentality, linguistic personality, and cultural keywords. They will be discussed in turn.

The following two quotes from O. D. Kornilov, a prominent proponent of this approach, illustrate the point.

Любой национальный язык выполняет несколько основных функций: функцию общения (коммуникативную), функцию сообщения (информативную), функцию воздействия (эмотивную) и, что для нас особенно важно, функцию ФИКСАЦИИ И ХРАНЕНИЯ ВСЕГО КОМПЛЕКСА ЗНАНИЙ И ПРЕДСТАВЛЕНИЙ ДАННОГО ЯЗЫКОВОГО СООБЩЕСТВА О МИРЕ. Такое универсальное, глобальное знание – результат работы коллективного сознания – зафиксировано в языке, прежде всего в его лексическом и фразеологическом составе. Но существуют разные виды человеческого сознания: индивидуальное сознание отдельного человека, коллективное обыденное сознание нации, научное сознание. ... Таким образом, следует говорить о МНОЖЕСТВЕННОСТИ ЯЗЫКОВЫХ КАРТИН МИРА: о научной языковой картине мира, о языковой картине мира национального языка, о языковой картине мира отдельного человека.

[Every ethnic language fulfills several basic functions: the function of communication (communicative), the function of informing (informative), the function of influence (emotive), and, what is of particular importance for us, the function of FIXATING AND STORING THE ENTIRE COMPLEX OF KNOWLEDGE AND REPRESENTATIONS OF THE GIVEN LINGUISTIC COMMUNITY ABOUT THE WORLD. Such universal, global knowledge is a result of the work of collective consciousness fixated in the language, primarily in its lexical and phraseological components. However, there are various forms of human consciousness: individual consciousness of a particular person, collective consciousness of an ethnic group, scholarly consciousness ... Thus, one should talk about a MULTIPLICITY OF LINGUISTIC IMAGES OF THE WORLD: about a scientific linguistic image of the world, about a linguistic image of the world of the ethnic language, about a linguistic image of the world of particular persons.] (Kornilov, 2003:4)

Каждый народ видит ИНВАРИАНТ БЫТИЯ в своей особой, неповторимой ПРОЕКЦИИ. Специфика этой проекции запечатлевается в языке, образуя ЯКМ национального языка, и передается вместе с ней от поколения к поколению.

[Every ethnic group sees the INVARIABLE PART OF ITS EXISTENCE in its separate, unique PROJECTION. The specificity of that projection is sealed in language, forming the LIW of the ethnic language, and it is transferred along with it from one generation to the other.] (Kornilov, 2003:325)

Clearly, the key concept, that of the linguistic image of the world, further develops the original Humboldt's Weltansicht hypothesis, often erroneously called *Weltanschauung* (Trabant, 2007:263). Humboldt (1841, VII:53) claims that language is "das bildende Organ des Gedanken" (a constitutive organ of thought) and further that: "Das Denken ist aber nicht bloss abhängig von der Sprache überhaupt, sondern, bis auf einen gewissen Grad, auch von jeder einzelnen bestimmten" (Thinking is dependent not just on language in general but, to a certain degree, on each individual language) (Humboldt 1841, IV:21). Most importantly, he states that: "So liegt in jeder Sprache eine eigenthümliche Weltansicht" (Consequently, in each language there is a peculiar view of the world) (Humboldt 1841, VII:60). A further step in the development of the concept of a linguistic image of the world was the work of Leo Weisgerber (1962), who further elaborated the idea about linguistic modeling of the world by providing a more detailed elucidation of language mechanisms that shape the worldview of their speakers. However, it is in Russian linguistics that this concept has gained its full recognition, becoming a central component of what seems to be a dominant linguistic approach in present-day Russia. The other two constituents of this theory, the idea of a "linguistic personality" and the notion of "cultural keywords" are derived from the linguistic image of the world – *linguistic personality* is largely its embodiment at the level of individual speakers and *cultural keywords*, also called *cultural concepts*, are its lexical expressions.

Russian linguistic personality in this approach is connected with the Russian image of the world through Russian "national character" or "national mentality." National images of the world are derivatives of national mentality, as suggested by Kornilov (2003). As Karaulov (2010:42) notes:

наличие общерусского языкового типа … базовой части общей для русских картины мира, или мировидения … и устойчивого комплекса коммуникативных черт, определяющих национально-культурную мотивированность речевого поведения … и позволяют говорить о русской языковой личности.

[the existence of the common Russian language type … the basic part of the image of the world common to Russians or their worldview … and a stable complex of communicative features, determining national-cultural motivation of verbal behavior … are indeed what allow us to speak about the Russian linguistic personality.]

Karaulov (2010) sees linguistic personality as a three-level construct comprising verbal, linguo-cultural, and pragmatic levels. It is at the linguo-cultural level that the linguistic image of the world plays a central role.

Radbil' (2013:68) postulates an even closer relationship between linguistic personality and national linguistic mentality: "Мы исходим из определенного изоморфизма языковой личности и структуры языкового менталитета этноса в целом." (We assume a certain anisomorphism of linguistic personality and the structure of linguistic mentality of the ethnos at large.) The concept of "national, linguistic mentality" is divided into four layers comprising perception, logical thinking, emotions, and values. For this author, a linguistic image of the world is central at the linguo-cognitive level.

As can be seen in Šmelev (2005), cultural keywords are those lexemes that carry information about the "Russian character" and worldview. He distinguishes the following lexical spheres of particular importance:

1. Words relating to certain aspects of universal philosophical concepts (e.g., two words for 'truth' in Russian: *правда* and *истина*);
2. The words for concepts existing in other cultures, but having particular significance in the Russian culture (e.g., *душа* 'soul');
3. The words for specific Russian concepts (e.g., *тоска* 'a specific type of melancholy, yearning, etc.'); and
4. Modal words, particles, and interjections with specific Russian meanings (e.g., *авось* 'perhaps, maybe').

Perhaps the most systematic overview of this approach along with the implications for cross-linguistic lexical contrasting is provided by Kornilov (2014). Kornilov (2014:147–164) posits three classes of national-specific vocabulary: lexemes referring to nation-specific entities, those representing universal concepts with nation-specific prototypes, and those signifying nation-specific abstract concepts. He bases cross-linguistic lexical contrast on the following four spheres of universal human cognition: sensory-receptive, logical-conceptual, emotional-evaluation, and value-ethical (Kornilov 2014:282). One example of the first sphere is exemplified by the fact that languages divide the space of colors differently, while the second sphere is exemplified by different conceptualizations of body parts in various languages, and the final two categories by differences in idioms.

While linguistic culturology represents the dominant approach in present-day Russian linguistics, important work in this vein has been conducted in other Slavic linguistic traditions. Thus, Bartmiński (2005, 2014) and Bartmiński and Chlebda (2008) offer a model for an ethnolinguistic study of Slavic identities within this general approach. Bartmiński and Chlebda (2008:19) identify four data sources for this research: dictionary data, public discourse corpus data, general corpus data, experimental data. Bartmiński (2005:274) proposes the comparison of the following range of concepts:

Postulowałem, by porównywać:
1) sposób określania tożsamości zbiorowej: kim jesteśmy "my" (autostereotypy);
2) sposób postrzegania i językowego ujmowania innych, kim są "oni" (heterostereotypy sąsiadów);
3) sposoby konceptualizacji własnego miejsca, tj. własnej lokalizacji w świecie;
4) sposoby konceptualizacji czasu wspólnotowego, w którym żyjemy;
5) wartości funkcjonujące, tj. obowiązujące (deklaratywnie i faktycznie) w świecie społecznym uznanym za „nasz" (wspólnotowy, społeczny, narodowy);
6) stosowane środki wyrazu w postaci typów wypowiedzi zróżnicowanych wedle kryteriów stylowych i gatunkowych

[I postulated that the following should be compared:
1) The manner in which collective identity is determined: who "we" are (self-stereotypes);
2) The manner of construing and linguistic expression of others, who "they" are (hetero-stereotypes of neighbors);
3) The ways of conceptualizing one's own place, i.e., one's own localization in the world;
4) The ways of conceptualizing the collective time, in which we live;
5) Functioning i.e., obligatory values (declarative and factual);
6) Utilized means of expression in the form of the types of utterances differentiated by style and genre.]

Bartmiński goes on to provide examples of the concepts (concepts being the ground for comparison, *tertium comparationis*, for him) to be compared. The following semantic groups are relevant for him: contemporary political concepts (e.g., democracy, the left, freedom, independence), social concepts (e.g., home, family, honor, fatherland), moral values (e.g., justice, solidarity, courage, and others), personal traits (e.g., decency, fidelity), general concepts (e.g., the individual, work, faith), and cognitive concepts (e.g., truth, lies). He proposes a list of seventy-five keywords for cross-Slavic comparison.

Dragićević (2010b) addressed verbal associations as an expression of the link between the Serbian language and culture, and, similarly, Piper (2003) saw association dictionaries as valuable datasets for the study of ethnocultural stereotypes. A number of similar investigations can also be found in Dragićević (2016).

To sum up, the intellectual tradition of linguistic culturology introduced the ideas of a national linguistic personality, defined by a specific linguistic image of the world widespread among the speakers who share that linguistic personality. They have also proposed that certain culture-specific words, phrases, their meanings, groups of words, and links between them (most notably associative) testify to that specific national linguistic personality.

This stream of scholars should be given their due credit for drawing the attention of the linguistic community to the nexus of language and culture. This was an enormous achievement in light of the fact that the dominant, so-called formal approaches, such as the minimalist program (Chomsky, 1995) or optimality theory (Kager, 1999), completely excluded these phenomena from linguistic analysis, concentrating exclusively on what is common in the languages of the world.

However, in the present research, the postulates of linguistic culturology can be used only as a starting point. The features of linguistic culturology that separate it from the present research are as follows:

a. Isolationism: cultural practices in language are analyzed as having no connection to cross-cultural psychology and other similar approaches, for example, a well-known parameter of collectivism versus individualism is not of interest to "linguoculturologists";

b. Particularism: there is no connection to other fields of Slavic scholarship, e.g., the study of loanwords, which may have established certain culturally relevant distinctions in the lexicon;

c. Elitism: this approach exaggerates the role of literature, intellectuals, and so on – some cultural features may exist in literature, or a narrow elite population group, and be absent from the mental lexicons of the majority of the population;

d. Atomism: as the analysis is often overly fine-grained to be applicable, it goes into very peculiar features of one or several words;

e. Determinism: authors commonly postulate a possible cause of a feature, leaving no room for random events;

f. Ethnocentrism: authors seem to be equating an ethnic group with a particular language, such as talking about Russian, or any other, national mentality, while in reality every language is used by various ethnic groups with their distinct cultures;

g. Arbitrariness: only words that supposedly prove the claim are chosen, while other cases that do not confirm the claim remain disregarded.

I will return to these differences at the end of this section.

Natural Semantic Metalanguage (NSM) theory, proposed by Anna Wierzbicka and further developed by Cliff Goddard, is the second relevant research approach. Wierzbicka's central claim is that "in natural language meaning consists in human interpretation of the world" (1988:2, repeated in Wierzbicka 1992 and elsewhere). She also went on to say that "It is subjective, it is anthropocentric, it reflects predominant cultural concerns and culture-specific modes of social interaction as much as any objective features of the world 'as such.'" To add to this, in a relatively recent statement about the theory, Goddard and Wierzbicka, its two most prominent representatives, state the following (2002a: 1–3):

The NSM framework is based on evidence supporting the idea that there is a set of simple, indefinable meanings – universal semantic primes – which have concrete linguistic exponents in all the world's languages. By using universal semantic primes as a vocabulary for semantic description, we can achieve semantic analyses which are maximally intelligible, testable, and untranslatable, as well as enabling the maximum possible resolution of semantic analysis.

In a later publication, Goddard identifies the current set of semantic primes (the original set was established in Wierzbicka 1972), exemplified by their exponents in English, such as substantives (*I, you, someone* . . .), quantifiers (*one, two, much/many* . . .), evaluators (*good, bad*), and so on (see Goddard, 2008b: 33).

The second major component of the NSM theory is the way in which the primes combine:

> The Natural Semantic Metalanguage consists not just of a lexicon, but also of a syntax. Semantic primes are hypothesized to have certain universal combinatorial properties, and the available evidence indicates that these properties also manifest themselves in all or most languages . . . To give a very brief indication of the kinds of properties involved, it can be mentioned that they include: (a) basic combinatorics: e.g., that substantives can combine with specifiers – 'this something~thing', 'someone else', 'one place', 'two parts', 'many kinds'; (b) basic and extended valences of predicates and quantifiers, e.g., that *do* has patient and instrument valences such as 'do something to something' and 'do something with something', and that one allows a partitive option, in a expressions such as 'one of these things'; (c) the complement options of the mental primes, *know, think* and *want.* (Goddard, 2012:714)

The third important element of the theory is that of semantic molecules: "semantic molecules are complex meanings which are decomposable into combinations of semantic primes but which function as units in the structure of other, more complex concepts. For example, explications for sparrow, owl, and eagle include 'bird' as a semantic molecule; explications for fork, spoon, and plate include 'eat'; explications for walk and run include 'feet' and 'ground'" (Goddard, 2012:720).

Fourth, the theory relies on what the authors call templates, as proposed in Goddard (2012:724): "in NSM theory, a semantic template is a structured set of component types shared by words of a particular semantic class." Goddard goes on to describe the activity templates as follows: "for bodily locomotion and routine physical activities, the Manner section describes a coordinated set of body-part movements. For complex physical activities, the Instrument section describes an Instrument and how it is used, and the nature of the incremental effect that this exercises on the object (what is happening to the object)" (2012:725–728).

The theory also relies on the cultural scripts: "one of the key techniques for ethnopragmatic description, used extensively by contributors to this volume, is the 'cultural script.' Essentially, this refers to a statement – framed largely or entirely within the non-ethnocentric macrolanguage of semantic primes – of some particular attitude, evaluation, or assumption, which is hypothesized to be widely known and shared among people of a given speech community" (Goddard, 2011:5) and "'cultural scripts' as understood in this article are representations of cultural norms that are widely held in a given society and that are reflected in language, in culture-specific keywords, phrases, conversational routines, and so on" (Wierzbicka, 2002:401).

Goddard (2002:15–16) expressly discusses some lexical differences between the primes in various languages. Similarly, Goddard (2012:728–733) features section 5, titled "Crosslinguistic comparison using semantic templates," where NSM templates are used to demonstrate the similarities and the differences in action verbs between English and several other languages.

It would follow from the NSM theory that the root of cross-linguistic variation lies in the fact that different languages build different semantic molecules, and that their semantic templates as well as their cultural scripts differ too.

Differences in the molecules and frames, in addition to the cultural scripts, are what definitely affect a large number of cases where Slavic languages exibit peculiarities. This encompasses the cases where they differ from one another and those where they have something in common but different from non-Slavic languages. To exemplify the molecules: *hands* is *ręce* in Polish, which can also be *arms*; *long* is either *долгий* or *длинный* in Russian, depending on what it is applied to, *money* in Serbo-Croatian is *novac* (more formal) or *pare* (more colloquial but still standard). While we can clearly see that at the level of the molecules, markers of cultural identity abound, the categories of molecules, established in Goddard (2012:723), cannot be seen as a predictor of the types of differences in Slavic languages or their probability. There is no evidence that the level of differences in, for example, body parts is any higher than in topological items or mechanical objects. Additionally, the fact that the molecules are anisomorphic does not necessarily mean that the lexical item described in such a manner to include that particular molecule will also be different from its equivalent in another language.

Let us now turn to the templates. They comprise four components: a lexico-syntactic frame, a prototypical motivational scenario, the manner (for any routine activity) or instrument (for a complex activity), and the potential outcome. Comparing the English word *drink* with Kalam *ñb* 'eat/drink', Goddard (2012:728–730) has demonstrated that the differences can be found in motivational scenarios. The one in Kalam does not include something like water, and the manner; something stays in the mouth for a short period in Kalam, and for a very short period in English. It is thus quite clear that the differences in the frames can lead to certain types of cross-linguistic differences (in this case application splits). One can also find examples for the differences in lexico-syntactic frames, e.g., the Slavic perfective and imperfective verbs, when compared to the English aspect-neutral verbs. The same perfective versus imperfective verbs, if they are resultative as in Czech *dĕlat* 'to be doing' and *udĕlat* 'to get done, to finish doing', show the difference in the potential outcomes segment of the NSM template. We see that all segments of the proposed templates are relevant to pinpointing the differences. However, it is impossible to see the link between the differences relevant here and particular segments of the templates.

Similar is the situation with NSM cultural scripts. While we can see the differences based on incongruent prototypes and concept-based zero equivalence, which can be seen from the analysis of Russian cultural scripts (Wierzbicka, 2002), the scripts cannot be used as predictors of general Slavic cross- and intercultural differences. They can, however, certainly be included in such analysis but across a complete dataset, including those that are shared with other cultures.

To sum up, NSM theory proposes tools for cross-linguistic comparison, consisting of universal constituent semantic elements that are organized in individual languages in culture-specific and language-specific configurations. The theory has first proposed semantic primitives, the most elementary semantic constituents (e.g., *this, bad, I*) and added other elements such as molecules, frames, scripts, etc. in the course of the further development of the theory.

One problem leading to the incompatibility of the present approach with the NSM theory (some points of difference have already been indicated in the review of the theory) is that practical endeavors, like the one in this book, need to minimize the amount of information at the level of description. In sharp contrast to that, NSM is most intricate at the level of concrete descriptions at the surface, to use a spatial metaphor, due in part to the fact that NSM operates with a very limited number of elements at its deepest level. The detail of its descriptions makes them undeployable.

To exemplify this, let us look at the extremely long explication of the Polish word *ojczyzna* (roughly 'fatherland'). The approach relies on some fifty semantic primes (the elements at its deepest level), which makes the description of lexical items too long to be deployed in the kind of endeavors envisaged here, as seen from the following example of an exceptionally long explication, adapted from Wierzbicka (1997:190):

ojczyzna
  (a) a country
  (b) I was born in this country
  (c) I am like a part of this country
  (d) I can't be like a part of any other country
  (e) this country is like a part of me

(f) when I think about this country, I feel something good
(g) if I didn't, this would be very bad
(h) I think something like this when I think about this country
(i) this country is not like any other country
(j) this country is like a person
(k) many bad things happened to this country
(l) I don't want bad things to happen to this country
(m) this country did many good things for me
(n) like a mother does good things for her children
(o) I want to do good things for this country
(p) if I feel something bad because of this I don't want not to do these things because of this
(q) many other people think the same when they think about this country
(r) these people feel something good when they think about this country
(s) these people are like one thing
(t) I am like a part of this thing
(u) these people say things in the same way
(v) these people do many things in the same way
(w) these people think about many things in the same way
(x) these people often feel in the same way
(y) when I think about these people, I feel something good
(z) these people are like a part of this country
(z′) before this time, for a long time many other people were like a part of this country

The epistemological construct proposed here would be much more attuned to an information-reduction theoretical approach, based on establishing a set of standard situations and deviations from a default parameter setting, which would be a replacement for markedness, following the suggestion of Haspelmath (2006). In other words, rather than assuming that Slavic languages share some components in common (which eventually makes the descriptions overly intricate to be deployed), one could assume that all of them are unique with a great deal of overlap between them, much greater than with other languages. If that overlap is the default parameter setting, then all we need in a description of cross-linguistic differences is the deviation from this default.

Cultural linguistics is the third relevant research approach to be examined here. Palmer (1996), an early proponent of cultural linguistic research, sees this line of research as stemming from the traditions of anthropological linguistics and cognitive linguistics. For Palmer, a central concept of cultural linguistics (in addition to language itself) is imagery:

In my own view, language is the play of verbal symbols that are based in imagery. Imagery is what we see in our mind's eye, but it is also the taste of a mango, the feel of walking in a tropical downpour, the music of *Mississippi Masala*. Our imaginations dwell on experiences obtained through all the sensory modes, and then we talk. (Palmer, 1996:3)

He identifies the following topics of particular importance in this approach: cultural knowledge embedded in metaphor and metonymy, cognitive models and schemas in recurrent topical areas (e.g., body parts), shared understanding of conventional scenarios, which govern traditional narratives, folk taxonomies that define the essence of things, and semantic imagery of sociolinguistic events. Concrete examples of this kind of analysis are provided throughout Palmer's book.

Obviously, Palmer continues a well-established tradition of cross-cultural study of metaphors in cognitive linguistics, as presented in Steen (2007), Kövecses (2005), Lakoff and Johnson (1999), and earlier in Lakoff and Johnson (1980), and lastly Langacker (1987 and 1991). In the rich body of cognitive linguistic literature on this subject, Kövecses (2005) is of special importance, and especially the three sections on variation in metaphors (pp. 65–294). Kövecses establishes the dimensions along which metaphors vary (cross-cultural variation and within-culture variation), which elements of metaphors are affected (e.g., experiential basis, source domain, target domain), and the causes of variation; differential experience, which includes sociocultural context, history, human concerns, and cognitive preferences and styles, whereby the latter includes experiential focus, metaphors and metonymy, as well as blending.

The close relation between language and culture in Humboldt's Weltansicht hypothesis was further developed in American anthropological linguistics of the twentieth century, another important source of present-day cultural linguistics. The idea of linguistic relativity (also known as linguistic determinism) comes very strongly in the Sapir–Whorf hypothesis, the best-known intellectual product of this school of thought. This notion is succinctly expressed in Whorf (1940:247):

We cut nature up, organize it into concepts, and ascribe significances as we do, largely because we are parties to an agreement to organize it in this way – an agreement that holds throughout our speech community and is codified in the patterns of our language. The agreement is, of course, an implicit and unstated one, *but its terms are absolutely obligatory*; we cannot talk at all except by subscribing to the organization and classification of data which the agreement decrees.

This set of ideas was given further elaboration in Sapir (1921) and Whorf (1956), among others. If we leave aside the controversial direction of influence, if and how much a language influences its culture, and the fact that numerous findings of twentieth-century American anthropological linguistics have now been refuted, what is important in this intellectual tradition is its strong emphasis on cross-cultural and cross-linguistic anisomorphism. This tradition concurrently offers numerous examples of lexical anisomorphism between English and indigenous languages of the Americas (most notably Hopi and

Navaho). Thus, for example, Whorf (1956:57) discusses "An American Indian Model of the Universe," finding that in Hopi there is no notion of dynamic time, while subjective and objective time is of paramount importance. Similarly, discussing "A Linguistic Consideration of Thinking in Primitive Communities," he finds out that Navajo classifies realities into static objects and dynamic objects, and static objects can be round or long (Whorf, 1956:65).

This general approach evolved into a theoretical model of cultural conceptualizations and language developed by Farzad Sharifian. This interdisciplinary model concurrently relates to several areas of applied linguistics, including intercultural communication, world Englishes and English as an international language, political discourse analysis, and a cluster of theoretical approaches, including distributed cognition, cognitive psychology, cognitive linguistics, cognitive anthropology, complexity science, and anthropological linguistics (see Sharifian, 2011: xvii). He distinguishes the following two segments of this central concept. "Cultural cognition is composed of cultural schemas . . . and cultural categories . . . that can be described as patterns of distributed knowledge across the cultural group" (Sharifian, 2011:5).

A central concept in this model is that of cultural conceptualizations. It is important that the author recognizes the mix of individual and collective factors. "Human conceptualisation is as much a cultural as it is an individual phenomenon" (Sharifian, 2011:3). The author adopts a distributed model of cultural conceptualizations: "cultural cognitions may be best described as networks of distributed representations across the minds in cultural groups" (Sharifian, 2011:3). He further notes: "cognitive networks do not necessarily end with the individual . . . they often enter into larger networks of cognitive interconnection with those of others in a group." He distinguishes the following two segments of this central concept: "cultural cognition is composed of cultural schemas . . . and cultural categories . . . that can be described as patterns of distributed knowledge across the cultural group" (Sharifian, 2011:5). Sharifian (2011:8–11) also mentions the following cultural conceptualizations often discussed in the subject literature: event schemas, role schemas, image schemas, proposition schemas, and emotion schemas. This author characterizes cultural cognition as an emergent complex adaptive system: "cultural cognition is emergent in the sense that it is a gestalt that is more than the sum of its parts and cannot be reduced to the cognition of a single individual in the group." Furthermore, "cultural cognition is also a complex system in that an individual's cognition does not comprise the cultural group's collective and emergent cognition as a whole" (Sharifian, 2011:35). "Because the interactions between the members of a group are not mirror images of each other, the emergent cognition is constantly evolving, making the system adaptive" (Sharifian, 2011:38).

Language is a conduit of cultural conceptualizations: "language is shaped by the cultural conceptualisations that have prevailed at different stages in the history of a speech community and these can leave their traces in current linguistic practice. In this sense language can be viewed as one of the primary mechanisms which stores and communicates cultural conceptualisations. It acts as both a memory bank and a fluid vehicle for the retransmission of these socioculturally embodied cultural conceptualisations" (Sharifian, 2011:39).

To sum up, stemming from the previous traditions of anthropological linguistics, cultural linguistics proposed that cross-cultural differences are expressed in mental imagery (culture-specific metaphors, narratives, etc.) and cultural conceptualizations (culture-specific schemas and categories widely distributed among the members of that culture).

The approach of cultural linguistics offers important and interesting insights. It is much broader than the two previously discussed streams of thought, Slavic linguistic culturology and the NSM theory, in the sense that cultural linguistics does not focus on a narrow set of content or methodological issues. However, it shares the areas of incompatibility with the present project that one can find in the former two approaches. First, the choice of material is rather arbitrary – authors typically select interesting culture-specific examples rather than analyzing a broader dataset and establishing which segments are culturally specific and which are not. Second, there is a related problem that the ground for comparison is not established. Comparison between languages and cultures is performed ad hoc without a clear *tertium comparationis*. Third, cultural linguistics is still isolated and linguocentric, in the sense that it does not tie into a rich body of cross-cultural psychology. Finally, here too, we find an overgeneralized view of an ethnic group or a nation as linguistically and culturally unified.

A final approach to be mentioned here is cross-cultural psychology and cultural anthropology. Although not a linguistic approach, this line of research offers ample opportunity to establish solid ground for linguistic comparison. This line of research includes the authors focusing on concrete and measurable dimensions that vary from one culture to another. The tradition of relevant cross-cultural research can be traced to Hall's classic patterns (see Hall, 1959 and 1966). In cross-cultural psychology, Triandis's opposition of collectivism and individualism gave an early boost to this line of thinking (see Triandis, 1972, 1994a, 1994b, 1995). The field of cross-cultural psychology became a well-established scholarly field, as evidenced, for example, by Berry et al. (1997). Leaving some of its field aside, I will focus on certain culturally relevant oppositions established in cultural anthropology and cross-cultural psychology which can be of use in the cross-cultural linguistic research pursued in this book.

The first two relevant distinctions stem from Hall (1959 and 1966). He distinguished between polychronic cultures in which there are multiple timelines and the monochronic ones, where time is one distinct timeline. One consequence of such a construal of time is that in monochronic cultures personal relations are subordinate to the schedule of activities with inflexible appointment time, while in polychronic cultures the schedule of activities is subordinate to personal relations and the appointment time is flexible. Furthermore, personal and work time are separated in monochronic cultures and fused in polychronic cultures; members of monochronic cultures complete one task at a time and the members of polychronic cultures juggle many tasks at one time. Finally, time is tangible, inflexible, and activities are measurable on a timeline in monochronic cultures, while it is fluid and flexible in polychronic cultures, with activities measured as they contribute to the overall goal rather than on a timeline. Hall's other classic pattern relates to how much needs to be stated in a given culture and how much needs to be inferred from the context. We can then distinguish high-context cultures, where a great deal is inferred from the context rather than expressly stated and low-context cultures, where overt statements are more common.

Hofstede and Hofstede (1994) established the following distinctions: power distance (the level of tolerance for unequal distribution of power in the society), individualism/collectivism, masculinity/femininity, and uncertainty avoidance. A certain degree of overlap exists between this approach and that of Trompenaars and Hampden-Turner (1997). The latter approach will be excluded from this analysis given that they are tailored primarily to the business environment and that many dimensions result in effects, rather than underlying patterns.

Finally, the Schwartz Value Inventory (Schwartz, 1994) distinguishes between values at the individual level and those at the level of the culture. Only the latter is relevant in the present analysis. Schwartz distinguishes seven value types and three value dimensions. He arranges values in a circle, placing diametrically opposed values opposite each other in the circle. Conservatism is opposed to individual autonomy and affective autonomy (the three value types on one dimension), a harmonious relationship with the environment is opposed to mastery of the environment (the second dimension with two value types), and hierarchy is opposed to egalitarianism (the third dimension with two value types).

In social psychology, there are also numerous studies devoted to narrower issues in cross-cultural differences. A good example is Nisbett (2003) where a number of such studies is presented in a non-technical manner.

Summing up, one can say that various authors in the fields of cultural anthropology and cross-cultural psychology have established a number of broad dimensions (mostly construed as scales between two polar opposites such as individualism and collectivism) that assume different values in different cultures.

All previously discussed value types established by Hall, Hofstede and Hofstede, and Schwartz can be used as a ground for a consistent internal and external comparison of Slavic lexicons at large. The first step in each dimension would be to establish the predominant value type in the Slavic languages in question and then look for linguistic expression of such value types.

2.2 The Research Traditions of the Exchange Layer

The research on lexical transfer is a well-established field of research in all Slavic linguistic traditions. On the one hand, there exists a tradition of documenting foreign words in general and from particular languages or language groups in dictionaries and monographs. On the other hand, there is a growing body of research in the field of contact linguistics that addresses loanwords. The review of the relevant research traditions will commence with more theoretically oriented approaches to linguistic contact (quite naturally, focusing on those in the lexical sphere). I will then proceed to the monographs about lexical borrowing.

The overarching approach for the study of lexical borrowing is linguistic contactology. Globally, a rigorous scholarly study of linguistic contact was initiated by Weinreich (1953), who certainly incorporated all earlier important contributions. Of particular importance for lexical borrowing is Haugen (1950). The line of work he had initiated has spread into a variety of directions as evidenced, among others, by Goebl et al. (1996/1997), Coetsem (2000), Thomason (2001), Myers-Scotton (2002), Winford (2003, 2005), Matras (2009), Hickey (2012), Paulasto et al. (2014), and Comrie and Golluscio (2015). One should note that a significant portion of this research tradition is not pertinent to the present study, as it addresses phenomena such as bilinguals, creoles, etc., but practically every publication will at least briefly discuss lexical borrowing. The study of linguistic contact in Slavic linguistics is equally strong. It is particularly strong in the Slavic south, where one should mention the seminal work of Filipović (1986), which influenced numerous studies in Ivir and Kalogjera (1991), and a more recent Ajduković (2004a). The latter author provides an excellent review of the field of contactology, distinguishing five phases in its development that have led to the current body of knowledge (Ajduković, 2004a:9–47). Further contributions include Russian authors Rozencvejg (1972a and 1972b), Zhluktenko (1989), Karlinskij (1990), Bazilev (1999), Zahvataeva (2010), and others. The field of linguistic contactology comprises various other areas, such as bilingualism, code-switching, creoles, pidgins, grammatical borrowing. Lexical transfer is just a very limited area of research within linguistic contactology. In the field of lexical transfer, there is a preponderance of one single topic – the adaptation of the loanwords or their meanings in the recipient language. The topics within contactology other than lexical borrowing are generally not of interest here given that my concern here lies in what lexical elements determine the cultural identities of the speakers of certain standard languages and macrolanguages. There will certainly be some bilinguals among those speakers, some of them will code-switch, and there will even be some creole-like language forms like *trasyanka* and *surzhyk* in the Slavic East. However, these are just marginal phenomena which generally remain outside of the scope of the present monograph. My main focus here lies in borrowed lexical stock, its sources and subject-matter fields, in which one particular source may be more prominent than another and where each source shapes the cultural identity of the speakers of a given language or group of languages.

The specific set of research topics relevant in this monograph is the theory of lexical borrowing. The body of literature about lexical borrowing is vast. Thus, the Modern Language Association (2017) records 2,021 bibliographical units under the subject-matter heading "loanwords." Such units have been present since 1895 and their sharp increase takes place in the 1980s (from 16 records in the previous decade to 382 in the 1980s). One should emphasize again the fact that a great deal of this research tradition busies itself with the adaptation of borrowings (Simonović, 2015 offers a good example with a review of the previous research tradition in the field of adaptation), which is generally not of interest here. The number of relevant publications is thus considerably narrower than the previously mentioned MLA numbers would suggest.

Ever since Haugen (1950), the following types of borrowing have been distinguished: direct loanwords, where the whole word is borrowed, e.g., Russian *офис* from English *office*, and loan blends, where domestic and borrowed material coexists in the same word, e.g., Serbo-Croatian *samoreklama* – *samo-* 'self', inherited, and *reklama*, from German *Reklame*, and loan shifts, such as semantic shifts, e.g., Polish *mysz* 'mouse, rodent > computer implement' and loan translation, e.g., Serbo-Croatian *neboder* (lit. 'skyripper') based on English *skyscraper*. These distinctions are still relevant, as demonstrated by Haspelmath (2009:38–40).

As early as in Bloomfield (1933), an important distinction between cultural and contact borrowing was established. Bloomfield devotes one chapter of his book to cultural borrowing (in which new concepts and ideas are adopted) and another to what he calls intimate borrowing (where languages in contact exchange words that do not have to be related to "cultural novelties"). The third type of borrowing (dialectal) is not of interest here because it remains within the same language (between two dialects or the standard and dialects). This distinction between cultural and contact borrowing is crucial here given that the first kind of borrowing has a much higher prominence in building cultural identity. For example, Greco-Latin lexical heritage is what creates the cultural identity of numerous European cultures, dividing them from other cultures such as Japanese and, even more so, Chinese.

Very early on, researchers were considering the relation between inherited and borrowed lexical items. Thus Deroy (1954) distinguishes causes and pretexts of borrowing to differentiate between practical necessity (discussed in chapter 6, titled "Nécessité pratique," in French – this is commonly called "necessary loans") and emotional reasons (chapter 7, "Raisons de cœur"), which are known as "luxury loans," where there already exists an inherited word that covers the concept. Obviously, the contemplation of borrowing moved away from this initial distinction. In a recent publication, Onysko and Winter-Froemel (2011) distinguish two types of borrowings, based on their semantic and pragmatic effect, where catachrestic means 'not used in the strict sense':

We apply the terminology of catachrestic and non-catachrestic innovations to two complementary types of incremental or additive language change. The fundamental linguistic criterion to distinguish between these two types of innovations is tied to the question of whether the concept designated by the new expression (the innovation) is already expressed by another lexical unit in the language or not. This essentially means taking an onomasiological perspective. (Onysko and Winter-Froemel, 2011:1554)

In Haspelmath (2009) necessary loans evolve into *cultural borrowings* and luxury loans into *core borrowings*. He also adds a third type, namely *therapeutic borrowings*, which include taboo borrowing and borrowing to avoid homonymy. Capturing the relationship between inherited and borrowed lexical items is crucial in studying lexical layers of cultural identity. As will be seen throughout the text of this monograph, the competition between inherited and borrowed is often an important contributor to shaping the cultural identity of speakers.

There were also attempts to determine the degree of borrowability, as in Van Hout and Muysken (1994). Studies like Poplack et al. (1988) have demonstrated the link between borrowing and various social factors (such as integration, etc.). While such studies are only tangentially relevant there, one should be aware of the fact that the cultural and geographical aspects of borrowing interfere with various constraints to borrowability and that they are modulated by diverse social factors at the level of the person.

Coetsem (2000) has proposed *A General and Unified Theory of the Transmission Process in Language Contact*. Although his theory comprises a broader set of phenomena such as bilingualism, language learning, creoles, etc., numerous points relevant for the present research have been distinguished. Coetsem's (2000:49–104) integrated model assumes two principal types of lexical transfer, between the source and the recipient language: borrowing with recipient language agentivity, i.e., the pull transfer, and imposition with source language agentivity, i.e., the push transfer. These two transfer types are affected by a stability gradient, where borrowing concerns generally less stable elements of the recipient language, while imposition influences more stable elements. Two basic transmission operations are imitation, in which the recipient language imitates the pattern of the source language, and adaptation, where the source language pattern is adapted to the recipient language. Borrowing can lead to inclusion and eventually integration. While this theory strives to elucidate a wider set of phenomena, for the purposes of the present study these distinctions are important, as they can explain the role of the lexical strata in shaping cultural identity. That role is fundamentally different in each of the established categories. Furthermore, they help us to understand the attitudes toward transfer-related lexical items, as those in consequence of imitation are judged by normative linguists, especially in Slavic countries, not to be, as they would put it, "in the spirit of the language." This line of research goes on, as demonstrated by Winford (2005), who mostly concentrates on bilingualism and creoles.

One further relevant concept is that of motivation for borrowing. Hock (1986:408–421) distinguishes the following types of motivation: need, prestige, linguistic nationalism, and taboo. Needless to say, these categories have been discussed ever since Weinreich (1953). Other studies point out the factors that need to be addressed in analyzing the lexicon in contact situations. The three discussed are: "(1) the pertinent sociolinguistic factors at play in given contact situations; (2) the pertinent cognitive processes that mediate between the languages in contact; and (3) the pertinent dynamic processes of lexical unit formation" (Mathiot and Rise, 1996/1997:129). A number of review articles in Goebl et al. (1996/1997) have discussed relevant sociolinguistic factors. What seems to be most pertinent to language-to-language borrowing (as opposed to those at the level of the speaker) is nationality (Olivesi, 1996/1997), ethnicity (Devetak, 1996/1997), language policy (Labrie, 1996/1997a), territoriality (Labrie, 1996/1997b), and identity (Haarman, 1996/1997). A number of articles in Goebl et al. (1996/1997) offer language-contact reviews of various Slavic countries and languages (Neweklowsky, 1996/1997 for Federal Republic of Yugoslavia; Nečak-Lük, 1996/1997 for Slovenia; Pupovac, 1996/1997 for Croatia; Kovačec, 1996/1997 for Bosnia and Herzegovina; Fielder, 1996/1997 for Bulgaria; Friedman, 1996/1997 for Macedonia; Kramer, 1996/1997 for Bulgarian-Macedonian relations; Rokoszowa, 1996/1997 for Poland; Treder, 1996/1997 for Polish-Cashubian relations; Zeman, 1996/1997 for Czech-Slovak relations; Ondrejovič, 1996/1997 for Slovakia; Nekvapil, 1996/1997 for the Czech Republic; Gustavsson, 1996/1997 for Belarus; Britsyn, 1996/1997 for Ukraine).

Lexical exchange was also addressed in anthropological linguistics. Sapir (1921:ch. 9, s.v.) thus makes the following important observations: "When there is cultural borrowing there is always the likelihood that the associated words may be borrowed too. … It is generally assumed that the nature and extent of borrowing depend entirely on the historical facts of culture relation … It seems very probable that the psychological attitude of the borrowing language itself towards linguistic material has much to do with its receptivity to foreign words."

Summarizing, one can say that in the vast body of contact linguistic literature, only works on lexical borrowing bear direct relevance to the present project. Within lexical borrowing, a prolific line of research on adaptation is generally not of interest here. I therefore reviewed several key distinctions, including but not limited to cultural versus contact borrowing, core versus cultural borrowing, and various categories of motivation for borrowing.

All the aforementioned distinctions are relevant in the study of lexical layers of identity. The cultural circles from which words are borrowed (e.g., Near Eastern, Western European) clearly profile linguistic and cultural identities of the languages in question. Equally important is the relationship between inherited and borrowed words, which additionally creates an interface with the surface lexical layer. When addressing cultural aspects of loanwords, it is important what the substance of borrowing is, what type of borrowing is at stake, and what are the mechanisms determining the process of borrowing.

2.3   The Research Traditions of the Surface Layer

There are two main topics of interest in lexicological sociolinguistics: standardology and lexical variation. In the field of standardology, the delimitation of standard and non-standard in the lexicon is based here on Ammon (2004), having in mind the complexity of the issue, as also demonstrated by Smakman (2012), and its embeddedness in the culture, as shown by Dittmar (2004). Equally important in the light of the present project are the attitudes toward the lexical stock of the standard language, most notably the attitude of purism (see in particular Thomas, 1991) and nationalism in language policies (see Kordić, 2010).

Ammon (2004) points out the complexity of the idea of standardness.

An entire language (L), then, is a set of varieties (V): $L_1 = \{V_{1a}, \ldots, V_{1n}\}$. Such a set can be dubbed a *standard language* if it contains at least one standard variety; otherwise it is a *non-standard language* or a *vernacular language*. (Ammon, 2004:274)

This begs a more general question of what makes a linguistic form, especially a variant, standard as opposed to non-standard. The answer does not necessarily have to be a strict yes–no distinction, but it could lead to gradations of standardness of linguistic forms, thereby disclosing in detail why there is no clear-cut distinction between standard and non-standard varieties. Another important question is: what exactly makes a standard variety coherent so that it may be regarded as a system, though perhaps an open one and not precisely delimitable. Finally, it remains to be asked: what provides an entire standard language with the coherence that justifies placing standard and non-standard varieties together into a single language? (Ammon, 2004:275)

He then goes on to answer the questions by distinguishing two factors in the configuration. The first is roofing, where only the standard varieties can roof, and only non-standard varieties can be roofed. The term "roof" refers to the language of culture that forms over a dialect. He also talks about mutual distance between the varieties. He differentiates the following possible configurations of these two factors:

If the linguistic distance between two varieties is great, they belong to different languages . . .
  If the linguistic distance between two varieties is medium: . . .
  If one variety roofs the other, or both are roofed by the same variety with no more than medium distance between the roofing variety and the varieties being roofed, then all belong to the same language . . .
  In case of two standard varieties (where neither can roof the other), they belong to different languages. . . .
  If the distance between two varieties is small . . .
  In the case of two standard varieties (where neither can roof the other), both belong to the same language . . .
  In case of two non-standard varieties, each of which is roofed by a different standard variety with both standard varieties belonging to different languages . . . they belong to different languages. (Ammon, 2004:275)

In the context of this monograph, Ammon's approach has a twofold importance. First, it emphasizes the elusiveness of the difference between standard and non-standard. This is most prominent in the lexicon, where there may exist a large area of overlap between the two. Second, it underlines the complexity of the classification of linguistic varieties. The distance between them largely hinges on the differences between their respective lexicons.

In discussing the complexity of the relation between standard and non-standard language forms, one should in particular mention Smakman (2012) who surveyed over one thousand non-linguists from England, Flanders, Japan, the Netherlands, New Zealand, Poland, and the United States and concluded that, although the ideas about the standard language have very little in common, one can recognize a socially distinctive (exclusive) notion of the standard language and socially cohesive (integrative) one. The former notion pertains to the language form that is used only in formal communication (such as the news, official documents, etc.). One should also be aware of the interplay of standardization and ideology, as discussed by Armstrong and Mackenzie (2013).

The topic of lexical variation is connected to that of standardology given that standard languages are both delimited and internally differentiated by the lexicon belonging to different registers, territories, connotative values, etc. One should have in mind the general parameters of sociolinguistic variation outlined in Trudgill (2001), Apte (1994), and others. More specifically, of particular importance here is lexical variation, as discussed in Geeraerts at al. (1994). These authors distinguish the following types of lexical variations:

Semasiological variation
the situation that a particular lexical item may refer to distinct types of referents.

Onomasiological variation
the situation that a referent or type of referent may be named by means of various conceptually distinct lexical categories

Formal variation
the situation that a particular referent or type of referent may be named by means of various lexical items, regardless of whether these represent conceptually different categories or not.

Contextual variation
the situation that variational phenomena of the kind just specified may themselves correlate with contextual factors such as the formality of the speech situation, or the geographical and sociological characteristics of the participants in the communicative interaction. (Geeraerts et al., 1994:3–4)

The most relevant type of variation here is the contextual one. What is particularly important is that variation is a function of speakers' choice. The dynamics of the interaction between elites and the general speaker population stems from the interventions of the elites into speakers' choices and the speakers' compliance or non-compliance with these interventions.

Following this sociocognitive approach, I argue in the present monograph that one should go beyond a purely linguocentric approach to variation and look into the successful attempts to implement certain values, most notably using monolingual dictionaries. That kind of research would connect the topic of variation to the topic of attitudes versus standard and non-standard forms and thus supplement intercultural research by looking into the maneuvers in the surface lexical layer of cultural identity.

An important distinction between restricted and elaborated codes was established by Bernstein (2003:11):

I now had distinguished between two types of speech variants. I have suggested that restricted speech variants are context-dependent, give rise to particularistic orders of meaning, where principles are verbally implicit or simply announced; whereas elaborated speech variants are context-independent, give rise to universalistic orders of meaning, where principles are made verbally explicit and elaborated. I have also suggested, that restricted and elaborated speech variants possess distinctive linguistic features and so by implication the resources of the grammar and lexes will be differently explored.

Dittmar (1976:12) builds upon Bernstein's ideas to come up with a coherent model in which linguistic rules are influenced by social structure and via planning strategies realized as speech forms. The importance of these distinctions is similar to that of later sociocognitive approaches: linguistic variation is inextricably connected to the social structure.

An important contribution is made by Edwards (1985), who studied the relationship between language, society, and identity. He points out that the change is a matter of course in the interface of language and society, and identity is an evolving concept. Any interventions, according to him, are seriously limited. For our purposes, the following conclusion seems to be of particular importance, as it points to the futility of certain language planning efforts (some of which will be mentioned in Chapter 10):

> Language shift and decline have an historical inevitability and have proved impossible to halt or reverse without widespread, draconian or undemocratic methods. As an objective marker of groupness, language is highly susceptible to change; despite its obvious claims on our attention, its continuation is not necessary for the continuation of identity itself. There is evidence to suggest that the communicative and symbolic aspects of language are separable during periods of change, such that the latter can continue to exercise a role in group identity in the absence of the former. Failure to recognise this separability and inaccurate notions of the indispensability of communicative language for group continuity may lead to unwise and fruitless intervention attempts. (Edwards, 1985:169)

Slavic scholars have contributed to the study of standardology and lexical variation research in Slavic scholarship. One can mention in particular Vinogradov (1967), Brozović (1970), and Jedlička (1978), Daneš (1979), Havránek (1980), Tolstoj (1988), and Ondrejovič (2011), who elucidated the emergence of Slavic standard languages and standard languages in general and who have established important concepts in delineating standard language forms from their non-standard counterparts and understanding the range of planning activities around those standards.

Cvrček (2006) discusses the scope, content, and criteria of normative codification. The criteria of codification are of particular importance given that they are directly applicable to lexical choices. The criteria are normativity, functionality, systematicity, and all-national character. Čermák (2006) discusses prescriptivism as an important ingredient in the surface layer of Slavic languages through the lens of stability in relation to variation. He concludes his paper with the following reasonable warning to the prescriptivists (and the fact that such a warning needs to be issued is telling): "Stabilita jazyka je dána přirozeným územ, a nikoliv diktátem" (Language stability is given by natural usage, and not by a dictate) (Čermák, 2006:44).

An important ingredient of the surface layer in Slavic languages is the notion of the culture of language or culture of speech (*культура речи* or *культура языка* in Russian, *kultura języka* in Polish, *jezička kultura* in Serbo-Croatian). The literature on the culture of language is vast (e.g., in Russian: Vinokur, [1929] 2006; Uspenskij, 1976; Skvorcov, 1980; Strel'čuk, 2012; and many others), which demonstrates that this notion is part and parcel of Slavic normative linguistics. Of particular importance for us here is the work of the Polish linguist Andrzej Markowski (2004–2005, 2005), who discusses lexical correctness (i.e., lexical usage consistent with the standard language norms) in the second half of his 2005 book. Among other things, he develops a very precise classification of the deviation from lexical norms. The categories of deviations from lexical norms include superfluous words and idioms (those that are used although better lexical solutions exist), erroneously understood words and idioms, words mixed with others, the extension of meaning as a consequence of lexical errors, modification of the form of words and idioms, words and idioms used in an inappropriate context. These categories will be of particular importance in the analysis of the dynamics between the elites and the body of speakers discussed in Chapter 12.

One should also note that the consequences and the social impact of lexical planning that are pertinent here are those in general vocabulary and those spheres of terminologies accessible to the general speaker population. Temmerman (2000), presenting a sociocognitive approach to terminology, showed very convincingly that terminologies are not so far away from general vocabulary as previously postulated in the classical approaches of the Vienna (see Felber, 1984, 2001; Felber and Budin, 1989) and Soviet school (see Danilenko, 1977). However, one can still see that terminologies, especially specialized ones that remain out of the reach of the general body of speakers, may feature norming maneuvers that may be based more in practicality and less in ideology than those in the general lexicon.

To summarize, sociolinguistic lexicology has brought various important categories to our attention. Of these, only those categories that connect lexical use to relevant collective identities are on the backdrop of broader social and historical phenomena. Most notably, the contributions that elucidate the idea of standardness in the use of vocabulary and those that explain certain types of lexical variation are relevant here. The review in this section was then focused on those categories. They will be embedded in the analysis of the surface layer, most notably in the degree that they show the integration and the interaction of this layer with a wider sociohistorical background through the interplay of standardizing elites with the general body of speakers.

2.4   Confrontation of Slavic Languages

The dawn of present-day Slavic studies falls in the late eighteenth and early nineteenth centuries. National revival movements in various Slavic countries brought about the nascence of present-day Slavic linguistic studies, in many environments as a pushback against Germanization or as geopolitical maneuvers against German political influences. It should also be mentioned that Slavic languages played an important role in early Indo-European studies. The role of Slavic languages among Indo-European languages was well elaborated in the work of Karl Brugmann (most notably Brugmann and Delbrück, 1886–1900) and Antoine Meillet (see in particular Meillet, 1903), who followed in the footsteps of Franz Bopp (in particular Bopp, 1853), August Schleicher (1861), and others. That tradition leads to the comparative study of Slavic languages which remained very strong in the late nineteenth century and throughout the twentieth century, in particular in its first six decades, when comparativism was a dominant approach in Slavic studies. The interest was equally strong in non-Slavic countries (e.g., Miklosich, 1875; Vaillant, 1950–1977; Shevelev, 1965) and in Slavic countries (e.g., Nahtigal, 1952 and Bernštejn, 1961, 1974). The Indo-European and the Slavic comparative linguistic tradition alike used biological metaphors of family, kinship, etc., thus promoting the idea of communality in each "linguistic family." Further contributions to this line of thinking were works such as Lehr-Spławiński (1946), who searched for the origin and the ancestral lands of the Slavic people. Even the historiography of the Slavs was initiated by these philological studies. Curta (2001:6) thus notes: "Slavic studies began as an almost exclusively linguistic and philological enterprise." One should also mention the rich tradition of Slavic philology, mostly the study of Slavic historical texts and authors such as Jagić, Sreznevski, Šahmatov, and others as well as publications such as *Archiv für Slavische Philologie.*

The aforementioned period of intense interest in comparing Slavic languages leads to a rich philological tradition, based on the idea of Slavdom, but that tradition started to meander into linguistics (addressing general linguistic rather than specifically Slavic issues) and comparative literature, or more broadly, comparative cultural studies, where comparison goes well beyond Slavdom. How complex the issues are and how much research has evolved since the early comparatist days can be seen in the studies of Slavic enclaves, borderlands, and microlanguages in Kamusella et al. (2016) and Duličenko (2005), which show a high level of sociolinguistc diversity and entanglement with neighboring cultures. The same is true about various reviews of Slavic languages and their lexicons, such as Warchoł (1989), Comrie and Corbett (1993), Sussex and Cubberley (2006), Kamper and Warejko (2007), and Kempgen et al. (2007, 2014). Obviously, the previous tradition of historical approaches to Slavic languages continues, as demonstrated by Gołąb (1991).

There exists a long and prolific tradition of comparative grammars of Slavic languages (Vaillant, 1950–1977; Nahtigal, 1952; Bernštejn, 1961, 1974;

Bošković, 1977; Ivšić, 1979; Stieber, 1979; Mihaljević, 2002–2014; Seliščev, [1919] 2010; to name a few). There is also a tradition of providing reviews of Slavic languages (e.g., Horálek 1955; Kondrašov 1986; Comrie and Corbett 1993; Dalewska-Greń 1997; Sussex and Cubberley 2006; Kempgen et al. 2007; Gutschmidt et al., 2014). The former, as the name would suggest, do not preoccupy themselves with the lexicon, the latter normally do feature sections on the lexicon, but that section is just a fraction devoted to grammatical and other features (for example, in Comrie and Corbett, 1993, the sections devoted to the lexis of each Slavic language constitute on average only some 7 percent of the text devoted to that language).

An early comparison of Slavic core lexical repertoires was conducted by Lekov (1955). If we disregard ideological components of his text characteristic for its time, we can appreciate the attention that it turned to contrasting the lexicons of Slavic languages. Lekov identifies the following fields in the core vocabulary: general nature terms; sky and celestial bodies; natural phenomena; surface of the Earth; metals, geological and mineralogical entities; bodies of water; directions of the compass; seasons; years, months, weeks, days; fauna; flora; birds; fish; human body parts; kinship terms; most frequent actions; adjectives; color terms; basic abstract terms; adverbs; pronouns; numerals; prepositions, conjunctions and particles. He concluded the following about the size of the core vocabulary:

Численоста на основния речников фонд на отделните славянски езици надминава 1300 думи и се доближава до 1600.

(The core vocabulary in each Slavic language surpasses 1300 and approaches 1600 words.) (Lekov, 1955:99)

Lekov also identified the semantic fields of similarities and differences between Slavic languages:

Единството на славянските езици в техния основен речников фонд е само понякога относително, а много често бива и пълно. Най-добре е подчертано то в следните семантични области: физическа природа, външни части на тялото, външни стари болести, елементарни действия, психически прости състояния и др. Освен това почти всички т. н. служебни думи показват старинна еднаквост и жива сегашна функция.

Националното своеобразие на славянските езици в техния основен речников фонд е обикновено относително и почти в никой отделен случай не е пълно. Най-вече то се проявява в наименованията на обекти или действия, свързани с нови страни на градския живот, с означенията на професиите, домашните и др. уреди, облекла, ястия и пр.

(Unity of Slavic languages in their core vocabularies is only occasionally relative, and it is very frequently full. This is most pronounced in the following semantic fields: physical nature, external body parts, external old illnesses, basic actions, simple psychological conditions, etc. Additionally, almost all so-called functional words exhibit ancient uniformity and vivid present function.

National peculiarities of Slavic languages in their core vocabularies is as a rule relative and in almost no particular case full. It is mostly expressed in the names of objects and actions related to new aspects of urban life, with the designations of professions, home and other appliances, garments, food, etc.) (Lekov, 1955:100)

Khodova (1960) talks about the lexical kinship of Slavic languages. She identifies the semantic fields of lexical similarity, largely consistent with Lekov's (1955) categories.

Среди многочисленных общих славянских слов древнего происхождения заметно выделяется ряд семантических групп слов, характеризуемых чертами особой устойчивости. Это названия родственных отношений, предметов и явлений природы, частей тела человека и животных, сельскохозяйственных культур, домашних и диких животных, рыб, занятий, важнейших простых действий и некоторые другие.

(Among numerous common Slavic words of ancient origin, there is a conspicuous layer of semantic groups of words characterized by the features of particular stability. These are kinship terms, objects and events in nature, human and animal body parts, farming cultures, domestic and wild animals, fish, occupations, the most important simple actions and some others.) (Khodova, 1960:14)

In a similar line of research Suprun (1983:43–44) established the following parameters for typological study of Slavic lexicons: quantitative characteristics of the size of the lexicon, representation of various semantic-thematic fields in the lexicon, statistical structure of the lexicon, lexical similarity of contrasted languages, part-of-speech classification, lexical and inflectional morphological characteristics of the lexicon, the semantic structure of the lexicon, stylistic stratification of the lexicon, associative characteristics, collocational characteristics, and external characteristics of the words (length, beginnings and ends, etc.). Although some of his measurements based on large monolingual Slavic dictionaries seem somewhat arbitrary, Suprun should be given credit for identifying the fields where lexical identity of Slavic languages can be studied. His fields are concrete and measurable and, as it will be seen further in this text, they are largely incorporated in the present approach.

Another important author is Bierich (2011), who turns attention to the need for a more comprehensive and systematic analysis of cultural linguistic facts in Slavic languages.

Die gesammelten sprachlichen und extralinguistischen Fakten müssen einer detaillierten Analyse unterzogen werden: etymologischen, ideographischen (anhand von semantischen Feldern), kontrastiven (im Rahmen der Varietäten einer Sprache bzw. verschiedener verwandter und nicht-verwandter Sprachen) usw. Nur durch solch eine umfassende Analyse kann man der Gefahr entgehen, dass einzelne isolierte sprachliche

Fakten zu nationalen kulturellen Schlüssel-Begriffen erklärt werden, ohne dabei zu überprüfen, ob ähnliche kulturelle Erscheinungen nicht doch in anderen Sprachen existieren.

(The totality of linguistic and extralinguistic facts have to be subjected to a detailed analysis: etymological, ideographical (because of the semantic fields), contrastive (between the varieties of one language and also different related and non-related languages), etc. It is only in such comprehensive analysis that one can avoid the danger to declare certain isolated linguistic facts to be key national cultural concepts without checking if similar cultural phenomena exist in other languages.) (Bierich, 2011:147)

Along with these general comparisons of the Slavic lexicon, one should note microanalyses of particular semantic fields. Thus Herne (1954) analyzes color terms in Slavic languages. However, this study is mostly concerned with etymological and semasiological aspects of these terms, most notably with establishing the timeline of their emergence. There are also analyses of the lexicon of one Slavic language against the backdrop of the Slavic language group. Thus Popowska-Taborska and Boryś (1996) analyze Kashubian in this manner and Jankowiak (1997) examines the status of Proto-Slavic lexical heritage in contemporary Polish. While these works do not strive to engage in a cultural profiling of the Slavic languages in question, the material they are presenting may constitute a starting point for such analysis.

A recent diachronic study of the development of Slavic lexicons is Markova (2016), who traced, using mostly Russian and Czech data, the semantic evolution of Proto-Slavic nouns in present-day Slavic languages. Among other things, Markova (2016:101–176) establishes the following taxonomy of semantic transformation types of the inherited Proto-Slavic lexical units: widening of the meaning, narrowing of the meaning, semantic widening of the etymological root, the development of distinctive features of a general semantics of the cognate, entantiosemy, metaphorical transfer, metonymical transfer, stylistic displacement of the lexeme, development of a connotative meaning of the lexeme, conceptual peculiarities of lexical units.

I have already mentioned Bartmiński (2005), who proposed the comparison of Slavic languages in the following segments: the expression of collective identity, the construal of others, the ways of conceptualizing one's own place, the ways of conceptualizing the collective time, obligatory and stylistic values, as well as style differentiation. Another kind of comparison, based on association networks is proposed by Piper (2003). Practical application of this method on Serbian can be seen in Dragićević (2010b and 2016). Occasionally, collections of papers, such as Alekseenko (2006) are devoted to the connection of broadly understood culture and Slavic languages.

Tolstoj (1997–1999) proposes a specific kind of analysis based on ethnocultural comparison in semantic fields and on semasiological analysis:

Выявление семантической разности слов конкретных диалектов (языков) может быть успешно проведено при обращении к семантической сетке с достаточной дробностью клеток (микрополя). Путем вычитания объема одной семемы из другой могут быть установлены разности, равные отдельным семантическим дифференциальным признакам (СДП, или семам).

(The expression of semantic differences of the words of concrete dialects (languages) can be successfully conducted utilizing a semantic network with an adequate differentiation of the cells (of the microfield). By matching the scope of one sememe from the other, one can establish differences equal to the separate semantic differential features (SDF, or semes).) (Tolstoj, 1997–1991, I:21)

What is important here is the emphasis on the density of semantic fields and on concrete semantic procedure for their comparison. One should also note that the *Slavic Linguistic Atlas* (www.slavatlas.org) offers rich lexical dialectal material for Slavic comparisons, as its questionnaire (MKS, 1965) contains lexical questions (pp. 60–65) and semantic questions (pp. 66–67).

Another field where important areas of differences between Slavic languages were identified are translation studies, such as an early contribution by Kosta (1986). He identified the problems of translating a Czech text into West and South Slavic languages, paying special attention to meaningful names, idioms, proverbs, and so on.

All the aforementioned contrastive studies of Slavic languages at the deep level point to various important areas of differences, thus building ground for a more comprehensive and systematic study of the deep layer.

There are important contrastive studies of Slavic languages in the exchange layer. Of special importance is Grenoble (2012), who surveyed contact phenomena between Slavic and non-Slavic languages (Iranian, Fino-Ugric, Western European) and internal Slavic phenomena (e.g., Czecho-Slovak, East Slavic). One aspect of the contact phenomena addressed in Grenoble's chapter is lexical transfer. The shaping of the Slavic lexicon by lexical borrowing is documented from the earliest Proto-Slavic periods. Balto-Slavic lexical contact commanded considerable attention starting initially as a small part of a larger debate about the possible existence of a Balto-Slavic protolanguage (which included too many voices to be listed here and which was considered essntially wrong by some such as Ivanov and Toporov, 1958). Intensive exploration of early Balto-Slavic contacts still goes on as evidenced, for example, by the volumes of *Балто-славянские исследования* (1972–, most recently Institut slavjanovedenia RAN, 2014). Early Germanic lexical borrowing in Proto-Slavic is documented by Pronk-Tiethoff (2013). Rozwadowski (1961) analyzed Iranian borrowings and Trubačev (1999), and Lehr-Spławiński (1957) did the same for Latin. Needless to say, there is a plethora of studies addressing lexical borrowing from non-Slavic and Slavic languages in each particular Slavic language. While the list of those

Standard Colloquial Language

Prestandard Literary Language   Dialects

Borrowed Literary Language   Literary Coine

Local Dialects

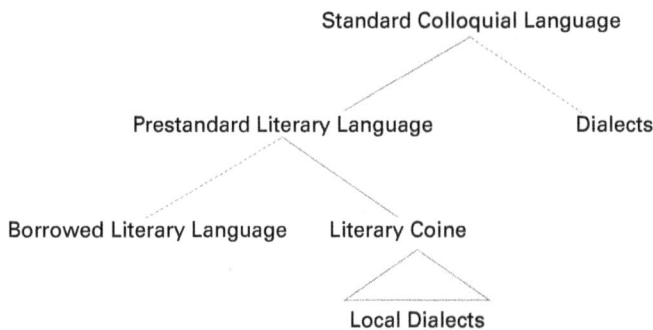

Figure 2.1 Sources of Slavic standard languages (adapted from Hill and Lehman, 1988:140)

studies is too long to be mentioned here, one should note that these studies along with Slavic dictionaries of loanwords constitute excellent material for the contrastive study of the exchange layer, for example by contrasting the status of German loanwords in Serbo-Croatian based on the material from Golubović (2007) with the same group of loanwords in Polish based on Vincenz and Hentschel (2010).

Of contrastive studies that created ground for the study of the surface layer, one should mention Hill and Lehman (1988). It is of particular importance that Lehman points out the regularities in the formation of standard Slavic languages, which involves the relationships with the language varieties shown in Figure 2.1.

Another important building block from this book is Peter Hill's analysis of lexical revolutions in the South Slavic realm as an expression of nationalism (1988:147–157). Yet another important contribution is Lučić (2002), where the lexical norm after the liberal revolutions of the 1989 in the Slavic world is explored through the prism of lexicographic activities.

An important division in the contrastive study of Slavic languages was introduced by Picchio (1984:3):

We may take as a point of departure for our considerations the division of historical Slavdom into two main areas, belonging to the jurisdiction of the Eastern Orthodox Churches (*Slavia orthodoxa*) and to that of the Roman Church (*Slavia romana*) respectively. This historiographic scheme is widely accepted. To avoid misunderstandings, we should only add a general remark: the boundary lines between the two cultural areas of Orthodox Slavdom and Roman Slavdom were never fixed in a definite way. Thus, we can speak of zones of mixed or overlapping influence (for example, Great Moravia, the Glagolitic area in Croatia, Bosnia, the Ukraine and Belorussia). This means that concepts of Slavia orthodoxa and of Slavia romana apply to cultural traditions rather than to territorial or administrative units.

This distinction has had considerable traction in Slavic studies and it is of particular importance for cultural identity. The areas of overlap and unclear boundaries between the two spheres are noteworthy, especially in Ukraine and the Balkans. Greenberg and Nomachi (2012) supplemented this division by talking about *Slavia islamica*.

One should also mention works like Panzer (2000) which gather reports on (mostly lexical) changes in Slavic languages after the fall of communism. There also exists a stream of research that explores the cultural identity of Slavic languages from the viewpoint of microlanguages and borderlands (Duličenko, 1981, 2005; Gustavsson, 1998; Stern and Voss, 2006). Finally, one should mention works like Bartschat (2009), Breu (2009), Hill (2014a and 2014b), Hinrichs (2014), Lubaś (2014), Marti (2014), Mokienko (2009a and 2009b), and Windgender (2014), which discuss various linguistic and socio-linguistic aspects in contrasting Slavic languages.

Summarizing, one can say that the Slavic research tradition offers numerous insights into the aspects of Slavic lexicons relevant to cultural identity of their speakers. Some are only tangentially relevant, others crucially. One should note that the mid twentieth century featured intense interest in contrasting Slavic lexicons, which ebbs with the flow of time, leaving important contributions by and large forgotten as the main focus of research moved elsewhere.

All of the aforementioned contributions introduce numerous important observations and the data for further research. I will now turn to proposing research methodology for the study of the three lexical layers of cultural identity, which includes important contributions from the literature reviewed in this chapter that also attempts to overcome the methodological shortcomings of the previously proposed approaches.

The review of the literature in the field leaves us with a wish list of sorts. Certain explorations could be possible, but they are missing crucial gear. What is needed for a comprehensive investigation of the lexical layers of cultural identity can succinctly be described as follows:

a. An approach that would encompass all lexical layers of cultural identity and all players involved in its creation;
b. Perspectives from various fields of linguistics and social sciences needed to elucidate the layers and their stakeholders;
c. Techniques that explore datasets in their entirety or consistent samples, that approach the language as a separate (albeit connected) entity from ethnicity, nation, etc., and that leave room for random events.

It is precisely that kind of approach and such perspectives and techniques that the present monograph is advocating, and that places this endeavor at an equidistance from each of the previously discussed approaches. Given the boundaries of what any pioneering exploration can do, I am trying to make a first step toward a more systematic exploration of Slavic cultural identities

(identities of speakers of particular Slavic languages and a more general Slavic identity) by sketching a general outline of an epistemological construct that I deem a promising tool for the explanation of Slavic cultural identities, applicable mutatis mutandis to other languages and language groups. The datasets used here are therefore primarily the tools of exemplifying the deployment of the construct.

3 Research Methodology

The epistemological construct proposed in this book strives to provide an inclusive and systematic tool for the study of lexical markers of cultural identity. The rich body of literature outlined in Chapter 2 has been making important contributions to our better understanding of the interplay of language and culture while raising intercultural awareness and sensitivity. However, large areas of cultural identity markers remain excluded from the analysis, and the analysis is often methodologically unsound. As discussed in the previous chapter, at least some of the following problems can be identified in practically every approach: isolationism, particularism, elitism, atomism, determinism, ethnocentrism, arbitrariness, and feasibility.

The proposal is intended to eliminate the aforementioned shortcomings of mainstream cross-cultural anthropocentric linguistics. First, the three layers require a methodological apparatus from cross-cultural linguistics (mostly in the deep layer), contactology (i.e., the study of linguistic contacts, in the exchange layer), and lexicological sociolinguistics (in the surface layer). Second, the methodological apparatus from all three linguistic approaches should be connected to the dimensions established in cross-cultural psychology and anthropology. In addition to these three innovations, the following principles of analysis are advocated and demonstrated:

a. Comprehensiveness – all members of the category are analyzed rather than just those individual cases that confirm research claims;
b. Stakeholders complexity sensitivity – the analysis distinguishes between the body of speakers and linguistic elites and sees both these entities as most diversified collectives;
c. Multi-perspectiveness – various linguistic and extra-linguistic perspectives are brought into the analysis;
d. Linguistic autonomism – recognizing that languages do not necessarily have to overlap with ethnic groups and that linguistic identity concerns speakers of languages rather than members of ethnic groups;
e. Sensitivity to linguistic complexity – recognizing the complexity of language varieties, such as dialects and ethnic variants;

Table 3.1 *The characteristics of the three lexical layers of cultural identity*

Layer	Focus	Structure	Changeability	Speakers' control	Elites' presence	Intervention type
Surface	features	random	Fast	real	dominant	direct
Exchange	features	thematic	Slow	potential	limited	indirect
Deep	words	core-periphery	Glacial	negligible	marginal	remote

   f. Limited determinism – understanding that some developments are random and the analysis can account for only a part of phenomena;

   g. Explanatory succinctness – the simplest possible explanatory tools are sought to encompass the broadest and widest fields of the phenomenon being explained.

As previously discussed, speakers are culturally defined in the lexicon by the way their language carves out the world, by their belongingness in certain cultural circles, and by their active role in negotiating their lexical choices. Consequently, in its core the model comprises the deep layer (which consists of relatively stable lexical distinctions and includes core research on language and culture), the exchange layer (which involves slowly evolving material from the lexical transfer between different languages and their cultures and includes linguistic contactology), and the surface layer (comprising engineered and a refereed lexicon susceptible to rapid changes, involving sociolinguistic research). The characteristics of the three layers are presented in Table 3.1.

The features of changeability, speakers' control, elites' presence and their influence are rather straightforward. Thus, it is clear that the changing stable elements of the vocabulary is close to impossible. It is also clear that speakers can reject newly introduced words. It is also clear that the elites are the force behind lexical interventions. Finally, the easily changeable surface layer clearly enables a direct type of intervention. However, the focus of analysis and the structure require some additional explanations.

The focus refers here to the subject of analysis and cross-linguistic comparison. In the deep layer, the focus is on the words, at the level of individual words, looking into culture-specific shaping of concepts into words and the inability to establish equivalence with other languages, and at the level of the lexicon, looking into the parameters of the culture, which make certain lexical fields less or more wide and deep. At the other two levels, the subject of analysis are features ascribed to the words (e.g., a borrowing from German, a non-standard word). In contrast to the dominant cultural linguistic approaches, in the proposed model, the analysis is conducted across the entirety of the criterion in question, taking into account the elites and regular speakers, and leaving room for random developments. The structure refers to the general organization of the layer. At the surface, features are included in the layer randomly; they are dependent on mostly political maneuvers of the elites and the speakers' attitudes toward them. In the exchange layer, the main principle of organization are lexical fields, so the organization is thematic, as in having a dominance of a certain language in one field. Examples of this include English for computer use, Italian in music, or using French to describe cuisine. In the deep layer, there is a core of inherited vocabulary that is supplemented by the lexemes from the exchange and surface layer. Lexical features and clusters in all three layers are explored with the simplest possible epistemological tools, thus making this construct applicable in various domains.

Proposed here are techniques to study each of the three layers and their interaction based on the previously mentioned principles. I will briskly outline these techniques here before they are discussed in detail and exemplified in the material from Slavic languages in Chapters 4–6 for the deep layer, 7–9 for the exchange layer, and 10–12 for the surface layer.

Three major research techniques are proposed for the deep layer: lexeme-level contrastive profiling, lexicon-level contrastive profiling, and divergence tracking. They will be discussed in turn.

Lexeme-level contrastive profiling rests on the idea (elaborated by Šipka, 2016) that the most parsimonious manner to account for lexical peculiarities of any particular language in relation to another is to document the cases of zero equivalence, multiple equivalence, and partial equivalence. Zero equivalence is found in the cases when a word that is present in one language does not have an equivalent in the other, e.g. Serbian *slava* 'family patron saint's day and feast' has no lexical equivalence in English. Multiple equivalence pertains to those situations where one word in one language has two or more equivalents in the other – for example, Polish *ręka* is either 'hand' or 'arm' in English. Finally, partial equivalence assumes that the equivalents in the two observed languages differ in some respect, e.g., Russian *пионер* is a true equivalent of the English *pioneer*, but in English the only prominent meaning has to do with the explorer of a new territory, idea, etc., while in Russian the meaning of the member of the communist pioneer movement is also very prominent. Some of these differences are random or purely mechanical, some are limited to certain periods of time, but a considerable proportion of them is culture-bound.

The natural dataset for conducting lexeme-level contrastive profiling are bilingual dictionaries. According to Zgusta (1971:294) the principal task of a bilingual dictionary is the coordination of lexical units of the source language with that of the target language. Bilingual dictionaries thus already offer word-to-word contrast of the source and target language. These kinds of datasets bring certain limitations – from the fact that even the best dictionaries do not fully reflect the situation in the languages they cover, to more or less prominent inconsistencies in lexicographic strategies. Comparing two bilingual dictionaries brings in additional challenges and requires additional solutions (this is exemplified in Chapter 4). All of these challenges should be kept in mind when determining what kinds of questions can be asked. Similarly, interpreting the results has to account for all those limitations.

What is proposed here is that the equivalence is explored in either the whole dictionary or in part, according to a coherent criterion. This may include the most frequent 1,000 lexical items featured in the bilingual dictionary at hand, a randomly selected 10% of a bilingual dictionary, or the most frequent 1,000 words in these languages, or one complete lexical field, for example kinship terms, body parts, movement terms, and other coherent criteria. The goal of the analysis is to find the patterns of differences between the two languages in question. These patterns then combine into a contrastive bilingual profile of these two languages. If similar patterns are found in comparing the source language with a number of target languages, what emerges is a lexeme-level profile of that source language. For example, if the analysis shows that the source language is consistently less precise in the sphere of body parts or kinship terms than the target language, that is one of the features in the bilingual lexeme-level contrastive profile of these two languages. Comparison with further languages eventually leads to a lexeme-level contrastive profile of the source language. The feature in question is shared with some languages and a separating point from others. The lexeme-level contrastive profile of the source language situates it in a certain cultural landscape. The results of this analysis along with the results of the lexicon-level analysis are matched with the dimensions established in cultural anthropology. The insights from the tradition of linguistic culturology (previously discussed in section 2.1) are incorporated in the proposed analysis in the qualitative analysis of the results. However, they are just a part of a broader picture, there is no cherry picking, and a range of lexical differences is investigated, both those that may confirm initial hypotheses about the cultural relevance of lexical differences and those that can refute them. The kind of analysis envisaged is exemplified in Chapter 4. Lexeme-level contrastive profiles based on lexical equivalence are supplemented by contrastive analysis of monolingual lexical relations, word formation, phraseological dictionaries, and associative norm dictionaries. The differences between the source and the target language of idioms, word-formation patterns, and associative networks are prominent ingredients of partial equivalence for which datasets are readily available in the form of monolingual phraseological lexical relations, word formation, and associative dictionaries. These datasets enable a more thorough analysis of the differences, unlike in the case of connotation where semantic differential data are normally not available across wide lexical ranges.

Lexicon-level contrastive profiling relies on the data derived from lexeme-level contrasting but also on analyzing and comparing thesauri and other monolingual dictionary datasets to explore if the lexicon of the language in question reflects a cultural anthropological dimension postulated for the culture that it serves. Its starting point are Hofstede and Hofstede's (1994) original dimensions of power distance, individualism/collectivism, masculinity/femininity, uncertainty avoidance, and long-term orientation, as well as Hall's (1959, 1966) classic patterns of polychronism versus monochronism and high- versus low-context cultures. For example, a collectivist culture is likely to have a higher density of the terms related to customs and kinship terms, and a lower density of the terms related to property and its transfer. The density of the semantic field in question is dependent on how precise semantic carving of the field is and how numerous are synonyms for various concepts within the field. If this field in a language of a collectivist culture is significantly denser (has more lexemes) than in a language of an individualist culture, the language with which one compares it, that difference in field density becomes a part of the lexicon-level contrastive bilingual profile. If the difference is consistent in the comparisons with various other languages, then that becomes a part of the lexicon-level contrastive profile of the language in question. The contrastive research of datasets from thesauri and general bilingual dictionaries brings even more complex limitations, which need to be considered when interpreting the results.

Divergence tracking is the final proposed research technique for the deep layer. To examine the emergence of culture-bound divisions, the datasets of historical dictionaries in general and in particular subject-matter fields should be analyzed. Two research techniques are proposed here. In the first exploration of divergence, the following questions related to semantic development from a protolanguage to present-day languages are examined: how many of the original senses of the Proto-Slavic stock have been lost, changed, or preserved in each language or language subgroup? Also, how many of the various subject-matter fields and other predictors differ in the ratio of loss, change, and preservation in relation to the group of languages that developed from the common source? Similarly, how do individual languages and language subgroups relate to each other in terms of this ratio? In other words, how often are the processes identical in each group and how often do they differ from one another? In the situations where a sense changes (one sense is replaced by another or there is another sense alongside the preserved one), what are the most common mechanisms of change?

The analysis relies on a simple taxonomy of semantic changes (loss, continuation, and modification) and a taxonomy of semantic fields and macrofields pertinent to the historical period in which divergence is tracked (presented in Figure 3.1).

Content

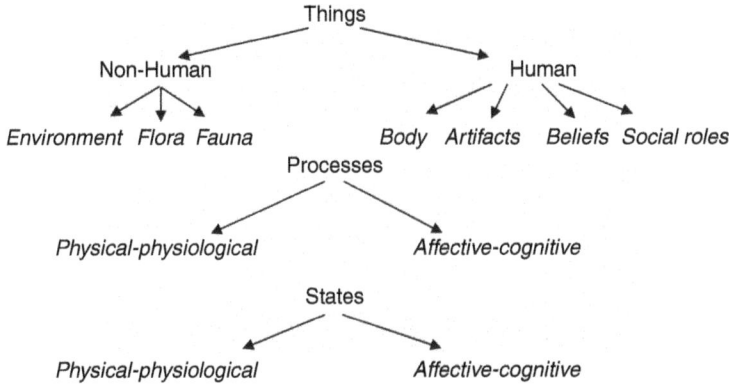

Function

Operators
Measures

Figure 3.1 A taxonomy of subject-matter fields in semantic divergence tracking

At its top level, the taxonomy of subject-matter fields relies on the distinction between things, processes, and states (as understood in Langacker, 1987:220). In things, the next distinction depends on whether the thing is non-human or human, while the final two categories distinguish between physical-physiological on the one hand and affective-cognitive on the other. In addition to these content-based fields, two additional function-based fields were used, for operators and measures. Obviously, the taxonomy deployed is rather eclectic in its nature. The top content–form distinction is the reflection of the well-known lexicographic distinction between content and functional words; the next level includes a cognitive-linguistic categorization, while the lower levels in each of the three main categories are commonly used in describing lexical fields in historical lexicology and other similar fields. While any taxonomy can be criticized for inconsistencies, the present one gives a reasonably consistent coverage of the fields found in the dataset. At the same time, its hierarchical organization ensures that the dataset is explored at several different levels of the taxonomy. The full taxonomy presents itself as follows with fifteen italicized terminal nodes used to code the field of the word.

The second proposed technique of divergence tracking focuses on lexemes rather than on meanings. A simple and manageable technique is proposed here, too, where the word has either retained its basic meaning, been replaced with another word, or undergone semantic or stylistic changes. The analysis uses the datasets of lists from the core of the lexicon (e.g., Swadesh, 2017) and contrasts two or more languages that developed from the same source.

The proposed techniques of divergence tracking supplement lexeme- and lexicon-level contrastive profiling in that they provide insights into the developmental side of the differences found in the contrastive profiles. Needless to say, the emergence of a certain lexical profile is a product of the processes in the deep layer and their interaction with the exchange and surface layers. Divergence tracking is thus an interface toward the other two layers. Divergence tracking is discussed in detail and exemplified in Chapter 6.

All proposed techniques of analysis could also be used to analyze dialects, not just standard languages, as proposed and demonstrated here.

As previously noted, the research in the exchange layer focuses on the features of words and phrases. The principal feature is the origin of a word or phrase and the pivotal division is between inherited and borrowed lexical items. Of interest here are all types of borrowed material discussed in section 2.2, i.e., loanwords (direct, where the whole word is borrowed, e.g., Russian *офис* from English *office*) and loan blends, where domestic and borrowed material coexists in the same word, (e.g., Serbo-Croatian *samoreklama* – *samo-* 'self', inherited, and *reklama*, from German *Reklame*) and loan shifts (semantic shifts, e.g., Polish *mysz* 'mouse, rodent > computer implement'), and loan translation (e.g., Serbo-Croatian *neboder* lit. 'skyripper', based on English *skyscraper*).

Here again, loanword dictionaries, etymological dictionaries that include loanwords, and even general monolingual dictionaries that note the origins of words are natural datasets for the analysis. The ratio and composition of borrowings situates the language in a certain cultural context – it forms its exchange lexical profile. Answering the following questions creates the profile. First, how much of the borrowed material is characteristic for the language under investigation and how much belongs to a broader linguistic environment (e.g., other languages that have developed from the same protolanguage)? Second, what is the ratio of the sources of borrowing in that language? A follow-up question can be formulated here as to which sociocultural and historical circumstances shaped the ratio of the sources of borrowing. Third, what is the distribution of borrowing in the general lexicon, relative to those in specialized fields? Finally, for each of the specialized fields, what is the proportion of each language of borrowing?

Answering the four aforementioned questions (general differences, the differences in the sources of borrowing, the differences in the structure of the sources, the differences in the participation of the loanwords in the general lexicon versus specialized fields of usage, and the differences in how the sources of borrowing profile specialized fields) assumes a ground for comparison in contrasting the language in question with another language. In an ideal situation, the two compared dictionaries would accurately reflect the body of loanwords in their respective language and the authors of the dictionaries use the same methodology (most notably, lexical selection, language and field labeling). Needless to say, the existing datasets of various languages deviate significantly from this ideal situation. If we set aside the sheer treatment inconsistencies that can be found in any dictionary, the following challenges can be distinguished.

Sampling bias – dictionaries of loanwords follow different sampling techniques, which produces the differences between them. First, there are differences between the body of loanwords in the dictionary and in the lexicon of that particular language. Second, any two observed loanword dictionaries exhibit different patterns of deviation from the general lexicon. To illustrate this bias, let us consider the terminology of philology (linguistics and theory/ history of literature). Being philologists, the authors of these dictionaries are prone to including very specific terminology in these fields, which is not the case with the fields with which they may be less familiar (e.g., quantum physics or genetic engineering). This generates the difference with the situation in the lexicon given that numerous terms of equal specificity in non-philological fields will be omitted. By the same token, the two dictionaries in question may exhibit different levels of depth in their coverage of various fields (e.g., the terminology of computing may be addressed exhaustively in one dictionary and only superficially in the other.

Language labeling bias – dictionaries of loanwords follow different strategies in labeling the languages of borrowing. The most conspicuous problem in this field is a different way of handling chains of borrowing and hybrids. For example, many European and even non-European languages feature a substantial number of loanwords that are adopted from French and/or German that are ultimately of Greco-Roman origin. In various loanword dictionaries, we can have the entire chain of borrowing labeled and even in those cases the order in the chain may differ (e.g., French from Latin or Latin via French), but we can also find the same loanword labeled using just the final or the initial link in the chain (e.g., French, the final link or Latin, the initial one).

Field labeling bias – dictionaries of loanwords follow different strategies in labeling specialized fields of usage. The most fundamental difference is that what may be labeled as a word belonging to a specialized field in one dictionary may be left without a label in another dictionary. To exemplify this, numerous computing terms known to the general population (e.g., *keyboard, disk, port, monitor*, etc.) may be labeled as *computing* in one dictionary, *technical* in another, and without a label in yet another dictionary. More broadly, the strategy of one author may be to shy away from using specialized field labels while another author may be prone to using them profusely. A compounding problem is the fact that field labels are inherently inconsistent – they are used to mark the words common in a field of usage and words that are used exclusively in the field, but they are also used to segregate the different senses of the same word (e.g., *port* in computing and in shipping or seafaring).

I will now turn to the solutions intended to mitigate the three aforementioned biases. There is almost nothing that can be done about the sampling bias if one works with existing dictionary datasets. One natural solution is to acknowledge this research limitation. Furthermore, comparing percentages rather than numbers is an obvious solution to account for a different number of loanwords in the two contrasted dictionaries.

The language labeling bias can be mitigated in several ways. First, it can be done by taking into consideration just the last link in the borrowing chain, which makes the situation somewhat less complicated and mitigates some of the language labeling bias. Now the differences between the two languages are reduced to the difference in that language as opposed to the differences in establishing or not establishing the chain, differences in the ordering of the links in the chain, and so on. More importantly, establishing taxonomy of language groups which enables contrasting at a macrolanguage level significantly mitigates language-labeling bias. For example, establishing the following taxonomy in Figure 3.2 enables us to contrast the languages of borrowing at three different levels (e.g., European versus Near Eastern, living European versus classical European, Germanic versus Romance). Thus, if the contrast is between European and Near Eastern Languages, using just the final link in the chain of borrowing overcomes the problem of the differences of labeling the same entry as French, German, Greek, or Latin. It also eliminates a similar problem that in one dictionary Latin is a single category and in another it is divided into classical, medieval, and modern Latin. By the same token, this takes care of the practice of labeling the same entry as Turkish in one dictionary and Arabic in another (again, the former is commonly the final link in the chain and the latter the initial). Needless to say, the taxonomy is primarily cultural, based on external linguistic history and the sources of cultural influence, rather than on structural and/or genetic criteria.

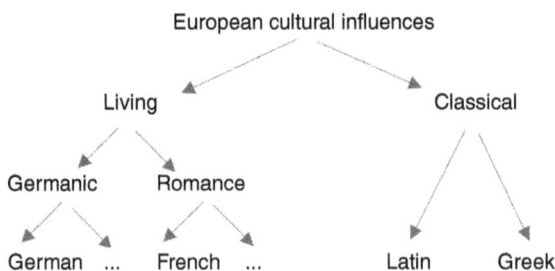

Figure 3.2 An example of macrolanguage hierarchy

The principal problem of the field labeling bias is that the two observed dictionaries may feature a different ratio of general versus specialized vocabulary, which stems from the authors' strategies (more versus less labeling) rather than from objective circumstances in the two observed languages. The answer to this challenge at the level of particular languages and language groups can be the use of the *language generality index*, which would measure the level of generality (and, by the same token, specificity) of a language relative to generality in the entire body of loanwords. This index is computed in the following manner: the percentage of unlabeled words in that language minus the average percentage of unlabeled words in the dataset. For example, if among the words borrowed from German there are 30 percent of unlabeled words, and if the average percentage for all languages in the dataset is 35, German in that dataset has a negative generality index of -5, which means that it is more specific. In other words, in that particular dictionary dataset, it is more tied to specialized lexical fields (as opposed to the general vocabulary). If we compare this index in two dictionaries, the effect of the authors' strategies would be eliminated. The *Language prominence index* is equal to the percentage of the language in the borrowed lexicon minus the average percentage for all languages. Thus, if German comprises 30 percent of the borrowed words in a given dictionary and the average for all languages is 15, the language prominence index for German is positive 15. The same index can be tabulated for each of the fields (*field prominence index*) as follows: the field prominence index is equal to the percentage of the field in the field-labeled lexicon minus the average percentage for all fields. Thus, if natural sciences comprises 30 percent of all labeled entries and an average percentage is 25, the field prominence index for natural sciences is 5. A similar index can be tabulated for the degree in which a language profiles a particular field. This *field profiling index* can be computed as the percentage of a language in a given field minus the percentage of the language in the entire dataset. If, for example, the percentage of Italian in the field of music is 20 and its percentage in the entire dataset is 15, Italian field profiling index for the field of music is 5, which means that it contributes to the profiling of that field more than it contributes to the profiling of the entire dataset. This index is not dependent on the authors' strategies. Another problem with the fields is that the same entry can be labeled differently in two dictionaries. Here, too, creating a hierarchy of macrofields (e.g., bringing psychology, sociology, anthropology, under the macrolabel of social sciences) eliminates labeling bias to some extent.

The following strategies of contrasting need to be deployed in the existing loanword dictionaries datasets.

a. All limitations (e.g., discrepancies between the language dataset and the dictionary dataset) should be clearly stated.

b. Contrasting the percentages of language and field macrocategories should be used to eliminate some of the existing labeling bias.

c. Using the indexes of generality, presence, and profiling further mitigates some of the existing challenges.

All these aforementioned elements (percentages and indices) contribute to the exchange language profile, just as the profiles in the deep layer are built through a series of bilingual exchange language profiles.

There are two additional important components of the exchange language profile. The first component relies on the fact that languages differ in the ratio of cultural versus geographical contact borrowing. The latter category comprises the following. First, there is horizontal geographical contact (i.e., lexical exchange with neighboring languages, for example between Serbian and Romanian). Second, there is concurrent vertical geographical contact of a dominant national language with a local language, e.g., Russian and Evenki, which is native to Russia and China. Finally, it is possible to distinguish the subsequent vertical geographical contact of a dominant language with a substrate language (e.g., Serbo-Croatian with its substrate language Dalmatian).

The second component comprises the direction of lexical transfer with its role in shaping the cultural identity of investigated languages. Practically all languages are both donors and recipients, but the ratio of inbound and outgoing transfer varies from language to language, and it can shift like a pendulum with time. The most notable example is English swinging from mostly inbound transfer after the Norman Conquest to the dominance of outbound transfer in the twentieth and early twenty-first centuries. A simple general *lexical transfer index* is proposed to measure the balance of lexical transfer in two languages. The lexical transfer index for language A is the percentage of the words in the total of this exchange that are lent to language B in the general lexicon of language B, minus the percentage of words borrowed from language B in the general lexicon of language A. For example, if language A lends 600 words to language B, and language A borrows 400 words from language B (i.e., the total volume of transfer is 1,000 words), then the lexical transfer index for language A is as follows: 60% borrowed minus 40% = positive 20. Conversely, language B features a negative lexical transfer index of −20. Positive values of the index mean transfer surplus; its negative values mean a deficit is clearly present. In addition, the two macrofield indices (the macrofield prominence index and the macrofield profiling index) that were used in the exchange profile are also proposed for the study of the direction of lexical transfer.

All these measures and profiles are discussed in detail and exemplified in Chapter 7, which concentrates on the general aspects of the exchange layer. Chapter 8 focuses on the geographical contact borrowing. In turn, Chapter 9 addresses the direction of lexical transfer. Again, the proposed measures can be applied to dialects. Needless to say, they will feature a different ratio of cultural versus contact borrowing, with the latter type being considerably more prominent than in the standard language.

The next part of the proposed research methodology is the study of the surface layer. Unlike the methodology intended for the deep and exchange layers, which can also be applied to organic dialects, the techniques proposed here are applicable to planned language forms only (such as standard languages considered in this monograph) given that the processes in the surface layer remain pertinent to planned language entities only. Dialects may feature prominent speakers as sources of authority and the speakers may have certain attitudes toward what they are doing, but there is no systematic agenda of lexical refereeing or engineering (i.e., declaring words non-standard or coining new words). Attitudes toward speakers of dialects are something completely different, as they are a part of general speakers' attitudes, not something that is primarily lodged in the lexicon (one's attitude can be about phonological, morphological, or any other linguistic features). The attitudes on the permissibility of certain dialectal words in the standard, in turn, are the preserve of the speakers of standard languages, i.e., something outside the organic dialect.

There are three interconnected components of this layer. The first component consists of macrolexical planning maneuvers (e.g., normativism, purism – these maneuvers are discussed in detail and exemplified in Chapter 10). The second component comprises microlexical planning maneuvers (e.g., normative and cryptonormative labeling in the dictionaries – discussed and exemplified in Chapter 11). The final component consists of speaker feedback, as in their attitudes toward planning maneuvers (discussed and exemplified further, in Chapter 12).

I propose two measures for the prominence of macro maneuvers. Both of them are burdened with methodological challenges, which need to be taken into account when interpreting the results. The first one, the *macro maneuver prominence indicator*, shows the percentage of the normative lexical content as compared to descriptive lexical content. For example, if one is to analyze published non-subject-matter monolingual dictionaries, what percentage of those published take account of lexical planning (e.g., orthographic dictionaries, loanword dictionaries, normative monolingual dictionaries), as compared to those general monolingual dictionaries without such intentions (e.g., general language dictionaries, historical dictionaries)? Depending on the maneuver and the time period, we can speak about broad and narrow maneuvers. The second is the *macro maneuver lexical volume indicator*, which shows the proportion of the lexicon affected by lexical planning. Here one can talk about deeper maneuvers, which affect more lexical mass, and shallow ones, which affect relatively narrow lexical strata. It is furthermore proposed that these values be linked with the aforementioned anthropological dimensions (individualism versus collectivism, etc.). Thus, for example, broader and deeper maneuvers may indicate a higher value of the power distance dimension and the uncertainty avoidance dimension.

Micro maneuvers are studied by looking into the proportion of a concrete micro-planning tool toward the elements of the same category, without a role in lexical planning. This is the *micro maneuver prominence index*. An obvious dataset for this kind of research are dictionaries. For example, each dictionary will contain a number of usage labels, a part of which are either overtly normative (stating that something is wrong, etc.) or crypto-normative (stating that something is obscene, obsolete, slang, etc.). The higher proportion of those (crypto)normative labels as compared to the labels without any normative value (e.g., subject-matter labels) means a higher value of that index. I also propose that this index be connected to the aforementioned anthropological dimensions of power distance and uncertainty avoidance.

Finally, the ultimate measure of the speaker feedback is the percentage of the words affected by lexical planning that are accepted by speakers. To study the acceptance of elite maneuvers among the speakers, I propose that the *lexical maneuver acceptance indicator* be used, a scale ranging from −100 (complete rejection of planned intervention) to 0 (the balance of the intervention with the status quo ante) to +100 (full acceptance of the intervention). This measure operates on the dataset of all lexical materials affected by the maneuver. At a point in time following the maneuver, that is reasonable enough for the usage to stabilize (e.g., ten years), the ratio of the lexical material introduced in the maneuver and the status quo material is tabulated.

The negative value of 100 means that no lexical material from the maneuver is in use at that point in time, and that everything found in the corpora belongs to the status quo lexical material that the maneuver strives to replace. The positive value of 100 means that there is no status quo material, in other words that the maneuver is fully accepted. The value of 0 means that the lexical material stemming from the maneuver is equal in size to that which the maneuver intends to replace. The index is calculated as the percentage of the lexicon from the lexical intervention that is accepted minus the status quo lexicon that survives after a certain period of time. Real-life values fall on both sides of the zero, which enables comparison of the maneuvers across time and languages. Given that this measure requires longitudinal studies, another indicator, measuring speaker attitudes at one moment in time, is also proposed, namely the *speaker attitude direction indicator*. This indicator is calculated in the following manner. Using a representative sample of texts which advocate lexical changes, and which enable comments (e.g., on Facebook or in online newspapers), one tabulates the ratio of positive and negative comments. The value of +100 is assigned if all comments are positive, the value of −100 is assigned if all of them are negative, and zero means the balance of positive and negative comments. Again, the index is calculated as the difference between positive and negative comments. This indicator can point to the prospects of a maneuver being eventually accepted or rejected. Attitudes at the speaker's side can point to an anthropological dimension. For example, a high rate of the lexical maneuver acceptance indicator can point to a high level of the uncertainty avoidance dimension and collectivism.

The outcome of the dynamics between elite maneuvers and speaker feedback is a surface-level lexical profile of the standard language, which is based on three components and their corresponding indicators: fragmentation, internal distance (vertical and horizontal), and external distance (vertical and horizontal). *Fragmentation* is a measure of the distinguishable subcomponents a standard language has (e.g., ethnic, geographical variants, etc.). The crudest possible numerical measure would be as follows. The value of 0 means no such subcomponent exist. Then, the higher the number, the higher the fragmentation (the value of 1 is assigned for a two-way split, the number 2 for a three-way split, etc.). However, as will be demonstrated in Chapter 12, this may lead to insurmountable problems, and my ultimate proposal is to use the effective number of components calculated via the Herfindahl–Hirschman Index.[1] *Internal vertical distance* refers to the lexical distance between formal and colloquial standards (the indicator shows the percentage of the words from a colloquial standard which cannot be used in a formal standard). *Internal horizontal distance* pertains to the lexical distance between distinct subcomponents of the standard language. Its indicator comprises the percentage of the words that are not common to the subcomponents, i.e., those words that are marked as belonging to one of the other variants of the standard language. *External vertical distance* pertains to the lexical distance between a standard language and its urban and rural dialectal base. Its indicator points to the percentage of the words that are used in these forms but not in the standard language. Finally, *external horizontal distance* pertains to the distance between the standard language in question and the lexically most closely related standard language (e.g., Czech to Slovak, see Ondrejovič, 1996/1997, Short, 1993a and 1993b; Macedonian to Bulgarian, see Fielder, 1996/1997; Friedman 1996/1997; Kramer 1996/1997). Its indicator is the percentage of words that are different in these two standard languages.

Needless to say, all proposed research techniques are supplemented by qualitative insights where the evidence from linguistic culturology is used at

---

[1] For an accessible explanation of the measure, see Taagapera and Goffman (1981).

the deep level, the findings of linguistic contactology (and theory of lexical borrowing in particular) are included at the exchange level, and the socio-linguistic lexicology is utilized at the surface level. More detailed discussion of the proposed methodology will be provided in Chapters 4–6 (the deep level), 7–9 (the exchange level), and 10–12 (the surface level).

Part II

The Deep Layer

4 Lexeme-level Culture-bound Words, Divisions, and Features

In Chapter 2 I note some methodological inconsistencies of the common approaches to the deep layer. I will start here by providing the nuts and bolts of my own proposal and then discuss several concrete examples, pointing out possible controversies arising from an arbitrary treatment of individual examples.

Wierzbicka (1997:156–195) has devoted considerable time to discussing the differences between the words for *homeland* and *fatherland* in Polish, German, and Russian. While her observations may be true, the question is whether we can draw any conclusions from these isolated examples. If we take another language, Serbo-Croatian, we will find that its Serbian variant features two words of this kind: neutral *domovina* 'homeland' and the somewhat outdated and definitely poetic *otadžbina* 'fatherland', while its Bosnian and Croatian variants use only the former. Now, it would be rather problematic to draw any conclusions of cultural differences between the variants of Serbo-Croatian (or Bosnian, Croatian, Serbian languages, and most recently Montenegrin, if we follow political divisions). The difference is a result of rather unpredictable historical events. Namely, the existence of the four Serbo-Croatian-speaking ethnic groups in the same country of Yugoslavia from 1918 to 1992, the obsolescence of the word-formation pattern of the word *otadžbina*, etc. almost erased the difference between the three variants. The initial difference itself was most likely a maneuver of the intellectuals (e.g., linguists, writers), starting from the early nineteenth century, who introduced those words on the wave of early nationalism, possibly influenced by other European languages. We cannot really infer anything about the way Serbs, Croats, Bosniaks, and Montenegrins think based on this difference.

In another famous example known to practically every introductory learner of Russian or Polish, we find that the English verb *to go* in its basic meaning and neutral register has at least the following four equivalents: *идти, ехать, ходить, ездить* in Russian and *iść, jechać, chodzić, jeździć* in Polish. These Russian and Polish equivalents read roughly: to go continuously and on foot, to go continuously by means of transportation, to go intermittently on foot, and to go intermittently by means of transportation. We may be tempted to draw conclusions based on these two languages and this particular example that Slavs are more precise in the semantic field of movement than the speakers of English. We would, however, be confronted with contradicting data from Serbo-Croatian, which is exactly the same as English (you would use *ići* 'to go' for all these four Russian and Polish words). The point is that, in Serbo-Croatian, this verb spread over the others, and these other forms retained only specialized meanings (*jahati* means 'to ride a horse', *hodati* means 'to walk, to stroll', and *jezditi* is a poetic word for 'to soar'). Further differences between Serbian and Russian in the field of movement are illustrated by Okano (2015).

To sum up, we cannot conclude, absolutely, anything about cultural differences based on this single example. However, if we find a range of examples where the concepts of movement are expressed more precisely in Slavic languages than in English (where some Slavic languages may be more precise in some spheres, and others in other spheres) and if that relates to a parameter established in cultural anthropology or psychology (in this case the aforementioned Hall's pattern of polychronism in Slavic languages versus monochronism in English), then we may have valid evidence. As seen, building of this evidence requires painstaking work, i.e., considerably more than pointing to single words.

Sometimes, one may be tempted to interpret the presence of proverbial elements such as "Человек предполагает а бог располагает" (lit. Man assumes, God distributes) in Russian, "Człowiek strzela, Pan Bóg kulę nosi" (lit. Man shoots, God carries the bullet) in Polish, and "Čovjek snuje, Bog određuje" (lit. Man dreams, God determines) in Serbo-Croatian as a linguistic expression of the external locus of control in Slavic culture (as opposed to the internal one in Germanic cultures, where a person is always in control). However, when we dig deeper, we will find out that German has: "Der Mensch denkt, Gott lenkt" (lit. Man thinks, God drives) and that English features: "Man proposes, but God disposes," all of which are translations of the Latin phrase "Homo proponit, sed Deus disponit," from Book I, Chapter 19, of *The Imitation of Christ* by the German cleric Thomas à Kempis. It is obvious that this particular linguistic element is a result of a rather unpredictable historic event, something that can be traced to one particular author rather than to the cultures of any present-day languages. This particular example can still be used as partial evidence for a different construal of the locus of control in Slavic and Germanic languages, but one would have to prove that these proverbs are used with a considerably higher frequency in Slavic than in Germanic languages and that they are known to a much broader circle of speakers of the former than the latter languages. Needless to say, a sine qua non would be other corroborating evidence to that effect.

The three concrete cases suffice to illustrate various pitfalls of using individual examples as evidence assuming a deterministic viewpoint, disregarding contrary evidence, and not linking them to other linguistic and extra-linguistic evidence. The first building block intended to start solving these problems is lexeme-level contrastive profiling.

Lexeme-level contrastive profiling rests on the idea (elaborated in Šipka, 2015) that the most parsimonious manner of accounting for cross-linguistic equivalence is to count the number of equivalents. If we are lexically contrasting two languages, the following four situations are possible:

a. Full equivalence (1=1 equivalence)
b. Zero equivalence (1=0 equivalence)
c. Multiple equivalence (1=2+ equivalence)
d. Partial equivalence (1≈1 equivalence)

The first situation, full equivalence, is extremely rare. It is found mostly in technical terminologies and nomenclatures, e.g. English *neutron* versus French *neutron*.

The second situation, zero equivalence, is also marginal in its size and it includes some of the cases commonly discussed in mainstream anthropological linguistics (linguistic culturology, natural semantic metalanguage, and cultural linguistics). Such is the equivalence between Serbian *slava*, which can only be explained in English as 'family (or profession, municipality, church, and so on) patron saint day and feast', as there is no English equivalent.

Multiple equivalence comprises a significant number of cases and is found in cases like: Polish *ręka* versus English *hand* and *arm*.

Finally, partial equivalence, also a very frequent situation, happens when there exists one-to-one equivalence, but the equivalents differ in some important respect. For example, English *oxygen* is opaque for most of its speakers, and its German equivalent *Sauerstoff* is immediately recognized by its speakers as 'sour matter', just like the term кислород in Bulgarian, Macedonian, and Russian.

Full equivalence is generally not of interest in cultural linguistic studies. It is marginal in scope and what it demonstrates is obvious – languages from similar technological background will be likely to feature this kind of equivalence, be it information technologies in one group of languages or hunting and gathering in another.

Zero equivalence is frequently in the scope of interest in linguistic culturology. While qualitative analysis of individual cases may have value in a wider scheme of things, it is imperative that the analysis be conducted over a consistent range of data. A good source for such analysis, at least for Slavic languages, are borrowings from Slavic languages in other, otherwise dominant, languages in lexical exchange. Thus, most borrowings from Slavic languages into English are de facto zero equivalents. The word is borrowed (and attested in most comprehensive dictionaries but unknown to the vast majority of speakers and used in the texts of that language italicized and explained) because there

Table 4.1 *The distribution of source languages*

Language	Example	Count	Percent
Russian	*borsch, pirog, samovar*	481	74.92
Polish	*Mazurka, Sejm, szlachta*	56	8.72
S-Cr	*dinar, polje, ponor*	33	5.14
Czech	*dobro, koruna, robot*	29	4.52
General Slavic	*knez, tsar, vaivode*	24	3.7
Bulgarian	*lev, Gamza, Pomak*	13	2.02
Slovenian	*Slovene*	3	0.47
Slovak	*Tauberian*	2	0.31
Ukrainian	*Gley*	1	0.16
		642	100.00

is a lexical gap for that word in English. My own analysis of Slavic borrowings in the *Oxford English Dictionary* (*OED*; Šipka, 2004) points to such cases. Obviously, this is only a subset of zero-equivalence vocabulary between any of the Slavic languages and English. However, especially in the case of Russian where numerous such cases are attested, such analysis provides an insight into what type of words these are. The analysis of Slavic words in English has been performed using the material from the *OED* (1989), which, with its 231,100 main entries, offers the most comprehensive insight into the English vocabulary. Following the procedure described in Šipka (2004), 642 entries were extracted, some of which could be linked to particular Slavic languages, while others were general Slavic. These entries were consequently manually filtered to exclude the instances where the etymological labels relating to Slavic languages are used only to corroborate the Indo-European origin of Old English words and to eliminate repeated entries. A rather liberal criterion was used, whereby the word is considered a Slavicism (i.e., borrowing from a Slavic language) if one of the Slavic languages was a member of the borrowing chain. The lexical stock of Slavicisms encompasses the words borrowed in the English directly, the non-Slavic lexemes borrowed through a Slavic language, and Slavic words borrowed through a non-Slavic language. The distribution of these cases per language is shown in Table 4.1.

I will now describe the characteristics of each subject-matter field featured in Table 4.2.

History: There are two major groups of historisms. First, there are the terms such as *hussar, szlachta, boyar, heyduk, tsarevich*, etc. related to the pre-twentieth-century, often medieval past of various Slavic peoples. Second, there are items such as *Bolshevik, commissar, Gosplan, kolkhoz, sovkhoz, subbotnik, udarnik*, etc. related to the Soviet communist experiment. The

Table 4.2 *Subject-matter fields of borrowings*

Field	Count	Percent
History	141	21.96
Ethnic designations	92	14.33
Geography, geology, mineralogy	75	11.68
Science and technology	61	9.50
Food	46	7.17
Zoology	34	5.30
Music	28	4.36
Literature and art theory	27	4.21
Politics	27	4.21
Social relations	27	4.21
Objects	23	3.58
Garments	20	3.12
Religion	17	2.65
Measures	15	2.34
Botany	9	1.40
	642	100.00

most recent loanwords in this group, e.g., *perestroika* and *glasnost* come from the practice of abandoning the communist system. Most lexemes in this group are so-called culture-bound words, i.e., the definition will contain a reference "in Russia," etc. In addition to being culture-bound words and historisms, these lexemes are also period-bound, which is reflected in the usage label "Hist." A natural result of this limited reference is the low frequency of practically all items in this group. It suffices to say that out of 141 lexemes in this group, only 27 (or 19.15%) were recognized by the English spell-checker in Microsoft Word 2003. Only in rare instances will a lexeme assume a general meaning. The entry *tsar* with the following two meanings exemplifies this point:

a. Hist. The title of the autocrat or emperor of Russia; historically, borne also by Serbian rulers of the 14th c., as the Tsar Stephen Dushan., b. transf. A person having great authority or absolute power; a tyrant, 'boss'. orig. US. (*OED*, 2004:s.v.)

Ethnic designations: There are two major groups of designations in this category: a. the names of the Slavic peoples, such as *Bosniac, Czech, Slovak*, etc., and b. the names of minority groups inhabiting Slavic lands, e.g., *Koryak, Mordvin, Nenets*. The first group of ethnic names is considerably more frequent than the second one. The high frequency is particularly observable with the Russian ethnic name, which has even developed its derivational nest, e.g., *Russify, Russianize, Russianist, Russianism*.

Geography, geology, mineralogy: One section of the lexemes in this category refers to the morphological features of terrain and types of soil, while the other designates various minerals. The terms from the first group refer to specific morphological configurations and soil types of Russia (e.g., *chernozem, sierozem, step, taiga*) and the Balkans (e.g., *ponor, polje, uvala*). Terms for minerals (e.g., *nenadkevite, nifontovite, nordite, obruchevite, samarskite*) refer to the minerals and their components found in the Slavic countries, mostly Russia and/or discovered by the Slavic scholars.

Science and technology: Most lexemes in this category belong to either Soviet space-era vocabulary (e.g., *lunokhod, sputnik*, etc.) or various discoveries of scientists from the Slavic countries, e.g., *kurchatovium, mendelevium, Tesla, Markov*. The most central vocabulary item in this category, the word *robot*, demonstrates the role of the so-called butterfly effect in the process of borrowing. As stated in the *OED* (2004:s.v.), the word comes from "Czech, f. robota forced labour; used by Karel Čapek (1890–1938) in his play *R.U.R.* (Rossum's Universal Robots, 1920)." This particular item defies the general pattern of borrowing both in this thematic category and in general. An unpredictable act of creative use of language has yielded a highly frequent borrowing.

Food: Vocabulary items from this category fall under the general pattern of the culture-bound nature of the borrowings. The lexemes are either food products (e.g., *borsch, kielbasa, pierog, shashlik, stroganoff*) or spirits (e.g., *rakia, vodka, zubrowka*) characteristic for Slavic cultures. Some of these items (e.g., *vodka* and *paprika*) have gained general popularity in the English-speaking countries.

Zoology: This category comprises fauna, such as *beluga, borzoi, zubr*, endemic to or characteristic for biomes of the Slavic countries. The structure of this subject-matter category is akin to the botanical field.

Music and dance: There are two groups of lexemes in this subject-matter area. First, there are traditional music forms and instruments, and dance formations such as *gusle, balalaika, tamburitza, kolo, kazachoc*, etc. Second, there are the terms related to the most prominent Slavic classical composers, e.g., *Chopinesque, Dvořakian, Tchaikovskian*.

Literature and art theory: This group contains the lexemes relating to the traditional Slavic literary traditions, such as *bylina, skaz, Glagolitic*, those belonging to the arsenal of the twentieth-century avant-garde artistic movements, e.g., *Constructivism, Cubo-Futurism, Suprematism*, etc., and items relating to philological theories (*defamiliarization, Dostoyevskian, Trubeckoyan*, and others).

Politics: This category comprises names of the parliaments and territorial units in Slavic countries, e.g. *duma, Sejm, Sobranie, Skupština, oblast*, etc. as well as Soviet-era general political terms which are still being used (unlike previously mentioned historisms), e.g., *apparatchik, disinformation, nomenklatura, residentsia*, etc.

Social relations: This category comprises mostly marginal vocabulary used to describe features and social roles, e.g. *babushka, kulturny, niekulturny, specialist*. The category falls out of the general pattern of borrowing in which the Slavic words refer to culture-bound entities. The only non-marginal lexeme in this group is *vampire*, a general Slavic borrowing, which is far more frequent than other lexemes and which has developed a rich polysemic structure.

Objects: This category follows the general pattern of the culture-bound character of the borrowings and contains names of edifices and other objects related to Slavic and their neighboring cultures, e.g., *dacha, isba, terem, troika*. The group in general remains marginal, with the only exception of *troika*, which has developed a new sense "a group or set of three persons (rarely things) or categories of people associated in power; a three-person commission or administrative council. Also attrib." (*OED*, 2004:s.v.).

Garments: Similar to the previous category, this group of words comprises garments specific to Slavic and their neighboring cultures, e.g., *rubashka, shapka, shuba, parka*. The latter item is the only one which gained popularity beyond the borders of the Slavic cultures.

Religion: This category contains items relating mostly to Orthodox Christianity, different schools of thought, customs, and sacral objects, e.g., *starover, slava, iconostas, riza*. These lexemes follow the general pattern of borrowing.

Measures: There are two kinds of lexemes in this category. First, parochial measures, such as *arsheen, verst, tchetvert*, and second local currencies, e.g., *dinar, koruna, rouble, zloty*. The entire category is practically destined to become obsolete. The measures are replaced with the metric system and the currencies will eventually be replaced by the Euro.

Botany: This category comprises faunae, such as *badiaga, kamish, zelkova*, etc. endemic to or characteristic of biomes in the Slavic countries. The structure of this subject-matter category is akin to the zoological field.

It is clear that only a very small number of these lexemes influence "the way people think" (most of all, the groups devoted to social relations and religion can be thought to have such effect). Most commonly, these zero-equivalence borrowings into English paint the general cultural landscape of the speakers of Slavic languages: common objects, food, garments, musical instruments, common collective memory, known items of cultural and scholarly production, surrounding ethnic groups, flora, fauna, geology, etc. – all of which are not common in other cultures.

One should repeat here that what is borrowed in English does not fully overlap with what would in fact be zero equivalent in English, but there is definitely a great deal of overlap, and even this limited sample shows a muted presence of zero equivalence in the general lexeme-level contrastive profile. The present analysis also clearly demonstrates that most of these words paint the general culture-specific environmental and sociocultural backdrop rather than influence "the way people think." Some supporting evidence is found in the fact that similar data have been found in Alvarado (1989, 1990), who studied Slavic borrowings in Spanish.

I will now turn to other types of equivalence, most notably multiple equivalence. In order to preliminarily explore the degree of difference in equivalence between two Slavic languages and between Slavic and non-Slavic languages, a list of the 1,000 most frequent words in Russian was used (Ljaševkska and Šarov, 2009). The equivalents of these words were then analyzed in Polish (Bogusławski, 1985) and Serbian, a variant of Serbo-Croatian (Stanković, 1998) – two Slavic languages – as well as English (Korolev, 2017) and German (Rimaschewskaja, 1998) – two European non-Slavic languages. The same procedure was repeated with a list of the 1,000 most frequent Polish words (Kazoić, 2009), compared with Russian (Bogusławski, 1985) and English (Fisiak, 2011). The logic behind this was to choose the words that are central to each speaker of these languages and that even intermediate learners of these languages will know and encounter on a daily basis. That way the comparison is made at the core lexical level rather than in the spheres of lofty concepts and ideas that only intellectual elites commonly encounter. Russian, Polish, and Serbo-Croatian are selected as the most populous members of the three groups of Slavic languages. English and German are selected as two Indo-European languages from the neighboring Germanic branch, which are very strong sources of lexical influence on Slavic languages.

A simple coding schema was used for these words. There were essentially four theoretical possibilities (for further details see Šipka, 2015): full one-on-one equivalence, zero equivalence (a word in the source language does not have an equivalent in the target language), multiple equivalence (there is one word in the source language versus several in the target language), and partial equivalence (there is one-to-one equivalence but the equivalents differ in some important respect, e.g. in this Russian–English example *красный*: red ~ *дерево*: mahogany (lit. red wood). The difference is that the color name is used in a term for mahogany in Russian but not in English. Zero equivalence is practically not found in this cohort of the most frequent lexemes, which then gave three options: full, multiple, and partial equivalence.

The type of equivalence was determined solely on the data provided by the author(s) of the dictionary, which is definitely a limitation of this analysis (the ways to cope with this limitation will be discussed later on). Given that multiple equivalence is the most dominant type, an additional classification of the types of multiple equivalence was created and tabulated for each of the analyzed dictionaries. A pilot analysis has shown that there are four main types of generators of multiple equivalence: semantic differentiation, semantic transfer, the co(n)textual split, and the form-related split. They will be explained in turn.

A classic example of differentiation are body part names in Slavic languages versus English, e.g., Polish *ręka*, which is both *hand* and *arm*, or *noga*, which is both *foot* and *leg*. In this case a conceptual sphere that is covered with one word in the source language is divided into two or more words in the target language. How this division is configured varies. For example, the following Polish–Russian example is different from the aforementioned Polish–English, given that the target language has one word that covers the whole semantic range and one which is specified: *fala* 'wave' vs. (wave in general) *волна* (sizable sea wave) *вал*. This variation is at the next level of specificity and I will not address it here.

Semantic transfer is mostly metaphorical, as in the following Polish–English example: Polish *czoło* versus English *forehead* (część twarzy 'part of the face') and *front* (przód 'front part'), where forehead is metaphorically transferred in Polish to mean 'front' (e.g., of a table), which is not the case in English. Here too, at a more specific level one can note a number of different types of transfers – for example, the following Russian–English example is not metaphorical but rather metonymical: Russian *бумага* is in English *paper* and *document*. Again, I will not analyze that more specific level here.

Co(n)textual splits are found in the situations where the text type (context) or surrounding words (co-text) require two different words in the target language, as in Polish *sędzia* versus English *judge* (in court), *referee* (in soccer, boxing, wrestling), *umpire* (in tennis, baseball, cricket), *judge, juror* (in a competition). This is a Polish–English example of a contextual split. Similarly, in Russian *золотой* versus German *Gold-, golden -ая медаль Goldmedaille* 'gold medal', *-ые часы goldene Uhr* 'gold watch', a Russian-German co-textual split is exemplified. Here, the Russian adjective for gold is rendered with two German lexemes, and that choice is determined by the type of noun head which that particular adjective modifies.

Finally, form-related splits occur when the internal structure of a word in the source language has several interpretations. Polish *pociąg* 'train/inclination', being related to the verb *pociągać* 'pull', can mean both *train* and *inclination* in English, given the structural feature of the form of this Polish word. Similarly, Russian *данные* literally means 'the given ones', so it is split into *data* (they are given, which is the Latin etymology of the English word) and *capabilities* (that, what is given to a person) in English.

The categories of full and partial equivalence and the subcategories of multiple equivalence are illustrated in Table 4.3, using the examples from all six analyzed dictionaries.

The frequency of these categories and subcategories was then analyzed for the top 1,000 most frequent words in the six aforementioned dictionaries. Needless to say, these dictionaries differ in size, they belong to different lexicographic traditions, and each author has his or her own style of establishing equivalence.

Table 4.3 *Examples of equivalence categories*

	Russian–Polish	Russian–Serbian	Russian–English	Russian–German	Polish–Russian	Polish–English
1. Full equivalence	вера : wiara 'faith'	два : два 'two'	вместе : together	дверь : Tür 'door'	generał : генерал 'general'	ciotka : aunt
2. Multiple equivalence						
a. Differentiation	здание 'building' : budynek (общественное, больших размеров 'public, of large proportions'): gmach	гражданин 'citizen, national' : држављанин 'national'; грађанин 'citizen'	берег : (моря, озера) shore; (морское побережье) coast	говорить : разговаривать 'talk, speak' reden 'talk' высказывать, произносить 'to express, to utter' sagen 'say'	fala 'wave': волна; (wielka fala morska 'large sea wave') вал	profesor : (na uniwersytecie 'at university') professor; (w szkole średniej 'in high school'); teacher
b. Transfer	воля 'freedom' : wola; (свобода 'liberty'); wolność	голова 'head' : глава 'head'; грло 'head of cattle'	бумага : paper, (документ) document	борьба 'fight' : Kampf, спорт 'sport' Ringen	północ 'north, midnight' : север 'north'; (czas 'time') полночь 'midnight'	czoło : (część twarzy) forehead; (przód) front
c. Form-related	среда 'Wednesday, environment': środa 'Wednesday'; środowisko 'environment'	данные 'data, capabilities': подаци 'data'; способности 'capabilities'	единый : (один, единственный): a single (объединённый) united	всякий 'every, different' : каждый jeder 'every'; разный verschieden 'different'	pociąg 'train, drive' : поезд 'train'; (skłonność) влечение 'drive'	pociąg : train; (skłonność) inclination

d. Co(n)textual	*словно* : 'as, as if' *jak gdyby*; (с сущ. при сравнении с данным предметом 'with a noun in comparison with a given object'); *jak*	*воздух* 'air' : *ваздух* 'air, Serbian'; *зрак* 'air, Croatian'	*врач* : *doctor*; *physician* книжн.	*золотой* : *Gold, golden*; *~ая медаль* : *Goldmedaille*; *~ые часы* : *goldene Uhr*	*chętnie* 'gladly' : *охотно*; (w odpowiedzi 'in an answer'); *с удовольствием*	*sędzia* : (w sądzie 'in court') *judge*; (w piłce nożnej boksie, zapasach 'in soccer, boxing, wrestling'); *referee*
3. Partial equivalence	*врач* : *lekarz* 'doctor'; *зубной ~* 'lit. tooth doctor': *dentysta* 'dentist'	*дверь* : *врата* 'door'; *день открытых ~ей* 'day of the open door': *дан слободног приступа* 'lit. day of free access'	*красный* : *red*; 'red' *~ дерево* 'lit. red tree': *mahogany* 'mahogany'	*автор* 'author': *Autor*, (литературного или научного произведения тж. *Verfasser* 'of a literary or scholarly work, also Verfasser'; музыкального произведения тж. *Komponist* 'of a musical work, also Komponist')	*papier* 'paper' : *бумага*; *~у* 'papers'; (dokumenty osobiste 'personal documents') *документы* 'documents'	*tytuł* : *title*; *tytuł szlachecki knighthood*

Table 4.4 *The frequency of equivalence types*

Category	Russian–Polish % (N)	Russian–Serbian % (N)	Polish–Russian % (N)	Russian–English % (N)	Russian–German % (N)	Polish–English % (N)
Multiple	60.4 (604)	60.7 (607)	54 (540)	74.0 (740)	69.2 (692)	65.6 (656)
Partial	7.6 (76)	5.8 (58)	3.2 (32)	8.7 (87)	6.6 (66)	12.8 (128)
Full	32.0 (320)	33.5 (335)	42.8 (428)	17.3 (173)	24.2 (242)	21.6 (216)
Total	100.0 (1000)	100.0 (1,000)	100 (1000)	100.0 (1,000)	100.0 (1,000)	100 (1,000)

This imposes certain limitations as to what in the data can and cannot be interpreted as significant. The frequency of the three types of equivalency (zero, multiple, and partial) is presented in Table 4.4.

Two matters are noteworthy here. First, multiple equivalence is dominant, compared to other types of equivalence. Second, the level of full equivalence is somewhat higher between Slavic languages (on average 36.1% in the three dictionaries, Russian–Polish, Polish–Russian, and Russian–Serbian) than between Slavic and non-Slavic languages (on average 21% in the other three dictionaries, Russian–English, Russian–German, and Polish–English). This does not come as a surprise given the common heritage of Slavic languages. Certainly, the authors can disagree as to when the need exists to signal partial equivalence. However, the data is consistent in the three dictionaries on both sides of the Slavic–non-Slavic divide, which likely means that the influence of that factor was only marginal.

The distribution of the subcategories of multiple equivalence is presented in Table 4.5.

The most striking difference between Slavic–Slavic and Slavic–non-Slavic equivalence (bolded in the table) is that in the former case the differentiation is the dominant subtype of multiple equivalence (on average 58.2%) and in the latter it is transfer (on average 47.8%). It seems that Slavic languages share more common semantic transfers (mostly metaphors) and that their internal lexical divergence rests mostly on the need of each particular language to carve out more precise semantic domains. In contrast, numerous semantic transfers in Slavic languages are not shared in non-Slavic languages. This can be explained by the common heritage of Slavic languages – semantic transfers were active in Proto-Slavic much later than in Proto-Indo-European, so their effects are likely to be stronger in the languages sharing Proto-Slavic linguistic heritage.

A simple way to measure what seems to be a key difference between Slavic and non-Slavic languages is to calculate the *DT index* (differentiation versus transfer) which is equal to the percentage of differentiation divided by the percentage of transfer. In this particular case Slavic–Slavic

Table 4.5 *The distribution of multiple equivalence types*

	Russian–Polish % (N)	Russian–Serbian % (N)	Polish–Russian % (N)	Russian–English % (N)	Russian–German % (N)	Polish–English % (N)
Differentiation	**60.4%** (365)	**55.7%** (338)	**58.30%** (315)	27.6% (204)	20.3% (141)	28.90% (192)
Transfer	23.3% (141)	23.4% (142)	20.70% (112)	**47.8%** (354)	**54.2%** (377)	**41.40%** (275)
Co(n)textual	13.7% (83)	17.5% (106)	17.00% (92)	20.3% (150)	22.4% (156)	24.10% (160)
Form-related	2.5% (15)	3.5% (21)	3.90% (21)	4.3% (32)	3.0% (21)	5.70% (38)
Total	100.0% (604)	100.0% (607)	100% (540)	100.0% (740)	100.0% (695)	100.0% (665)

dictionaries have a DT index of 2.6 (i.e., above 1.0, which is the equilibrium of the two subtypes) and the Slavic–Non-Slavic value is 0.54, i.e., below the equilibrium point.

The second item of interest is a lower percentage of co(n)textual splits in Slavic–Slavic dictionaries (16% on average) than in Slavic–Non-Slavic dictionaries (22.3% on average). This disproportion might point to the fact that Slavic languages share some contexts and co-texts that are different in non-Slavic languages. Again, given the differences between the dictionaries and their limited number, all findings here should be taken only as indicators of possible trends.

Given that the differentiation versus transfer seems to be the key distinguishing feature, I investigated whether these values differ in the words associated with the three lexical layers of cultural identity – deep (the words inherited from Proto-Slavic), exchange (borrowed words), and surface (engineered words). These words were analyzed in Russian–Polish and Polish–Russian dictionaries and also in Russian–English and English–Russian. In the sample of 1,000 Russian words, the following ratio of these words was found: 89.6% were inherited (e.g., *рука*), 10.1% borrowed (e.g., *автор*), and 0.3% engineered (*самолёт*). The Polish ratio was very similar: 93.6 % were inherited (e.g., *ręka*), 6% borrowed (e.g., *autor*), and 0.4% engineered (e.g., *samolot*). The results are presented in Table 4.6.

No real trend emerges from these data, which would mean that once the word is borrowed, it becomes susceptible to the same trends occurring with inherited words. We can see that the values are very close among inherited and borrowed words. This reveals some clues about the interaction of the three layers (further discussed in Chapter 13), namely that the adaptation of the borrowings from the exchange layer into the core of the deep layer pertains not

Table 4.6 *Differentiation and transfer in inherited and borrowed words*

	Russian–Polish		Russian–English		Polish–Russian		Polish–English	
	B	I	B	I	B	I	B	I
D	27.70%	37.60%	19.80%	20.50%	21.70%	32.30%	18.30%	19.20%
	28	337	20	184	13	302	11	180
T	7.90%	14.80%	31.70%	35.90%	13.30%	11.10%	31.70%	27.40%
	8	133	32	322	8	104	19	256

only to general morphological and phonological parameters (which is well-known from various contactological studies) but also to the deeper semantic functioning of those words and their role in profiling cultural identity.

To summarize, the present analysis of the lexical mass of Slavic and non-Slavic bilingual dictionaries selected using a coherent criterion of frequency demonstrates a technique for possible coherent analyses while hinting at a trend in the field of multiple equivalence, where metaphorical extensions unite Slavic languages and semantic differentiation divides them. Needless to say, the idea of addressing these data was to provide an introductory example and hopefully stimulate further research, which would dig deeper into these and other possible trends.

One promising field of research may lie in contrasting unrelated languages from substantially different spheres of cultural influences. An interesting question concerns whether the patterns of differences of these languages may reveal more about cultural identity than contrastive data with related languages and/or those from similar cultural spheres. In order to initially explore this issue, I conducted a pilot survey of Japanese Slavists in August of 2017, asking those colleagues to provide examples of lexical anisomorpism between Japanese and Slavic languages (most were Russian, but there were also Polish and Serbo-Croatian examples). What is characteristic of these examples is that while concrete lexeme pairs may differ from the Slavic–English ones, general principles of anisomorphism remain the same.

We can thus find examples of zero equivalence, such as Russian *скучно* 'boring', which does not have a Japanese equivalent. According to one of the informants, it includes the feelings that the Japanese describe as *sabishi* 'sad', *kodokuna* 'lonely', and *muina* 'idle'. There are also examples of multiple equivalence, such as Serbo-Croatian *voda* 'water' vs. Japanese *mizu* 'cold water' and *yu* 'hot water', or Russian *жизнь* 'life' vs. Japanese *jinsei* 'person's life', *seikatsu* 'everyday life', *seimei* 'physical life'. These examples show different carvings of the conceptual sphere, but there are those related to different metaphoric patterns, as in Russian *горло* 'throat, neck of a bottle' vs. Japanese *nodo* 'throat' and *kubi* 'neck of the bottle'. We can see that, unlike in the previous examples where Slavic languages were aligned with English, in this case, Japanese is aligned with English and Polish. The concept of 'neck' is used as a metaphor to describe a part of the bottle in those languages, unlike in Russian where it is literally 'throat of the bottle'. There were also examples of contextual splits as in numerous kinship terms where Japanese, depending on the nature of the situation, uses a more nuanced system of terms of address than any of the Slavic languages.

Finally, there were examples of partial equivalence, as in Russian *соборность* (the rough Japanese equivalent is *wa*), both being roughly translated in English as 'the belief in a universal bond of sharing that connects all humanity'. However, the Russian and the Japanese word exhibit profound differences in their cultural background (as they are partially related to different religious settings).

What follows from this survey is the hypotheses that general mechanisms of lexical anisomorphism between Japanese and Slavic languages are identical to those between Slavic languages and English and between any two Slavic languages. In contrast to that, concrete pairs of equivalents are often peculiar to Japanese–Slavic lexical relations, and their thorough study in bilingual dictionaries may lead to a more detailed picture of Slavic lexical markers of cultural identity. For example, the aforementioned word for 'boring' would simply be disregarded if we only use the material from European languages, given that all of them have that concept. Further contributions to lexeme-level markers of cultural identity may come from bilingual dictionaries between Slavic languages and African, Asian, and South American languages, which are only moderately exposed to European cultural influences.

I will now turn to a brief discussion of the relationship beween partial and multiple equivalence. A productive way in which ongoing microanalyses in linguistic culturology can be incorporated into the present analysis would to select a coherent semantic category in one language and analyze partial equivalents in other languages. Babenko (1989), a dictionary of the lexical means of expressing emotions in Russian, constitutes an excellent source of the semantic field of emotions. If one of the conceptual fields from that source is selected, e.g., that of *грусть* (which is a kind of culture-specific state of sadness), one can conduct a consistent analysis of what makes the words from that field culture-specific, how many of them are culture specific, how many of them are universal, and so on. In that way, we are not simply cherry-picking those examples that allegedly confirm our ideas but, rather, confronting our ideas with a bulk of consistently selected data. Babenko (1989:151–152) divides these words into the following categories: *Эмоциональное состояние* (the emotional state), *Становление эмоционального состояния* (a formation of the emotional state), *Эмоциональное воздействие* (emotional impact), and *Эмоциональное отношение* (emotional attitude), *Внешнее выражение эмоций* (external expression of emotion), *Эмоциональная характеризация* (emotional characterization), *Эмоциональное качество* (emotional property). Under each category, the following types of meanings are differentiated: (1) basic form, (2) referential derivative, and (3) metaphorical derivative.

To demonstrate a possible analysis of partial equivalence, I took only the basic meanings for the emotional state. It comprised the following lexemes. Many of them are culture-specific and most of them have multiple English equivalents, so I am not providing their translations: *безнадежность, безотрадность, безысходность, грустить, грустный, грусть, депрессия, журиться, задавленность, затосковать, ипохондрия, кручина, кручиниться, кручинушка, крутиться, кукситься, меланхолия, назола, наскучаться, натосковаться, невеселый, нерадостный, ностальгия, отчаяние, пессимизм, пессимистический, печалиться, опечалиться, печаловаться, печаль, печальный, подавленность, подосадовать, покручиниться, понурость, поскучать, потомиться, потосковать, потужить, сгрустнуться, сетовать, посетовать, скука, скучать, скучища, скучный, сожаление, сокрушаться, соскучиться, сплин, томный, тоска, тоскливость, тоскливый, тосковать, унылость, унылый, уныние, утепление, хандра, хандрить, хмуро, хмурь.*

One can see that many of these words (e.g., *грусть, печаль, тоска*) belong to those that are commonly purported to be the keywords of Russian culture. It is, then, interesting to see what their equivalence would look like in another Slavic language. On the one hand, one may expect that most words would have one equivalent, which would have some specific features. In other words, some features of the Russian words would make that cross-cultural difference. On the other hand, one may expect multiple equivalents, which would mean that the Russian word is broader than any of its equivalents in another Slavic language (i.e., the scope of semantic coverage is culture-specific). Each of these words was thus checked in Stanković (1998), a Russian–Serbian dictionary, and the general patterns of equivalence shown in Table 4.7 were found.

Table 4.7 *The equivalence between Russian and Serbian*

	Frequency	Percent
Full equivalence	2	3.2
Multiple equivalence	41	65.1
Partial equivalence	1	1.6
Not attested	19	30.2
Total	63	101.0

We can clearly see that, in this case, the culture-specific element actually shows the wide semantic scope of the Russian words, the fact that, in Serbian, they are covered by different words with different meanings in different contexts. The number of non-attested items is relatively high because many of the words on the list are derivatives, where their basic word is attested but the derivative is not, as all relevant information about the derivative can be inferred from the basic word.

If we take a qualitative look at the examples, we can note the following. First, some multiple equivalence (not more than 10%) is affected by the fact that there are alternative Serbian suffixes for some abstract nouns or that there are co-text and context-based synonyms in Serbian. Thus, the entire mass of multiple equivalents should not be ascribed to cross-cultural differences. Second, in the vast majority of cases in multiple equivalence, Serbian covers the field of the Russian word with semantically nuanced equivalents. Third, it is remarkable that this field shows a much higher level of multiple equivalence than the general sample from the same dictionary (over 60% in the general sample and over 90% in the attested entries from this semantic field). Finally, the number of unattested items is a potential indicator of a higher density of that field in Russian than in the Serbian language. This is definitely not true for all unattested entries, given that some are not included as the base word was present, so the compiler did not see the need to list predictable derivatives. Field density will be discussed in detail in the next chapter.

This brief look into one Russian semantic field demonstrated a possible manner of systematically approaching cross-cultural differences. Rather than arbitrarily selecting a group of cultural keywords, one can identify consistently selected vocabulary areas (e.g., words for specific emotions, geographical concepts, kinship terms, etc.) that build a lexical profile of a given language's cultural identity. If this is confirmed in contrasting equivalency with a range of related and unrelated languages, that can definitely constitute proof that lex-emes from that particular vocabulary area contribute to the cultural profile of that language. The merger of lexeme-level analysis with lexicon-level analysis will be further explored in the next chapter.

5   Lexicon-based Culture-bound Field Density

I will now turn to discussing lexicon-based culture-bound field density, the second proposed approach to studying the deep layer of lexical identity. There are two principal ways in which a higher or lower lexical field density can be construed. First, multiple equivalence (the principal factor in lexeme-level contrasting, as demonstrated in Chapter 4) can be more prominent in certain lexical fields. Second, certain lexical fields can feature more lexical relations in one language than in the other. There is some degree of overlap between the two, but not even all synonyms in the language that is lexically richer in that field need to be in the relation of multiple equivalence. For example, some members of the synonymic nests may be so infrequent that they would realistically never function as equivalents of the words from the less rich language in that field. In addition, there may be more words in idioms, lexical relations, word-formation patterns, association networks, etc., none of which are engaging in the equivalence relation. More importantly, the examination of these two types of field density is completely different. Field density stemming from multiple equivalents is related to lexeme-level equivalence in its nature and in the proposed manner of studying it. Lexical-relations-based field density, on the other hand, uses primarily monolingual data, linking it to the parameters identified in cultural anthropology and psychology.

Both types of culturally relevant lexical field density rely on the idea of the semantic field. The idea of lexical fields was introduced in a systematic scholarly manner by Trier (1931). His famous claim reads:

Das Wortzeichenfeld als Ganzes muß gegenwärtig sein, wenn das einzelne Wortzeichen verstanden werden soll, und es wird verstanden im Maße der Gegenwärtigkeit des Feldes. Es 'bedeutet' nur in diesem Ganzen und kraft dieses Ganzen. Außerhalb eines Feldganzen kann es ein Bedeuten überhaupt nicht geben.

(The lexical sign field in its entirety has to be present if one wishes to understand an individual lexical sign and it will be understood in the measure of the presence of the field. It 'means' only in this entirety and based on the entirety. Outside of the whole field there could be no meaning at all.) (Trier, 1931:5)

These ideas were de facto application of Saussurean structuralism (see Saussure 1972 [1916]) in the field of lexicology. While this general idea certainly bears importance, the issue of what exactly constitutes a semantic or lexical field is problematic. Lexical fields intersect, broader fields include narrower ones, they can be established based on various criteria, etc. For example, the field of car mechanic terms includes technical and general terms, it intersects with the fields of tools, mechanics, electrics, traffic, etc., and it is included in the field of motorization. All this shows us that lexical or semantic fields are not fixed and straightforward entities but rather one of the many possible ways in which words may be connected. They can thus be established as ad hoc epistemological tools and, in different approaches, different fields can be established. Some of the issues related to establishing lexical fields were discussed in Chapter 3 of this monograph. Now that the fields will be deployed to concrete data, one should be particularly aware of their non-fixed character.

The first dataset used in this chapter will exemplify a higher prominence of multiple equivalence in some semantic fields. It will also point to the manner in which the categories established in cross-cultural psychology and anthropology can be tied to lexical identity.

The first case study examines Serbo-Croatian–English lexical anisomorphism in light of Edward T. Hall's (Hall, 1959, 1966) classic pattern of polychronism vs. monochronism. Albeit largely supplanted by Hofstede's cultural dimensions (1994) and Schwartz's Value Inventory (1992), Hall's classic pattern still represents a parsimonious explanatory device that is relevant in theoretical and applied linguistics. If confirmed, Hall's aforementioned pattern can offer a simple predictor of areas where lexical anisomorphism commonly appears and thus contribute to the contrastive lexical profile of the two languages in question.

According to Hall's classic pattern of polychronism versus monochronism, various cultures exhibit the cross-cultural differences shown in Table 5.1 (table from Dahl, 2004:11):

The English language cultures are predominantly monochronic while the cultures of Serbo-Croatian belong to the polychronic camp.

Preliminary research reported here uses data from Benson (1993) and Filipović (1989) to explore the hypothesis of the polychronic nature of the Bosnian, Croatian, and Serbian cultures (that share the standard Serbo-Croatian, each in its own ethnic variant) as an indicator of the areas of multiple equivalence in English, which functions within monochronic cultures.

Initial observation points to the fact that the areas with broadly defined measures (e.g., *sat* 'clock, watch, hour ...'), body parts (e.g., *ruka* 'arm, hand'), work and social relations (e.g., *raditi* 'work, function, do, act, be about ...'), and others are prone to mistakes and errors induced by lexical anisomorphism (e.g., when a Serbo-Croatian learner of English refers to a skin bag rather than leather bag, uses bill to refer to a receipt, etc.).

Table 5.1 *Monochronic and polychronic cultures*

	Monochronic culture	Polychronic culture
Interpersonal relations	Interpersonal relations are subordinate to present schedule	Present schedule is subordinate to interpersonal relations
Activity co-ordination	Schedule co-ordinates activity; appointment time is rigid	Interpersonal relations co-ordinate activity; appointment time is flexible
Task handling	One task at a time	Many tasks are handled simultaneously
Breaks and personal time	Breaks and personal time are sacrosanct regardless of personal ties.	Breaks and personal time are subordinate to personal ties.
Temporal structure	Time is inflexible; time is tangible.	Time is flexible; time is fluid.
Work/personal time separability	Work time is clearly separable from personal time.	Work time is not clearly separable from personal time.
Organisational perception	Activities are isolated from organisation as a whole; tasks are measured by output in time (activity per hour or minute).	Activities are integrated into organisation as a whole; tasks are measured as part of overall organisational goal.

The present research discusses the following questions:

a. Is monochronism vs. polychronism a useful predictor of lexical aniso-morphism between Serbo-Croatian and English?
b. If (a) is true, what is the extent of this potential predictor and what are its relations toward other possible predictors?
c. If (a) is true, what are the ways of translating this predictor into a contrastive lexical profile descriptor?

In order to answer the above questions, the following procedure has been conducted. Šipka (2007a), a list of 1,542 Serbo-Croatian words, was used to extract entries from the electronic version of Benson (1993). Bauman (2007), a version of the General Service List (2,284 lexemes), was used to extract entries from the electronic version of Filipović (1989) with multiple Serbo-Croatian equivalents. This yielded two lists of dictionary entries, a Serbo-Croatian–English list (extracted from Benson, 1993), comprising 630 items, and an English–Serbo-Croatian list (extracted from Filipović, 1989), consisting of 567 items.

These two lists are then analyzed by assigning to the entries ad hoc semantic categories consistent with the cross-cultural differences as proposed by Hall. The purpose of assigning the categories was not to form a coherent taxonomy but rather to come up with areas of abundant lexical anisomorphism. The categories were thus data-driven, and the two lists were analyzed independently. In addition, part-of-speech labels were attached to each entry to test an alternative, purely formal criterion to lexical anisomorphism.

Table 5.2 *Serbo-Croatian categories with multiple*
English equivalents

Category	Frequency	Percent
Social roles and affective-cognitive processes (social interaction)	172	27.3
Artifacts (institutions)	65	10.3
Measures	159	25.2
Operators (logical operators)	58	9.2
Body parts	27	4.3
Other	149	23.7
Total	630	100

Potential confounding variables include the dictionary source (e.g., different defining styles, different defining depth), the lists used to filter the data (e.g., possible omissions, inconsistencies), the process of assigning categories (e.g., a tendency to overemphasize phenomena consistent with the intended explanation). However important, these external valuables are not likely to alter this preliminary non-statistical research. For example, if in this set of data, broadly understood measures account for 10 percent of the cases of Serbo-Croatian–English lexical anisomorphism, the fact that in real life this accounts for 7, 8, 9, 11, 12, etc. percent will not alter the general usefulness of this cognition in defining contrastive lexical profile.

The categorization of material where Serbo-Croatian is the source language and English the target language (with multiple equivalents of the source-language lexeme) shows that there are five categories consistent with Hall's classic pattern under discussion that can help identify areas of lexical anisomorphism (the categories from the taxonomy discussed in Chapter 3 are given first followed by non-technical narrower designations in parentheses). Table 5.2 shows the distribution of categories observed.

The following simple heuristics can be created based on this data. Serving polychronic cultures, Serbo-Croatian is less precise (more holistic) in expressing the concepts related to social interaction and institutions as well as broadly understood measuring concepts (and related logical operators and designations of body parts). The categories will be exemplified in turn.

Table 5.3 exemplifies the concepts related to social interaction.

As can be seen, socially performed concrete actions, categories of people, and abstract concepts seem to be more precisely carved in English. This, in turn, appears to be consistent with a less flexible and more compartmentalized organization of time. Similarly, in the related semantic field of institutions, Serbo-Croatian is more holistic, as shown in Table 5.4.

Table 5.3 *The field of social interaction*

Serbo-Croatian	English
raditi	work, do, act
dati	give, let, permit, allow, have something done
kultura	culture, cultivation
trgovina	trade, commerce, business, store
nauka	science, scholarly work, schooling
poslovođa	chief, manager, foreman
prijatelj	friend, follower, lover, son's (or daughter's) father-in-law
savet	advice, counsel, council
žena	woman, wife, cleaning woman
čovjek	person, human, man, male, husband
momak	young man, bachelor, helper, assistant, guy, boyfriend
građanin	city dweller, citizen
društvo	society, organization, association, club, company, croud

Table 5.4 *Institutions*

Serbo-Croatian	English
pošta	post office, mail
prodavac	seller, salesman
vlada	government, reign/rule
parking	parking space, parking lot

Along the same lines, whenever a lexeme refers to a broadly understood measure, Serbo-Croatian seems to be far less precise, as demonstrated in Table 5.5.

If one construes the measures category broadly enough, they can include logical operators (which measure an abstract space) and body parts (which segment the body and which are in fact primordial measures, e.g., inch, feet, yard, etc. still used in some parts of the world). Examples of these categories are provided in Tables 5.6 and 5.7.

As demonstrated, the categories that can help alert to the Serbo-Croatian–English lexical anisomorphism are largely derived from the differences along the polychronic vs. monochronic axis. English–Serbo-Croatian lexical anisomorphism seems to follow a different pattern, which could be expected, given that a monochronic culture is expected to feature a more precise segmentation of its various conceptual realms. The English–Serbo-Croatian lexical anisomorphism can be captured in the categories shown in Table 5.8.

Three general phenomena are observable here. The polychronic vs. monochronic distinction is a basis for only one category – movement. Segmental

Table 5.5 *Measures*

Serbo-Croatian	English
dan	day, daylight, date
dosta	enough, rather
mjesec	month, moon
veče	evening, soiree
par	pair, couple, match (to someone), partner (in school)
broj	number, numeral, figure, issue, size
visina	height, altitude, elevation, pitch, heaven
dužina	length, longitude, duration
cijena	price, value/worth, cost
greška	error, mistake, faux pas, fallacy
račun	arithmetic; mathematics; calculus, bill, check, account, receipt, calculation, plan
odmor	rest; pause, recess, vacation

Table 5.6 *Logical operators*

Serbo-Croation	English
a	and, but, while
kao	as, like
nego	than, but

Table 5.7 *Body parts*

Serbo-Croatian	English
ruka	hand, arm
noga	foot, leg
jezik	tongue, language
prst	finger, toe

Table 5.8 *English to Serbo-Croatian categories*

Category	Frequency	Percent
Environment and artifacts (rural world)	227	40
States (general features)	82	14.5
States (negative features)	30	5.3
Physical-physiological processes (movement)	54	9.5
Other	174	30.7
Total	567	100

Table 5.9 *Rural world concepts*

English	Serbo-Croatian
bed	krevet, postelja, ploha, ploča, podloga, ležaj, postolje, gredica, lijeha, temelj, podloga …
board	daska, drvena ploča, oglasna ploča, karton, ljepenka, stol, odbor, vijeće …
branch	grana, mladica, rukav rijeke, odvojak ceste ili pruge, ogranak, dio, loza (obitelji), odjeljak, odsjek, razred, struka, podružnica, filijala
horn	rog, ticalo, čuperak perja, roževina, čaša od roga, automobilska truba, gramofonski lijevak, vrh Mjesečeva srpa, rukav rijeke, rukavac
iron	željezo, gvožde, željezni alat, palica za golf sa željeznim vrškom, motka sa žigom, glačalo

construal of time in English means that the source of movement is always referred to using the preposition *from* regardless of the configuration of the landmark. The destination is marked with the preposition *to*, again, regardless of the configuration of the landmark. In contrast to this, Serbo-Croatian maintains the *in:on/at* distinction when talking about a source, about a destination, and about a location (the prepositions are, literally, *from-on/at, from-in*, etc.) The other two factors have to do with the longer and richer cultural history of the English language as well as with the higher context-sensitivity of the English language (i.e., the second of Hall's classic patterns). Thus, all old terms related to the rural world have developed numerous semantic extensions in English while Serbo-Croatian expresses them using separate lexemes. Also, the English language is less specific when talking about general and especially negative features (of people and things). These four categories are exemplified in turn in Table 5.9.

Thus, for example, the speakers of Serbo-Croatian have to use separate words for *bed* as a piece of furniture, as a stratum of rock or ore, platform supporting other objects, bed of a river. Similarly, *board* as material and as an institution, *horn* as a bony outgrowth and hooter, *branch* as division of a stem and administrative division, and *iron* as material, golf club, and pressing appliance. Here, the external history of the language rather than a cultural pattern influences the lexicon – earlier introduction of some technologies and the lack of external lexical influences in English.

The examples in Table 5.10 clearly show a plethora of very specific Serbo-Croatian terms for general and negative features, which are understated in English (being expressed "between the lines" in English). For example, Serbo-Croatian speakers would understand that "not a very good idea" is still good, as otherwise they would call it "horrible, catastrophic, idiotic" or something similar. This, in turn, can be linked to the second of Hall's patterns, that of belonging to a low-context culture in Serbo-Croatian and high-context culture in English.

Table 5.10 *Features*

English	Serbo-Croatian
free	slobodan, nepodložan, nezavisan, nevezan, neograničen, bezuvjetan, nesprječen, nesmetan, oslobođen, pošteđen, oprošten, bez okova, slobodan, nedoslovan, slobodan, dopušten, dozvoljen, otvoren, riješen zapreka, riješen nepoželjnog, ne protivan, neoprečan, nevezan, nespojen, besplatan, franko, pristupačan, neusiljen, naravan, dobrovoljan, izdašan, obilan, neograničen, koji uživa, darežljiv, iskren, otvoren, naravan, intiman familijaran, prost, besraman, neobuzdan, drzak, nepristojan, oslobođen special – specijalan, naročit, osobit, poseban, izvanredan, odličan, izvrstan,
safe	siguran, pouzdan, bezopasan, neškodljiv, zdrav, čitav, koji je u redu, neoštećen, neozlijeđen, koji je u dobru stanju
open	otvoren, slobodan, nezauzet, nepokriven, otkrit, izložen, nesložen, nesavijen, probušen, porozan, isprekidan, slobodan, nevezan, blag, očit, jasan, javan, otvoren, iskren, darežljiv, gostoljubiv, otvoren, tekući, neodlučan, neriješen, pristupačan
special	specijalan, naročit, osobit, poseban, izvanredan, odličan, izvrstan
comfort	utjeha, okrepa, olakšica, udobnost, lagodnost, komfor
bad	loš, bezvrijedan, nevaljao, škodljiv, pokvaren, neugodan, odvratan, zao, opak, loša zdravlja, bolestan, bolan, nedovoljan, nedostatan, težak, jak, nemio, grdan
broken	razbijen, razlupan, prelomljen, slomljen, prebijen, isprekidan, smrvljen, skršen, nepotpun, nesavršen, loš, preostao, slab, oslabljen, pokunjen, narušen, propao, uništen, neravan
poor	siromašan, ubog, oskudan, potrebit, potreban, bijedan, slab, loš, koji ne zadovoljava, mršav, neplodan, slab, nerodan

Finally, Table 5.11 shows lesser precision of the English movement-related lexemes, which includes not only aforementioned prepositional markers but also more complex concepts.

The previous examples offer a solid ground for a heuristic to help account for a substantial portion of lexical anisomorphism. The alternative, purely formal approach, utilizing the part-of-speech categorization, presented in Tables 5.12 and 5.13, does not offer much. The only useful information is the fact that verbs feature more Serbo-Croatian multiple equivalents of English terms. However, this phenomenon, being a consequence of the lesser precision in the sphere of the basic rural-life terms and movement in English, is already accounted for by these two semantic categories.

These results point to the conclusion that Hall's pattern of polychronism versus monochronism offers a useful lexical profiling tool. One can also see the limited role that the pattern of low- versus high-context cultures played in lexical profiling. The results demonstrate that both these patterns need to be taken into consideration along with other ingredients of anisomorphism.

Table 5.11 *Movement*

English	Serbo-Croatian
road	sidrište, rada, cesta, drum, put, staza, tračnice, željeznička pruga, putovanje
lead	vodstvo, vođenje, upravljanje, preticanje, prednjačenje, primjer, uzor, uputa, sport prednost, umjetan tok vode, prolaz u ledu, vod, uzica, remen, pravo kao prvi zaigrati, prednost, glavna, naslovna uloga, prvi glumac (glumica), prvak
to	k, ka, do, o, pri, kraj, kod, uz, blizu, sve do, u, u svrhu, radi, na, za
from	od, iz, po, o, s, kod, u, odakle

Table 5.12 *Serbo-Croatian to English parts of speech*

POS	Frequency	Percent
Nouns	332	52.6
Verbs	125	19.8
Adjectives	87	13.8
Adverbs	38	6.0
Prepositions	23	3.7
Pronouns	11	1.7
Conjunctions	8	1.3
Particles	5	0.8
Exclamation	1	0.2
Total	630	100.0

Table 5.13 *English to Serbo-Croatian parts of speech*

POS	Frequency	Percent
Nouns	285	50.3
Verbs	153	27.0
Adjectives	80	14.1
Adverbs	28	4.9
Prepositions	16	2.8
Conjunctions	3	0.5
Pronouns	2	0.4
Total	567	100.0

The following ingredients of a contrastive lexical profile can be presented.
1. The English equivalents of basic Serbo-Croatian vocabulary items will feature multiple equivalents in the spheres of social interaction concepts,

including institutions, broadly understood measures, encompassing logical operators and terms for body parts.

2. Serbo-Croatian equivalents of basic English terms will feature increased multiple equivalence with old rural-world terms, general and negative features, as well as movement terms.

It should be repeated that Hall's two classic patterns partially explain the phenomenon, but the contrastive lexical profile is formed by numerous other factors, for example, patterns of forming metaphors in the English language, which are not present in Serbo-Croatian. This, in turn, seems to be the matter of spontaneous historical development in English rather than a consequence of the need to carve lexical fields more precisely in Serbo-Croatian. This highlights the need to reduce the level of determinism in interpreting phenomena of this kind because, as discussed in Chapter 2, such determinism is often problematic with all major approaches to language and culture.

More broadly, the analysis of multiple equivalence between English and Serbo-Croatian demonstrates that the full picture about contrastive lexical profiles is a rather complex one. One needs to accept that some differences should be ascribed to random spontaneous development. Linguistic data need to be connected to the body of knowledge in anthropology. Moreover, all cases need to be taken into consideration in the fields accessible to the general body of speakers, rather than those used in the circles of writers and other members of linguistic elites. In other words, while the so-called cultural keywords may be a constituent of a cultural profile, the profile itself is much more complex and much less predictable than one might be tempted to believe, based on a set of arbitrarily selected lexemes.

The second example of the analysis of field density relying on multiple equivalence will be provided using English–Russian data from Hidekel' and Kaul' (2006). The authors selected very frequent Russian words that feature multiple equivalents in English. They determine the purpose of the dictionary as follows:

Словарь, исходящий из понимания специфики русского мышления, помогает изучающему не только понять особенности русско–английской эквивалентности, но и обучает формулированию исходно русской мысли на английском языке.

(This dictionary, based on the understanding of the specificity of Russian thinking, not only helps the learners to understand the peculiarities of Russian–English equivalence but also trains them to formulate source Russian thought in English.) (Hidekel' and Kaul', 2006:2)

Obviously, there is a certain degree of arbirtrariness in determining which words are frequently used and hence needed by the learners. However, this should not significantly influence the distribution of semantic fields, given that it would be hard to imagine that the authors systematically favored one field

Table 5.14 *General taxonomy fields in Hidekel'and Kaul' (2006)*

Category	Number	Percent
Processes – cognitive-affective	61	26.8
Processes – physical-physiological	43	18.9
States – cognitive-affective	19	8.3
States – physical-physiological	6	2.6
Social terms	37	16.2
Artifacts	14	6.1
Environment	5	2.2
Body parts	4	1.8
Measures	29	12.7
Operators	10	4.4
Total	228	100.0

over the other (they were selecting the examples based on the number of equivalents). What is important to note is that the authors selected words with an abundant number of equivalents – only exceptionally were there two or three, most commonly there were five or more equivalents, and not uncommonly more than ten of them. This data then does not point just to multiple equivalence in general but rather to highly fragmented cases of it.

Applying the macrocategories explained in Chapter 3 yields the results in Table 5.14.

Table 5.14 shows the following. First, affective-cognitive fields (in both processes and states) are much more prone to highly fragmented multiple equivalence than their physical-physiological counterparts. This is not surprising given that the former is more closely aligned with the culture than the latter, which is more rooted in general human faculties. Second, social things and measures are another two areas of concentrated multiple equivalence. This is consistent with the findings from the Serbo-Croatian–English dictionaries. Applying non-technical categories from that research yields the results in Table 5.15.

Generally, there is a great deal of alignment with the Serbo-Croatian–English data, with two exceptions. First, the number of other cases (i.e., those that do not belong to selected lexical fields) is somewhat higher. Second, the role of institutions is rather limited in the Russian case. Both these differences can be ascribed to the nature of the Russian dictionary – namely that it includes cases of highly fragmented multiple equivalence. In the fields of institutions, it is mostly just a case of binary multiple equivalence, e.g., building vs. institution (as post office and postal service). Also, many cases of multiple equivalence in other selected fields were cases of binary equivalence which would not have been treated in this dictionary.

Table 5.15 *Non-technical categories in Hidekel' and Kaul' (2006)*

Category	Number	Percent
Social roles and affective-cognitive processes (social interaction)	89	39.0
Measures	29	12.7
Operators (logical operators)	10	4.4
Body parts	4	1.8
Artifacts (institutions)	4	1.8
Other	92	40.4
Total	228	100.0

Hidekel' and Kaul' (2006) and similar dictionaries also offer material for qualitative analysis of the differences, as can be seen from the following example.

АРЕНДОВАТЬ, гл. – 1. to lease 2. to rent 3. to hire

Русские арендовать, брать в аренду, брать напрокат не предполагают различия по характеру нанимаемого и времени найма. Английские соответствия используются различно в зависимости от времени и характера нанимаемого объекта.

(Russian арендовать, брать в аренду, брать напрокат do not assume differences based on the nature of what is leased and the time of the lease. The English equivalents are used differently depending on the time of the leased object.) (Hidekel' and Kaul', 2006:7)

Conducting a qualitative analysis in select semantic fields can reveal possible repeated patterns of differences. The next step in the analysis would thus be to look into the underlying patterns of difference in each concrete case.

As one could see, a higher degree of multiple equivalence in some fields is at the same time a higher lexical density of those fields in the language that features multiple equivalents. If a considerably higher degree of multiple equivalence exists in one field when we go from language one to language two, then when we go in the opposite direction, that also means that language two features more words in that particular field than language one. In other words, non-reciprocal multiple equivalence in a lexical field is also a lexical imbalance in that particular field.

I will now turn to the comparison of lexical fields based on monolingual dictionary data. First, a comparison of idioms will be presented. Second, the size of lexical fields will be examined based on the network of lexical relations. Third, the density of word-formation networks will be examined. Finally, associative networks in certain fields will be explored.

Idioms and proverbs are often mentioned as expressions of cultural identity in the lexicon. At the very outset, one should be aware of the specific non-prototypical lexical status of both these elements – they are used in a limited set of situations and not as often as the core vocabulary (proverbs even less than idioms). Second, their content and literal meaning often stem from the previous stages of cultural and lexical development, and it can hence be less relevant for the current cultural profile of the speakers.

Nevertheless, a number of interesting questions can be asked about idioms and proverbs. First, which semantic fields typically feature more of this material. For example, do physical and physiological actions generally attract more idioms and proverbs than affective and cognitive actions, as may be inferred from cognitive linguistic research? Second, which words are most commonly found in the idioms? Third, what are quantitative markers of culture-specific beliefs and practices in proverbs? One can go on with questions of this kind, but this will suffice to illustrate the point. I will exemplify research of this kind by comparing Russian and Serbian idiom data and by summarizing prior research on Polish and Serbo-Croatian proverbs.

Idioms will be illustrated by Otašević (2012), a Serbian phraseological dictionary with over 11,000 idiom entries (many of which combine alternative forms of the idiom in one entry), and Larionova (2014), a Russian dictionary with over 4,000 idiom entries (many of which combine alternative forms of the idiom in one entry). Given significant differences in the size of these two monolingual dictionaries and differences in lexicographic strategies, the most reasonable contrasting would be to compare the percentages of certain words in the total body of idioms in each language. In this exploration, I used the following procedure. I extracted all idiom entries from both dictionaries, and I then created frequency lists of words in both of them. This procedure eliminated the effects of different size and mostly eliminated the effect of different lexicographic strategies. I then looked into the first 100 ranks in both frequency lists and extracted all semantic words in this frequency range, excluding functional words (e.g., prepositions, pronouns, forms of the verb *to be*). The remaining items show which words most commonly contribute to the lexical composition of the idioms in the two observed languages.

What is interesting in Table 5.16 is that, in both languages, the basis for the idioms are most frequently parts of the human body and basic physical and physiological actions, e.g., *put, throw, give, lift, enter, exit*. What is different between the two languages is that the ratio of these two categories is opposite. Serbian idioms are dominated by physical and physiological actions, while their Russian counterparts show a balance of this category with body parts (which are somewhat more frequent). This more dynamic character of Serbian idioms may be used to create a hypothesis that this difference follows a higher level of masculinity dimension (higher preference for achievement, heroism, assertiveness, success, etc.) in the Balkans than in the Slavic North. To prove it, one would need to conduct more comprehensive research, involving qualitative analysis of the idioms and also other segments of the lexicon. Further possible areas of contrasting can be explored based on works such as Mršević-Radović

Table 5.16 *Subject-matter fields in top-ranked words in Russian and Serbian idioms*

Serbian	Number	Percent
Physical-physiological actions	41	67.2
Body parts	9	14.8
Cognitive-affective actions	4	6.6
Social roles	3	4.9
Beliefs	2	3.3
Environment	2	3.3
Total	61	100.0
Russian	Number	Percent
Body parts	19	42.2
Physical-physiological actions	18	40.0
Cognitive-affective actions	3	6.7
Environment	3	6.7
Beliefs	2	4.4
Total	45	100.0

(2008), where the link between idioms and what the author calls "national cultures" are seen in the way mythology, space, time, demons, and the relation between God and man are mirrored in idioms. Contrasting lanuages in one or more of these fields may reveal relevant elements of the lexical profile in its idiomatic sphere.

Dobosiewicz (2002) conducted a contrastive analysis of Serbo-Croatian and Polish proverbs about gender relations. He analyzed proverbs about females, males, and gender relations. He found out a high degree of similarity between the two languages as to what is ascribed to these three entities, and considerable differences in how these predications are expressed in proverbs. Only around 30 percent of Serbo-Croatian proverbs feature direct Polish equivalents. For example, the features of malice, belligerence, stubbornness, authoritarianism, irresponsibility, stupidity, and so on are ascribed to women in both sets of proverbs, but each language finds its own linguistic forms of making the same or similar predications. The following hypothesis may be formulated based on these results. In some areas, related languages share deeper underlying cognitive structures. The differences between them are built on linguistic material – in the imagery or combination patterns specific to each particular language.

The size of lexical fields will be demonstrated by two Polish–Serbo-Croatian studies, one addressing computing terminology, the other obscene words.

Šipka (2002b) explored the field of users' computing terms in Polish and Serbian (just one ethnic variant of Serbo-Croatian to exclude ethnic variation as a potential factor for differences between the two languages). The analysis involved computing terms that are known by the general user population that are consequently attested in general dictionaries. This means that highly technical terms not known to the general body of speakers were excluded. A list of these concepts was established based on the English language and it turned out that an average number of words for these concepts is 1.21 in Polish and 1.41 in Serbian. Given that this research was conducted at the time when computing terminology was new in the general public discourse, one can hypothesize that the speakers of Serbian could not come to an agreemen on what should be used. This hypothesis can also be supported by the fact that Polish used less direct borrowing from English. A list of 387 terms from the *American Heritage Dictionary* labeled as "computing" was used to examine the way the two languages came up with new terms. The resuts were distributed in such a way that Polish had 93.64% terms based on internal resources (word formation, semantic extensions) and 6.45% borrowed directly from English. This ratio in Serbian was 89.66% from internal resources and 10.34 from borrowing.

Pecyna (1998) analyzed the field of obscene words in Polish and Serbo-Croatian. She collected synonyms in colloquial Polish and Serbo-Croatian, based on available studies, relevant dictionaries, corpus, and fieldwork. She found a consistently higher concentration of synonyms for basic obscene terms in Serbo-Croatian than in Polish (those terms based on primary sexual and excretion organs and activities). This was coupled with the higher diversity in the motivation and origin of those terms. For example, for two primary sexual organs, the distribution was as follows. 'Penis' had 30 synonyms in Polish versus 196 in Serbo-Croatian, 'vagina' had 28 Polish synonyms versus 117 in Serbo-Croatian. This clear lexical imbalance between the two languages shows higher prominence of these concepts in Serbo-Croatian over Polish. The fact that Serbo-Croatian comprises ethnic variants may have contributed to a smaller part of it, but even with that kind of variation taken into consideration, the difference is drastic. For this, again, I would propose a hypothesis about the link to a higher prominence of masculinity in the Slavic South than in the North.

It is clear from both previously mentioned pieces of research (on computing and obscene terms) that a lexical imbalance of the fields was attested. The next reasonable research question would be about cultural generators of these differences. One hypothesis may be that they are a reflection of Hofstede's masculinity vs. femininity dimension. Serbo-Croatian, being closer to the masculinity end of the scale, values agreement less and makes obscene words more prominent than Polish, which is closer to the femininity end of the scale. Obviously, to prove or disprove this hypothesis, one would need to conduct large-scale research at various levels. Nevertheless, data stemming from the analysis of the density of various fields can be used as evidence in conjunction with other pieces of information.

Table 5.17 *Negative and positive characterization of a person in Ćosić (2008)*

Lexical field	Number of headwords	Percent	Average size of the synonym nest
Negative characterizations	254	87	15.84
Positive characterizations	38	13	8.76

One way of exploring culturally relevant lexical field density is to compare the density of semantic fields containing polar opposites in monolingual dictionaries. To demonstrate this, I compared the number of entries for nouns that negatively characterize people versus those that positively characterize them in Ćosić (2008), a Serbian dictionary of synonyms. The first category can be exemplified by nouns like *bandit* 'bandit', *glupan* 'fool', *đubre* 'human garbage', while the second includes examples such as *altruista* 'altruist', *genije* 'genius', *lepotica* 'beauty (female)'. Only those meanings of these words that pertain to one of the two polar characterizations of persons were analyzed. In some cases, such as *mangup* (which means both 'ruffian' and 'cool guy'), the two meanings were polar opposites of each other. The number of headwords with negative and positive characterization was counted, along with the average number of synonyms in the nest. Numerous entries were cross-referenced, which means that they had only one synonym along with the main entry. The results are presented in Table 5.17.

As we can see, the lexical field of negative characterization is dominant in both the number of entries and the average size of synonym nests. Needless to say, there are dictionary factors that affect these numbers. Most notable of these factors is how often the dictionary compiler states members of synonym nests as separate entries as opposed to just listing them in the nest behind another entry. However, the dominance of the negative characterizations is preponderant to such a degree that dictionary strategies do not change the general picture in any significant way. The picture that emerges is one with a very clear focus on the negative when characterizing people. This would be consistent with the focus on negativity as a cross-cultural difference that was recently documented by Koopmann-Holm and Tsai (2014) on more negative German and less negative American condolences.

A similar imbalance between the negative and the positive can be found in other dictionaries. Thus, Jovanović and Atanacković (1980), a subject-matter dictionary of Serbo-Croatian, attest 125 words for sadness and 45 words for happiness (73% vs. 27%). For comparison, in Roget (1916), the ratio of dejection and cheerfulness is only 55% vs. 45%.

Lexical prominence of certain fields is determined not only by the number of synonyms, hyponyms, etc. in it, but also by more robust word-formation networks. To use a self-evident example, Slavic languages will feature many more derivations from the word *Slav* known to the majority of speakers than non-Slavic languages, in some of which even the central term in the word-formation network may be unknown. This is exemplified by the obscure word *Slavdom* in English that was discussed in the Introduction. The importance of word formation for the "linguistic image of the word" has already been discussed by Vendina (1998).

To demonstrate this line of research, I analyzed word-formation networks of basic body parts in Tihonov (2003), a Russian word formation dictionary, and Gortan-Premk et al. (2003), its Serbian counterpart. The following body parts from the Swadesh (2017) list attested in both of the aforementioned dictionaries were analyzed: *skin, bone, hair, head, ear, eye, nose, mouth, tooth, tongue, nail, foot, leg, knee, hand, belly, neck*, and *breasts*. In some cases, one word in one language was confronted with two in the other. Thus, *hair* is *dlaka* and *kosa*, *neck* is *šija* and *vrat*, and *breast* is *grudi* and *prsa* in Serbian, while *eye* is глаз and око and belly is живот and брюхо in Russian. The results of this analysis are presented in Table 5.18.

Table 5.18 *Word-formation networks of basic body parts in Serbian and Russian*

Word	Russian count	Serbian count	Russian to Serbian balance	Russian to Serbian balance as percentage of the total
skin	84	71	13	8%
bone	74	80	−6	−4%
hair	82	70	12	8%
head	204	375	−171	−30%
ear	65	76	−11	−8%
eye	132	178	−46	−15%
nose	78	32	46	42%
mouth	42	46	−4	−5%
tooth	100	120	−20	−9%
tongue	83	51	32	24%
nail	10	14	−4	−17%
foot	32	10	22	52%
leg	175	153	22	7%
knee	26	35	−9	−15%
hand	188	312	−124	−25%
belly	50	59	−9	−8%
neck	46	54	−8	−8%
breasts	57	78	−21	−16%
Total	*1528*	*1814*	*−286*	*−17%*
Average	84.89	100.78	−15.89	−1%

Table 5.19 *The frequency of word-
formation nests in Russian and Serbian*

Russian		Serbian	
head	204	head	375
hand	188	hand	312
leg	175	eye	178
eye	132	leg	153
tooth	100	tooth	120
skin	84	bone	80
tongue	83	breasts	78
hair	82	ear	76
nose	78	skin	71
bone	74	hair	70
ear	65	belly	59
breasts	57	neck	54
belly	50	tongue	51
neck	46	mouth	46
mouth	42	knee	35
foot	32	nose	32
knee	26	nail	14
nail	10	foot	10

We can see that body parts have significantly richer word-formation networks in Serbian than their Russian counterparts (the difference amounts to
17% of all attested members of word-formation networks in both observed
languages). We can also see that in several cases where Russian has richer
word-formation networks, the difference is drastic (52% for foot, 42% for nose,
and 24% for tongue, with some others in the lower figures). The two dictionaries used to extract this dataset were compiled using very similar methodology, so lexicographic differences could only have played a minor role.

Frequency count for the members of word-formation networks for each body
part is presented in Table 5.19.

We can see that at the top the two languages look very similar and then more
substantial differences develop as one goes down the list. A qualitative analysis
shows that richer word-formation networks correspond with richer polysemic
structures. For example, one case where Russian is richer, namely *nose*, corresponds with richer metaphorical extensions that the word has in Russian, which
are not common in Serbian (most notably the beak and the bow of a ship).
However, the difference in word-formation patterns is actually based on the fact
that the Russian word-formation network features a number of modifying pre-
fixoids focusing on the color and shape of one's nose. Why these qualitative
differences occur is something that can only be answered in a more complex

Table 5.20 *Associative networks of Russian and Serbian basic body parts*

Stimulus	Russian responses	Serbian responses
skin	рожа 'red skin (disease)' 9; белая 'white' 7; нежная 'tender' 6; загорелая 'bronzed', мягкая 'soft' 4; гладкая 'smooth', натуральная 'natural' 3	јакна 'jacket' 61; ципеле 'shoes' 23; животиња 'animal' 18; нежна 'soft' 17; тен 'complexion' 15
hair	длинные 'long' 12; дыбом 'stand on end', русые 'dark blond', рыжие 'red', светлые 'light' 5; густые 'thick' 4; голова 'head', коса 'hair', красивые 'beautiful' 3; блондинки 'of a blond', вьются 'fly', грязные 'dirty', мои 'my', на голове 'on the head', пышные 'fluffy', черные 'black' 2	дуга 'long' 92; плава 'blond' 39; глава 'head' 37; црна 'black' 35; длака 'hair (on the body)' 32
head	болит 'hurts' 66; умная 'wise' 43; садовая 'nonsense (idiom)' 23; светлая 'bright' 18; пустая 'empty' 12;	памет 'mind' 74; писмо 'tails (as in heads and tails)' 64; коса 'hair' 55; мозак 'brain' 46; шећера 'sugar (idiom)' 37
ear	болит 'hurts', горло-нос 'throat, nose' 7; большое 'big', слух 'hearing' 5; нос 'nose' 4; востро 'keep open', красное 'red', серьга 'earring', слышать 'listen', собаки 'of a dog' 3	слух 'hearing' 102; грло нос 'throat nose' 100; чути 'listen' 78; грло 'throat' 66; нос 'nose' 40
eye	алмаз 'jewel' 58; голубой 'blue' 23; зеленый 'green', око 'eye' 17; зоркий 'sharp' 16; острый 'sharp' 15; карий 'brown', очки 'eyeglasses' 12	вид 'sight' 127; плаво 'blue' 60; поглед 'view' 32; зелено 'green' 31; зеница 'pupil' 30
nose	длинный 'long' 68; больной 'sick', красный 'red' 38; курносый 'pug-nosed' 35; рот 'mouth' 30; прямой 'straight' 21	мирис 'smell' 76; лице 'face' 55; велики 'big' 40; уста 'mouth' 30; понос 'pride' 27
mouth	большой 'big' 67; губы 'lips' 33; до ушей 'up to ears' 28; красивый 'beautiful' 26; зубы 'teeth', нос 'nose' 25	пољубац 'kiss' 126; зуби 'tooth' 89; храна 'food' 85; језик 'mouth' 46; усне 'lips' 29
tooth	болит 'hurt' 28; больной 'sick' 17; боль 'pain' 14; белый 'white' 6; коренной 'root', рот 'mouth' 5	бол 'pain' 178; зубар 'dentist' 95; бело 'white' 46; каријес 'decay' 37; осмех 'smile' 28
tongue	длинный 'long' 14; русский 'Russian' 8; родной 'native' 6; без костей 'without bones', говяжий 'beef' 4; английский 'English', немецкий 'German' 3	говор 'speech; 80; уста 'moth' 72; српски 'Serbian' 66; енглески 'English', матерњи 'native' 30; пољубац 'kiss' 25
leg	рука 'hand' 92; болит 'hurts' 28; больная 'sick', человека 'of a man' 14; обувь 'footwear' 12; большая 'big', ботинок 'shoe', длинная 'long', красивая 'beautiful', кривая 'crooked', правая 'straight' 11	рука 'hand' 146; ципела 'shoe' 85; фудбал 'soccer' 29; стопало 'foot' 25; патика 'sneaker' 23
hand	нога 'leg' 78; друга 'other' 38; правая 'straight' 18; сильная 'strong' 16; об руку 'hand in hand (idiom)' 14; владыка 'his eminence' 11	нога 'leg' 73; пријатељство 'friendship', прст 'finger' 44; прсти 'fingers' 38; прстен 'ring' 37; помоћ 'help' 30

Table 5.20 (*cont.*)

Stimulus	Russian responses	Serbian responses
neck	длинная 'long' 19; тонкая 'thin' 10; голова 'head' 6; лебединая 'swan's' 5; грязная 'dirty' 4	глава 'head' 93; шија 'neck' 79; огрлица 'necklace' 73; жирафа 'giraffe' 52; ланчић 'necklace' 26
breasts	большая 'big' 14; колесом 'pumped up (idiom)' 8; женская 'female' 6; волосатая 'hairy', высокая 'tall', широкая 'broad' 4; женщина 'woman' 3	жена 'woman' 75; велике 'big' 41; тело 'body' 30; прса 'breast' 27; мајка 'mother' 24

investigation of various interconnected pieces of data. The idea that lexical features cannot be studied in isolation and by choosing only the kinds of examples that are convenient for the researcher is an ongoing idea throughout this book.

We saw that in addition to the different number of the members in word-formation networks, languages also differ in the nature of these networks, i.e., which words are included in word-formation networks and which particular body parts dominate the pool. A similar difference in the qualitative features can also be found in associative networks (which encompass the responses in association experiments, the words that speakers first think of when they hear the word in question, i.e., the stimulus). To exemplify research in this field, I analyzed associative networks of basic body parts from Swadesh (2017), which were attested in both Karaulov et al. (2002), a Russian associative dictionary, and Stefanović et al. (2005), its Serbian counterpart. The results of this analysis are presented in Table 5.20 with the number of responses given after each of them.

While there are some common associations between the two languages in question, such as lexical relations (synonyms, meronyms, etc.), sound similarity, idioms, and so on, what stands out as a remarkable difference is that Russian features many more descriptives that focus on the appearance. The number of those in both languages is presented in Table 5.21.

As can be seen, if one is to trust the soundness in the methodology of the two analyzed dictionaries, there is a clear difference in this regard between speakers of the two languages. This is coupled by a qualitative analysis of the Russian and Serbian word-formation patterns, where one can find numerous descriptive compounds (e.g., for the word 'nose'). Again, the place of this particular finding can only be fully understood in broader vocabulary ranges and confronted with other types of evidence. One additional problem with associative networks data lies in the fact that a great deal of associations may be influenced by current events. Thus, had the Serbian association network been studied in the 1990s (when an embargo on gasoline was imposed against Serbia), the word *benzin* 'gasoline' would

Table 5.21 *Visual descriptives in Russian and Serbian associative networks of body parts*

Stimulus	Russian appearance descriptives	Serbian appearanace descriptives
skin	6	1
hair	9	2
head	1	0
ear	1	0
eye	3	2
nose	3	1
mouth	3	0
tooth	1	0
tongue	1	0
leg	5	0
hand	2	0
neck	4	0
breasts	5	1
Average	3.38	0.54

Table 5.22 *A bilingual word sketch for* house/maison *from Kilgarriff (2013:3)*

modifier 24107 1.3	modifier 3467 0.8	object_of 9534 1.5	object_de 5965 2.3
white 702 9.65	paternal 112 47.29	build 726 9.06	habiter 220 42.58
opera 334 8.6	hanté 47 44.74	buy 533 8.7	bâtir 136 40.43
manor 236 8.19	familial 162 41.68	sell 306 8.02	quitter 320 39.26
guest 263 8.04	universel 233 38.6	own 138 7.77	construire 220 37.76
terraced 197 8.04	voisin 100 33.12	enter 171 7.59	acheter 139 31.84

house (noun) British National Corpus freq = 57976 (516.8 per million)
maison French web corpus freq = 36732 (289.6 per million)

[…]

likely have been associated with *nestašica* 'shortage', *embargo* 'embargo', *red* 'line, queue', *plastična boca* 'plastic bottle' (gasoline was so scarce that bottles were used to sell it in), etc.

The additional fields of research (lexical relations, word formation, idioms, and association networks) that were exemplified here are not the only possible lexeme and lexicon-level techniques for studying cross-cultural differences. Another possibility would be to include corpus data, and to compare bilingual word sketches, with an eye toward finding patterns in a given semantic field. Bilingual word sketches point to bilingual differences in common collocations, as demonstrated by the English–French example from Kilgarriff (2013:3) presented in Table 5.22. The words combining with the English word *house* and its French equivalent *maison* are provided in this example, along with the number of cases and their frequency per one million words. The first column contains the modifiers of the English word, the second, the modifiers of the French word, the third, the words that have the English word as their objects, and the fourth, the words that have the French word as their object.

If a pattern is found in the whole semantic field, for example that French (unlike English) consistently combines household items with people, such as family and neighbors, then that may be a piece of evidence pointing to a cross-cultural difference. The same can be done for Slavic languages. However, this kind of research is considerably more time-consuming, given that data need to be harvested (as opposed to being available in dictionaries). Additionally, representativeness is generally much more problematic for corpora than for dictionaries.

6   Stability and Change

Now that synchronic lexeme-level and lexicon-level study of the deep layer has been discussed and identified, I will turn to the diachronic aspects of the phenomenon. I will first discuss semantic divergence tracking to explore how culturally relevant lexical divisions in the deep layer are created by semantic splits of the inherited lexicon (section 6.1). I will then turn to lexical divergence tracking, including not only semantic but also usage sphere component (section 6.2). Divergence tracking is again illustrated by the material of Slavic languages, concentrating on the subgroups of Slavic languages in the former section and on the three most populous languages in each group in the latter.

6.1   Semantic Divergence Tracking

A key question in the analysis of the differences in lexical resources of present-day Slavic languages is that of what mechanisms caused the split of initially one Proto-Slavic system into a number of different systems. It goes without saying that this question can be applied to any group of genetically related languages (for example, one Indo-European language with another). However, Slavic languages represent a particularly interesting case, given that the number of languages in the Slavic branch is relatively low, they are culturally diverse, and their split is relatively recent (obviously, against a vast backdrop of diachronic linguistic and general historical development). Slavic material lends itself to analysis, then, much better than its counterparts in many other related language branches (e.g., those that have many more languages or those where the split is much earlier). The question about the separation of specific languages from the same source is concurrently a question about their unity. The factors that have influenced the lexical split of these languages have also left some subject-matter areas of the lexicon unchanged and thus common to some or all Slavic languages. These areas of the lexicon connect Slavic languages and often separate them from other language groups. That, in turn, contributes to creating the cultural identity of each particular language and of Slavdom.

Research presented in this chapter deals with the deep layer of Slavic cultural identity. It considers the mechanisms that have created differences in the three groups of Slavic languages. The diverging processes in the lexicon have often been mentioned but rarely studied. Vendina (2014:42) correctly notes:

Итак, картина общеславянских ареальных связей свидетельствует о том, что они относятся к истокам формирования славянского языкового единства. Однако в ходе исторического развития они оказались разрушены процессами, протекавшими в разных частях Славии самостоятельно и приведшими к последующему диалектному членению и образованию современных славянских языков.

(The picture of general Slavic territorial connections and witnesses are related to the sources of the formation of Slavic linguistic unity. However, in the course of historical development they were destroyed by the processes that happened separately in different parts of Slavdom and that brought about the ensuing dialectal differentiation and the formation of present-day Slavic languages.)

Initially a common set of roots and their senses has, with time, evolved in each of the three groups of Slavic languages. An umbrella question of this research is the extent to which the sense of original Slavic was preserved, how much was changed and how much completely lost. Finding answers to these questions gives us some insight into the historical processes that have transformed initial Slavic lexical mass and its related cultural identity into three separate groups (with further differentiation into separate languages, which is not the subject of the data analysis in this section).

A range of more sophisticated tools of semantic analysis in historical linguistics has been proposed (e.g., Geeraerts, 2010:233–239). Similarly, in Slavic studies Markova (2016:101–176) establishes a taxonomy of the types of semantic transformations of the inherited Proto-Slavic lexical units: widening of the meaning, narrowing of the meaning, semantic widening of the etymological root, the development of distinctive features of a general semantics of the cognate, entantiosemy, metaphorical transfer, metonymical transfer, stylistic displacement of the lexeme, development of a connotative meaning of the lexeme, and conceptual peculiarities of lexical units. However, I decided to use the simplest possible model. This decision is justified by the fact that it is not semantic change that is of interest in this research but rather how it shapes the lexical, and indirectly cultural, profile of the three groups of Slavic languages. In that light, more sophisticated taxonomies in the study of semantic change will be consolidated into a simpler scheme, which is more attuned to the goals of the present analysis.

The following questions, related to semantic development from Proto-Slavic to present-day Slavic languages, are examined.

1. What proportion of the words in each of the three groups of Slavic language have lost, changed, or preserved their original Proto-Slavic sense?
2. How much do the various subject-matter fields and word classes differ in the ratio of loss, change, and preservation in relation to Slavic languages as a whole and each of the three groups of Slavic languages?

3. How do the three groups of Slavic languages relate to each other in terms of this ratio (in other words, how often are the processes identical in each group and how often do they differ from one another)?

4. In the situations where a sense changes (one sense is replaced with another or there is another sense next to the preserved one), what are the most common mechanisms of change?

These questions were explored using the data from Derksen (2008), a dictionary of Slavic inherited lexicon, which provides Proto-Indo-European roots along with their senses and the continuants in four groups of Slavic languages (Church Slavonic, East, West, and South Slavic).

The following procedure was used with Derksen's (2008) dataset. The entries from Derksen (2008), 1,703 of them, were selected, where the Proto-Slavic sense was reconstructed. The rest of the entries, without the Proto-Slavic sense reconstructed, were discarded. For each of the selected entries, a database row was created with the following fields:

1. The word in Proto-Slavic
2. The sense of the Proto-Slavic word
3. The subject-matter area
4. The part of speech
5. The Church Slavonic reflex code
6. The East Slavic reflex code
7. The West Slavic reflex code
8. The South Slavic reflex code.

The first two fields were just taken over from Derksen (2008), while other fields contain self-created categories. The coding schema applied in each of them will be discussed in turn. Subject-matter fields were created to provide a simple generalization for the entities present during the Proto-Slavic time. The goal of this taxonomy is different from those known in Proto-Indo-European and Slavic studies, the goal of which was to provide thorough analyses of separate narrower lexical fields (see, e.g., Clarkson, 2007:196–209; Beekers, 2011:35–41). At its top level, the taxonomy of subject-matter fields relies on the distinction between things, processes, and states (as understood in Langacker, 1987:220); in things, the next distinction is whether the thing is non-human or human; while the three final categories distinguish between physical-physiological on the one hand, and affective-cognitive on the other. In addition to these content-based fields, two additional function-based fields were used, for operators and measures. Obviously, the taxonomy deployed is rather eclectic in its nature. The top content–form distinction is the reflection of the well-known lexicographic distinction between the content and functional words. The next level includes a cognitive-linguistic categorization, while lower levels in each of the three main categories are commonly used in describing lexical fields in historical lexicology, and other similar fields. While any taxonomy can be

Content

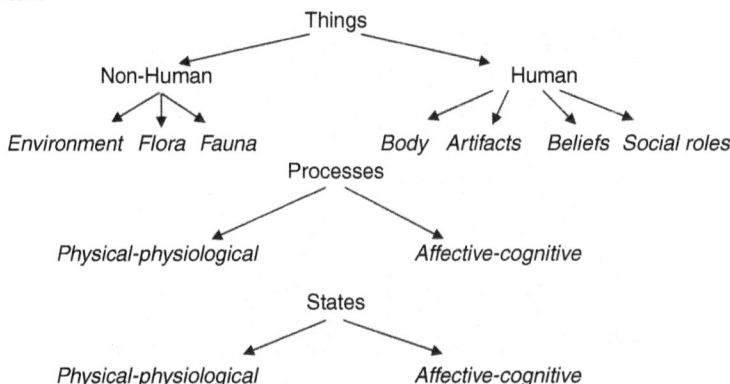

Figure 6.1 A taxonomy of subject-matter fields in the Slavic inherited lexicon

criticized for inconsistencies, the present one gives a reasonably consistent coverage of the fields found in the present dataset. At the same time, its hierarchical organization enables the dataset to be explored at several different levels of the taxonomy. The full taxonomy (already discussed in Chapter 3) presents itself as shown in Figure 6.1, with fifteen italicized terminal nodes used to code the field of the word.

Terminal nodes used will now be illustrated in Table 6.1, each with several roots that were assigned to that category.

A traditional word-class list was used in field 4 encompassing verbs, nouns, adjectives, adverbs, numerals, prepositions, pronouns, conjunctions, and exclamations.

Fields 5–8 contained the same values for all four groups of languages (Church Slavonic, East Slavic, West Slavic, and South Slavic). The following primary coding schema was used, with numbers and letters being arbitrary.

0 not attested (reduction) – this value was used when no language in the given group inherits the original sense or senses. For example, *volsti 'rule' is not attested in South Slavic languages.

1 attested (continuation), additionally: t – transfer, n – narrowing (specification), w – widening (generalization) – the value of 1 is assigned when the

Table 6.1 *Illustrated terminal nodes in a taxonomy of the subject-matter fields in the Slavic inherited lexicon*
Reconstructed forms are marked with *

Category	Explanation	Examples
Environment	words related to landscape, meteorological phenomena, etc.	*bagnò 'marsh', *padorga f. 'bad weather', *golot 'thin layer of ice'
Body	words related to human body	*golvà 'head', *palьcь m. jo 'finger', *mȏzgъ m. o (c) 'marrow, brain'
Flora	words related to plants and vegetables	*bèrza 'birch', *àblo; *àblъ 'apple', *mъxъ 'moss'
Fauna	words related to animal species and their body parts	*orьlъ 'eagle', *pьsь 'dog', *sòmъ 'sheat-fish'
Body	words related to the human body	*čelò 'forehead', *dòlnь 'palm of the hand', *palьcь 'finger'
Artifacts	words related to household, farming, crafts, etc.	*vьsь 'village', *gȏrdjь; *gȏrdja 'fence', *lemexъ 'ploughshare, plough'
Beliefs and traditions	words related to spiritual life and abstract concepts	*bȏgъ 'god', *čara 'magic, sorcery', *čùdo 'miracle'
Social roles	kinship and other social terms	drȗgъ 'companion, friend', *nestera 'niece', *sestrà 'sister'
Physical-physiological (PP) features	appearance of human and non-human subjects	*vȏrnъ 'black', *bridъkъ 'sharp', *bystrъ adj. o (a) 'quick'
Affective-cognitive (AC) features	human psychological features	*dȏrgъ 'dear', *durъnъ 'stupid, crazy', *dьrzъ 'daring, bold'
Physical-physiological (PP) processes	actions and other processes of human and non-human subjects	*dъržati 'hold', *ěxati 'go, ride', *ęti 'take'
Affective-cognitive (AC) processes	human psychological processes	*bojàti sę 'fear, be afraid', *golgolati 'speak', *gādàti 'guess'
Operators	words used to express logical, spatial, temporal, and other relations	a 'and, but', *jьz 'from, out of', *nizъ adv. 'down, below'
Measures	numbers, days, and other measures	*d(ъ)va 'two', *lěto 'summer', *pętъ 'fifth'

source sense is preserved and no additional senses developed (e.g., *vòńa; *vòńь 'smell' yields *woń* in Polish). If there are new senses, they are coded for the type of semantic change – continuation with transfer is found in Serbo-Croatian *kljuka* 'hook, door-knob' from *kļùka f. # (a) 'hook';

continuation with narrowing is found in Upper Sorbian *brać* 'take, steal' (stealing is a kind of taking) from **bьrati* 'take'; continuation with widening can be seen in Bosnian/Croatian/Serbian *ljeto* 'summer, year' from **lěto* 'summer'.

2 not attested, transformed (transformation): t – transfer (e.g., Serbo-Croatian *slatina* 'mineral spring' from **soltina* 'salt marsh'), n – narrowing (specification, e.g., Czech *jahoda* 'strawberry' from **àgoda* 'berry'), w – widening (generalization, e.g., Slovak *slatina* 'marsh' from **soltina* 'salt marsh') – this value was assigned when the original sense or senses are not present, but there are other senses that have developed from the original sense, again coded for the type of change.

3 split (bifurcation, where there are multiple senses in the source) – this value was used when the original root had at least two senses and at least one got lost (reduction for some senses and continuation for others, for example: **koterъ; *kotorъ* prn. 'who, which', which yields *koterý* 'which' in Slovak), additionally: t – transfer (e.g., Slovenian *drz* 'bold, impudent' from **dъrzъ* 'daring, bold'), n – narrowing (specification, e.g., Čakavian *breja* 'pregnant (of a cow), with young' from **bèrdjь* 'with young, pregnant'), w – widening (generalization, e.g., Slovenian *pásti* 'pasture, look after' from **pasti* 'pasture, herd') in cases where a new sense is attested alongside the lost and continued one.

As can be seen, a simple coding schema was used for semantic extensions – aside from narrowing and widening of the semantic domain, all other semantic extensions (e.g., metaphorical, metonymical) were coded as transfer.

The following table illustrates the initial dataset, with the aforementioned coding schema applied to each entry in it:

1	2	3	4	5	6	7	8
Ajьce	'egg'	Fa	N	1	1	1t	1

This basic table was used to recode in SPSS fields 3–8 into derived variables, and to conduct the investigation of the changes in the Slavic inherited lexicon. The way recoding was performed will be explained in the presentation of the results – its main purpose was to account for language and field macrocategories.

The following limitations of the procedure should be noted:

a. Source data
b. Coding schema
c. Church Slavonic data.

The first problem lies in the fact that the source data in Derksen (2008) are not compiled with an eye toward answering the questions of this research. In consequence, obscure dialectal words related to the root are attested, while the standard language uses a word not related to the word in question. A similar problem lies in the fact that something could be attested in a group of languages (even though it may be marginally retained in only one dialect of one language or widespread in most languages and their dialects). Finally, not all possibilities are included. For example, in the entry *žьrtva 'sacrifice' only Slovenian was attested, but the new sense 'victim' was not listed. In Serbo-Croatian, which has the same two senses, it is not listed at all. There are a number of further problems related to this dictionary dataset that were pointed out to me in private communication by Ilija Čašule, for which I am most grateful. These problems include further examples of unattested roots and meanings (e.g., in case of *šija 'neck', *udъ 'member, extremity', *trъbuxъ 'stomach, abdomen') and the fact that Macedonian remains almost unrepresented as is often the case with the Sorbian languages, the cognates are often incomplete and the meanings simplified. While all these deficiencies of the Derksen (2008) dataset have to be addressed, in its general evaluation and many other applications, in this particular case they affect the results only marginally. In the analysis that follows, therefore, I am interested in the proportions between the three groups of Slavic languages. The omissions in particular roots and their meanings and underrepresentations of some languages in any of the three branches can have only a very limited effect on the proportions between the three branches.

The second set of limitations stems from the coding schema. Along with possible omissions and mislabeling, one can mention the fact that the schema applied here is only one possible manner of categorizing the data, and that different categorizations can yield different results. Furthermore, there are always borderline cases for which one can argue that a different labeling would be possible. Finally, some cases can be assigned to several categories (e.g., two original senses belonging to two different subject-matter fields). These cases were always reduced to one of the two possibilities based on the first sense listed. The same is true about word-class labels.

Finally, Church Slavonic data includes an unsolvable confounding variable. Namely, the fact that something is not attested can mean that the word got lost and that the language in question uses another word instead (just as in other language groups), but it can also mean that the concept was not a part of the biblical setting or was simply not mentioned in sacral texts. Given that the loss of a sense cannot be accounted for, Church Slavonic data was excluded from this analysis.

All these limitations should be kept in mind when presenting and interpreting the results.

The aforementioned general questions (repeated below) were addressed in tabulating the results of this research.

1. What proportion of the words in each of the three groups of Slavic language have lost, changed, or preserved their original Proto-Slavic sense?

2. How much do the various subject-matter fields and word classes differ in the ratio of loss, change, and preservation in relation to Slavic languages as a whole and each of the three groups of Slavic languages?
3. How do the three groups of Slavic languages relate to each other in terms of this ratio (in other words, how often are the processes identical in each group and how often do they differ from one another)?
4. In the situations where a sense changes (one sense is replaced with another or there is another sense next to the preserved one), what are the most common mechanisms of change?

Each of these research questions will now be discussed in turn.

General Parameters of Development

Table 6.2 presents the general parameters of loss, preservation, and change.

In each group the ratio of loss, change, and preservation was as shown in Table 6.3.

Preservation can be thought of as a continuation of the original sense, with no new senses being developed. Change is either an emergence of a new sense

Table 6.2 *The general parameters of semantic development in Slavic languages*

Category	Number	Percent
Preservation in all three groups	471	27.7
Change in all three groups	436	25.6
Loss in all three groups	20	1.2
A combination of loss, change, and preservation	776	45.5
Total	1703	100.0

Table 6.3 *Semantic developments in East, West, and South Slavic*

	East Slavic		West Slavic		South Slavic	
Category	Number	Percent	Number	Percent	Number	Percent
Loss	175	10.3	204	12.0	168	9.9
Change	707	41.5	707	41.5	873	51.3
Preservation	821	48.2	792	46.5	662	38.9
Total	1703	100.0	1703	100.0	1703	100.0

alongside the old one or the replacement of the old sense with a new one. Loss happens when the root is not attested in that group of languages. The particulars of these changes will be discussed in the section "Mechanisms of Change" later in this chapter.

What can be seen is that less than one-third of the original stock of senses is preserved, so two-thirds of the vocabulary contribute to the differentiation of the three groups of Slavic languages. Given the previously mentioned limitations of this data (e.g., attestation in dialects, but not in the standard languages, attestation in one but not in all languages of the group), one can speculate that the differentiation between the groups, in terms of how much was left intact, is even higher than shown by this data. Obviously, some changes could have also gone in the same direction in two or all three groups, which in turn reduces the differentiation. Most of all, massive borrowing from Western European languages (to be discussed in Chapter 7) is a key factor of convergence between Slavic languages and their groups. Therefore, a relatively small percentage of fully retained roots does not mean that present-day Slavic languages are that far apart.

When comparing the three groups of Slavic languages, we can see that East and West Slavic languages show a higher degree of similarity, with South Slavic languages showing an outlying tendency with a considerably higher degree of change than in the other two more preserving groups.

Fields of Change

At the highest level of the aforementioned taxonomy of subject-matter fields, functional words show a considerably higher level of preservation in all three languages than content words (49% functional words preserved in all three language groups without changes compared to 24.1% in content words). The same holds true in each of the three groups (67.1% vs. 46.2% preserved without changes in the Eastern group, 63.4% vs. 44.7% in the Western branch, and 60.9% vs. 36.6% in the Southern group). If we further break down the category of content words into processes, states, and things, the differences in each of these fields are not dramatic (20.7% preserved without changes in processes, 24.4% in states and 28.6% in things). The differences are not dramatic in each group of Slavic languages (44.6% preserved for processes, 43.2% for states, 48.2% for things in East Slavic; 38.4% preserved for processes, 44.4% for states, and 48.7% for things in West Slavic; 31.9% preserved for processes, 38.0% for states, 39.0% for things in South Slavic). If things are further divided into human-related and non-human related, the differences are again not so dramatic: 27.3% of human-related, and 30.2% of non-human-related lexicon preserved without changes in all three groups, 45.9% human vs. 50.8% non-human in East Slavic, 48.0% human and 49.5% of non-human in West Slavic, 37.4% human and 40.7% non-human in South Slavic.

The distribution of the terminal nodes of the subject-matter taxonomy is presented in Tables 6.4–6.14. The relationship between the field and the processes was statistically significant. X^2 p value for cross-tabulation in each table was at 0.000.[1] In each of the tables two values are cross-tabulated: the type of process is in the columns and another value in the rows. For each row, the percentage number and percentage of loss, change, and preservation is given. Thus, for example, in the first row of the first table, there are two confirmed cases of loss (1.7%), 92 cases (80%) of change, and 21 cases (18.3%) of preservation. Tables 6.4–6.7 have macrofields in the rows, Tables 6.8–6.11 feature parts of speech in that position, while tables 6.12–6.14 cross-tabulate the type of process in one branch of Slavic languages with another.

Given that loss is only marginal (it represents the cases where the sense is continued, changed, or unchanged in Church Slavonic only), the interesting issue here is the ratio of preservation to change in various subject-matter fields. In addition to a higher preservation rate for function words (with measures having a higher rate than operators), one can notice several trends that also hold true in each group of Slavic languages presented in Tables 6.5–6.7. Physical-physiological states and processes exhibit a higher preservation rate than affective-cognitive processes. Beliefs and environment terms consistently show lower retention rates than other things. Fauna, body, social terms, and flora show the highest degree of preservation.

As previously noted, the trends of preservation versus change attested in the general development are also observable in each of the three groups. In addition, the level of preservation is understandably significantly higher in each of the three branches; however, the ratio of loss versus change seems to be erratic – one cannot notice any observable trends.

The pan-Slavic trends of development per world class are presented in Table 6.8. The next three tables show the same trends for each branch of Slavic languages.

What can be seen from Tables 6.8–6.11 is that there is a sharp division between functional word classes (numbers, pronouns, conjunctions, and prepositions; prefixes are too low in number to even be considered here, aside from the fact that they are not a word class) and content ones (all others). In the content group, the following hierarchy of preservation seems to exist, from highest to lowest: adverbs, adjectives, nouns, and verbs. Generally, the trends of preservation versus change or loss are not so strongly associated with parts of speech as they are with subject-matter areas.

---

[1] For more information about interpreting statistical parameters see Ross (2010).

Table 6.4 *The processes of semantic development in the three branches of Slavic languages*

| | | | Pan-Slavic processes | | | |
			Loss	Change	Preservation	Total
Field	AC processes	Count	2	92	21	115
		% Within the field	1.7	80.0	18.3	100.0
	AC states	Count	0	76	16	92
		% Within the field	0.0	82.6	17.4	100.0
	Artifacts	Count	2	167	50	219
		% Within the field	0.9	76.3	22.8	100.0
	Beliefs	Count	0	25	4	29
		% Within the field	0.0	86.2	13.8	100.0
	Body	Count	1	59	38	98
		% Within the field	1.0	60.2	38.8	100.0
	Environment	Count	2	138	30	170
		% Within the field	1.2	81.2	17.6	100.0
	Fauna	Count	0	66	54	120
		% Within the field	0.0	55.0	45.0	100.0
	Flora	Count	0	58	30	88
		% Within the field	0.0	65.9	34.1	100.0
	Measures	Count	2	30	39	71
		% Within the field	2.8	42.3	54.9	100.0
	Operators	Count	0	50	40	90
		% Within the field	0.0	55.6	44.4	100.0
	PP processes	Count	9	285	80	374
		% Within the field	2.4	76.2	21.4	100.0
	PP states	Count	2	111	45	158
		% Within the field	1.3	70.3	28.5	100.0
	Social roles	Count	0	55	24	79
		% Within the field	0.0	69.6	30.4	100.0
Total		Count	20	1212	471	1703
		% Within the field	1.2	71.2	27.7	100.0

Inter-Slavic Relations

The mechanisms of split between the groups of Slavic languages are presented in this section. The data are presented in Table 6.12. The rows show the process in one branch of Slavic languages, while each column shows what the

Table 6.5 *The processes of semantic development in East Slavic languages*

			Loss	Change	Preservation	Total
Field	AC processes	Count	20	47	48	115
		% Within the field	17.4	40.9	41.7	100.0
	AC states	Count	8	51	33	92
		% Within the field	8.7	55.4	35.9	100.0
	Artifacts	Count	19	113	87	219
		% Within the field	8.7	51.6	39.7	100.0
	Beliefs	Count	3	16	10	29
		% Within the field	10.3	55.2	34.5	100.0
	Body	Count	8	36	54	98
		% Within the field	8.2	36.7	55.1	100.0
	Environment	Count	13	97	60	170
		% Within the field	7.6	57.1	35.3	100.0
	Fauna	Count	8	31	81	120
		% Within the field	6.7	25.8	67.5	100.0
	Flora	Count	9	28	51	88
		% Within the field	10.2	31.8	58.0	100.0
	Measures	Count	2	18	51	71
		% Within the field	2.8	25.4	71.8	100.0
	Operators	Count	13	20	57	90
		% Within the field	14.4	22.2	63.3	100.0
	PP processes	Count	49	155	170	374
		% Within the field	13.1	41.4	45.5	100.0
	PP states	Count	19	64	75	158
		% Within the field	12.0	40.5	47.5	100.0
	Social roles	Count	4	31	44	79
		% Within the field	5.1	39.2	55.7	100.0
Total		Count	175	707	821	1703
		% Within the field	10.3	41.5	48.2	100.0

equivalent process in another branch of Slavic languages is. Thus, in the first row of the first table, the loss of a meaning is given for East Slavic languages. Out of all meanings that are lost in the Slavic East, 59 nine of them (33.7%) are also lost in the West, 63 cases (36%) are changed in the West, and 53 cases (30.3%) are preserved in the West.

Table 6.6 *The processes of semantic development in West Slavic languages*

			Loss	Change	Preservation	Total
Field	AC processes	Count	18	56	41	115
		% Within the field	15.7	48.7	35.7	100.0
	AC states	Count	14	49	29	92
		% Within the field	15.2	53.3	31.5	100.0
	Artifacts	Count	22	101	96	219
		% Within the field	10.0	46.1	43.8	100.0
	Beliefs	Count	4	14	11	29
		% Within the field	13.8	48.3	37.9	100.0
	Body	Count	6	35	57	98
		% Within the field	6.1	35.7	58.2	100.0
	Environment	Count	21	94	55	170
		% Within the field	12.4	55.3	32.4	100.0
	Fauna	Count	14	29	77	120
		% Within the field	11.7	24.2	64.2	100.0
	Flora	Count	5	28	55	88
		% Within the field	5.7	31.8	62.5	100.0
	Measures	Count	6	20	45	71
		% Within the field	8.5	28.2	63.4	100.0
	Operators	Count	12	21	57	90
		% Within the field	13.3	23.3	63.3	100.0
	PP processes	Count	56	171	147	374
		% Within the field	15.0	45.7	39.3	100.0
	PP states	Count	21	55	82	158
		% Within the field	13.3	34.8	51.9	100.0
	Social roles	Count	5	34	40	79
		% Within the field	6.3	43.0	50.6	100.0
Total		Count	204	707	792	1703
		% Within the field	12.0	41.5	46.5	100.0

We can see in Table 6.13 that the senses retained in East Slavic are retained at a higher rate in West Slavic than in South Slavic.

Table 6.14 also shows that what is preserved in West Slavic is preserved at a considerably higher rate in East Slavic compared to South Slavic.

One can see in Table 6.14 that South Slavic languages exhibit equidistance from West and East groups. Tables 6.12–6.14 seem to point out to a closer alignment of development in the Eastern and Western branches, which gives us some ground to

Table 6.7 *The processes of semantic development in South Slavic languages*

			Loss	Change	Preservation	Total
Field	AC processes	Count	18	69	28	115
		% Within the field	15.7	60.0	24.3	100.0
	AC states	Count	14	50	28	92
		% Within the field	15.2	54.3	30.4	100.0
	Artifacts	Count	27	122	70	219
		% Within the field	12.3	55.7	32.0	100.0
	Beliefs	Count	6	17	6	29
		% Within the field	20.7	58.6	20.7	100.0
	Body	Count	5	42	51	98
		% Within the field	5.1	42.9	52.0	100.0
	Environment	Count	12	112	46	170
		% Within the field	7.1	65.9	27.1	100.0
	Fauna	Count	11	41	68	120
		% Within the field	9.2	34.2	56.7	100.0
	Flora	Count	5	43	40	88
		% Within the field	5.7	48.9	45.5	100.0
	Measures	Count	2	25	44	71
		% Within the field	2.8	35.2	62.0	100.0
	Operators	Count	9	27	54	90
		% Within the field	10.0	30.0	60.0	100.0
	PP processes	Count	40	206	128	374
		% Within the field	10.7	55.1	34.2	100.0
	PP states	Count	18	73	67	158
		% Within the field	11.4	46.2	42.4	100.0
	Social roles	Count	1	46	32	79
		% Within the field	1.3	58.2	40.5	100.0
Total		Count	168	873	662	1703
		% Within the field	9.9	51.3	38.9	100.0

talk about North Slavic languages on the one hand and South on the other (which has been argued for other areas of a linguistic system in Mitrinović 2012).

The Mechanisms of Change

If we look at the mechanisms of semantic change using the previously described minimalist model, which distinguishes only three categories,

Table 6.8 *Pan-Slavic semantic development per part of speech*

			Loss	Change	Preservation	Total
POS	adjectives	Count	2	142	49	193
		% within the POS	1.0	73.6	25.4	100.0
	adverbs	Count	0	21	8	29
		% within the POS	0.0	72.4	27.6	100.0
	conjunctions	Count	0	5	4	9
		% within the POS	0.0	55.6	44.4	100.0
	nouns	Count	7	640	256	903
		% within the POS	0.8	70.9	28.3	100.0
	pronouns	Count	0	7	12	19
		% within the POS	0.0	36.8	63.2	100.0
	prefixes	Count	0	1	4	5
		% within the POS	0.0	20.0	80.0	100.0
	prepositions	Count	0	18	11	29
		% within the POS	0.0	62.1	37.9	100.0
	numbers	Count	0	0	22	22
		% within the POS	0.0	0.0	100.0	100.0
	verbs	Count	11	378	105	494
		% within the POS	2.2	76.5	21.3	100.0
Total		Count	20	1212	471	1703
		% within the POS	1.2	71.2	27.7	100.0

narrowing, transfer, and widening of the sense, we can notice that, yet again, East and West Slavic languages have very similar profiles with South Slavic languages being different. South Slavic languages are different in that their total number of changes is considerably higher and the proportion of transfer is higher. This data is presented in Table 6.15.

The results show that less than one-third of the senses of the original Proto-Slavic roots are preserved in all three language groups. This means that historical developments in the deep lexical layer of Slavic, cultural identity represent a crucial contribution to shaping present-day cultural identity of Slavic lexical systems. If we have in mind the previously mentioned limitations of the present dataset and the fact that the analysis addressed groups of Slavic languages rather than individual languages, one can state with some degree of confidence that the impact of this factor is considerably higher than the raw numbers from the present research demonstrate. One indicator of a wider scope of change, i.e., a lower presence of Proto-Slavic lexical stock,

Table 6.9 *East Slavic semantic development per part of speech*

			Loss	Change	Retention	Total
POS	adjectives	Count	26	81	86	193
		% within the POS	13.5	42.0	44.6	100.0
	adverbs	Count	5	7	17	29
		% within the POS	17.2	24.1	58.6	100.0
	conjunctions	Count	1	3	5	9
		% within the POS	11.1	33.3	55.6	100.0
	nouns	Count	69	402	432	903
		% within the POS	7.6	44.5	47.8	100.0
	pronouns	Count	3	2	14	19
		% within the POS	15.8	10.5	73.7	100.0
	prefixes	Count	0	0	5	5
		% within the POS	0.0	0.0	100.0	100.0
	prepositions	Count	2	9	18	29
		% within the POS	6.9	31.0	62.1	100.0
	numbers	Count	0	0	22	22
		% within the POS	0.0	0.0	100.0	100.0
	verbs	Count	69	203	222	494
		% within the POS	14.0	41.1	44.9	100.0
Total		Count	175	707	821	1703
		% within the POS	10.3	41.5	48.2	100.0

may be Jankowiak (1997:114) who analyzed the lexicon from the first seven volumes of Sławski (1974–2001), a Proto-Slavic dictionary in contemporary Polish, and found that Proto-Slavic lexemes are encountered once in sixty-six words in contemporary Polish frequency dictionaries and once in ten words in contemporary Polish texts. East and West Slavic languages show a considerably higher rate of preservation, 10 percent higher than in South Slavic languages. In general, East and West Slavic languages show distinct similarities in several areas and stay in contrast with South Slavic languages. This may point to the possibility of construing the opposition between North and South Slavic languages, at least in the lexicon. This would be consistent with the claims previously advanced by Mitrinović (2012). The analysis identified statistically significant differences between subject-matter fields, where functional words and several fields within content words (fauna, body, social terms, and flora) demonstrate a much higher degree of preservation than

Table 6.10 *West Slavic semantic development per part of speech*

			Loss	Change	Retention	Total
POS	adjectives	Count	29	75	89	193
		% within the POS	15.0	38.9	46.1	100.0
	adverbs	Count	4	6	19	29
		% within the POS	13.8	20.7	65.5	100.0
	conjunctions	Count	2	3	4	9
		% within the POS	22.2	33.3	44.4	100.0
	nouns	Count	89	384	430	903
		% within the POS	9.9	42.5	47.6	100.0
	pronouns	Count	1	5	13	19
		% within the POS	5.3	26.3	68.4	100.0
	prefixes	Count	1	0	4	5
		% within the POS	20.0	0.0	80.0	100.0
	prepositions	Count	4	7	18	29
		% within the POS	13.8	24.1	62.1	100.0
	numbers	Count	0	0	22	22
		% within the POS	0.0	0.0	100.0	100.0
	verbs	Count	74	227	193	494
		% within the POS	15.0	46.0	39.1	100.0
Total		Count	204	707	792	1703
		% within the POS	12.0	41.5	46.5	100.0

other content words fields. Similarly, and as expected, functional word classes (as generally a more conservative category) show a higher degree of preservation than content word classes. The most common mechanism of change is narrowing of the sense, followed closely by semantic transfer, while widening stays far behind.

6.2   Lexical Divergence Tracking

Another way of tracking divergence is at the lexical level. In order to demonstrate this approach, I analyzed semantic words from Swadesh (2017), to explore the similarities and differences between Russian, Polish, and Serbo-Croatian.

The following four possibilities were accounted for:
a. Retaining an inherited Proto-Slavic word;
b. Replacing the Proto-Slavic word;

Table 6.11 *South Slavic semantic development per part of speech*

			Loss	Change	Retention	Total
POS	adjectives	Count	20	93	80	193
		% within the POS	10.4	48.2	41.5	100.0
	adverbs	Count	5	12	12	29
		% within the POS	17.2	41.4	41.4	100.0
	conjunctions	Count	0	3	6	9
		% within the POS	0.0	33.3	66.7	100.0
	nouns	Count	80	475	348	903
		% within the POS	8.9	52.6	38.5	100.0
	pronouns	Count	0	5	14	19
		% within the POS	0.0	26.3	73.7	100.0
	prefixes	Count	1	0	4	5
		% within the POS	20.0	0.0	80.0	100.0
	prepositions	Count	4	10	15	29
		% within the POS	13.8	34.5	51.7	100.0
	numbers	Count	0	0	22	22
		% within the POS	0.0	0.0	100.0	100.0
	verbs	Count	58	275	161	494
		% within the POS	11.7	55.7	32.6	100.0
Total		Count	168	873	662	1703
		% within the POS	9.9	51.3	38.9	100.0

c. A semantic split of the original word, in which a new word is introduced instead of a part of the original meaning;
d. Stylistic differentiation, where another word is introduced for either stylistically neutral or marked connotation.

Table 6.16 shows the results obtained.

What can be seen is that over half of this basic vocabulary gets retained in its original meaning, while semantic differentiation represents the most robust mechanism of change in the remaining part of the vocabulary. This explains the high number of false cognates between Russian, Polish, and Serbo-Croatian in the vocabulary range included in Swadesh (2017).

The relation of the processes in language-to-language comparisons is presented in Tables 6.17–6.22. Again, the rows give the type of process in one language and the columns present equivalent processes in another. Thus, in the first row of Table 6.17 semantic differentiation is given for Russian. Out of all cases where semantic differentiation happened in Russian, in 19 cases (51.4%)

Table 6.12 *East Slavic processes versus West and South Slavic*

			West			
			Loss	Change	Preservation	Total
East	Loss	Count	59	63	53	175
		% Within the East	33.7	36.0	30.3	100.0
	Change	Count	79	506	122	707
		% Within the East	11.2	71.6	17.3	100.0
	Preservation	Count	66	138	617	821
		% Within the East	8.0	16.8	75.2	100.0
Total		Count	204	707	792	1703
		% Within the East	12.0	41.5	46.5	100.0
			South			
			Loss	Change	Preservation	Total
East	Loss	Count	47	78	50	175
		% Within the East	26.9	44.6	28.6	100.0
	Change	Count	68	546	93	707
		% Within the East	9.6	77.2	13.2	100.0
	Preservation	Count	53	249	519	821
		% Within the East	6.5	30.3	63.2	100.0
Total		Count	168	873	662	1703
		% Within the East	9.9	51.3	38.9	100.0

differentiation also happened in Polish, in 18 cases (48.6%) Polish inherited the Proto-Slavic word, and there were no attested cases for replacement or stylistic differentiation (0 cases and 0.0% in both categories).

The first interesting fact stemming from these tables is that Russian underwent considerably more changes (mostly semantic differentiation) than Polish and Serbo-Croatian.

Second, Russian is much better aligned with Polish, that is, when a word is inherited in Russian, it is more likely that it will also be inherited in Polish than in Serbo-Croatian. The same is true about the situations in which Russian words change. Serbo-Croatian is better aligned with Russian than with Polish, while Polish remains equidistant from the other two languages. Again, we find some, rather weak, supportive argument for closer lexical ties of Northern Slavic languages and also closer ties of Eastern and Southern languages. One should note that the analysis is limited to just three languages

Table 6.13 *West Slavic processes versus East and South Slavic*

			East			
			Loss	Change	Preservation	Total
West	Loss	Count	59	79	66	204
		% Within the West	28.9	38.7	32.4	100.0
	Change	Count	63	506	138	707
		% Within the West	8.9	71.6	19.5	100.0
	Preservation	Count	53	122	617	792
		% Within the West	6.7	15.4	77.9	100.0
Total		Count	175	707	821	1703
		% Within the West	10.3	41.5	48.2	100.0
			South			
			Loss	Change	Preservation	Total
West	Loss	Count	66	77	61	204
		% Within the West	32.4	37.7	29.9	100.0
	Change	Count	46	593	68	707
		% Within the West	6.5	83.9	9.6	100.0
	Preservation	Count	56	203	533	792
		% Within the West	7.1	25.6	67.3	100.0
Total		Count	168	873	662	1703
		% Within the West	9.9	51.3	38.9	100.0

from this group, so this would be a hypothesis rather than a claim, as is often the case throughout this monograph. Given that the present dataset is rather limited, and that its goal was just to demonstrate the proposed research technique, my findings can only be understood as a stimulus for further research on a broader dataset.

In the three chapters devoted to the deep lexical layers of identity, I demonstrated three areas of consistent data collection, using the material from Slavic languages. First, lexeme-level cross-linguistic contrastive analysis gathers the data that contributes to contrastive lexeme-level language profiles. Second, that data is integrated into lexicon-level cross-linguistic analysis of lexical fields. Lexicon-level analysis further spreads into the study of monolingual data – idioms, lexical relations in the field of interest as well as their word-formation and associative networks. Finally, semantic and lexical divergence-tracking techniques were demonstrated. The divergence analysis supplements the previous two techniques by providing

Table 6.14 *South Slavic processes versus East and West Slavic*

			East			
			Loss	Change	Preservation	Total
South	Loss	Count	47	68	53	168
		% Within the South	28.0	40.5	31.5	100.0
	Change	Count	78	546	249	873
		% Within the South	8.9	62.5	28.5	100.0
	Preservation	Count	50	93	519	662
		% Within the South	7.6	14.0	78.4	100.0
Total		Count	175	707	821	1703
		% Within the South	10.3	41.5	48.2	100.0
			West			
			Loss	Change	Preservation	Total
South	Loss	Count	66	46	56	168
		% Within the South	39.3	27.4	33.3	100.0
	Change	Count	77	593	203	873
		% Within the South	8.8	67.9	23.3	100.0
	Preservation	Count	61	68	533	662
		% Within the South	9.2	10.3	80.5	100.0
Total		Count	204	707	792	1703
		% Within the South	12.0	41.5	46.5	100.0

Table 6.15 *The types of semantic changes in three groups of Slavic languages*

	East		West		South	
Narrowing	357	52%	367	50%	478	47%
Transfer	277	40%	316	43%	452	45%
Widening	55	8%	51	7%	82	8%
Total	689	100%	734	100%	1012	100%

diachronic insights into possible causes for the differences in the deep lexical layer of genetically related languages.

Needless to say, all examples demonstrated by the dominant approaches discussed in Chapter 2 (linguistic culturology, NSM theory, and cultural linguistics) are welcome additions to the cultural profiles of languages they

Table 6.16 *Lexical diversion of semantic words from Swadesh (2017)*

Category	Number	Percent	Example
Proto-Slavic word retained in its basic meaning in all three languages	97	55.4	S-Cr. *ruka*, Pol. *ręka*, Rus. *рука* 'hand/arm'
Different word in at least one of the three languages	28	16.0	S-Cr. *desni*, Pol. *prawy*, Rus. *правый* 'right-side'
Semantic differentiation in at least one of the three languages	39	22.3	S-Cr. *zao* (evil) *loš* (bad), Pol. *zły*, Rus. *злой* (evil) *плохой* (bad) 'bad/evil'
Stylistic differentiation in at least one of the three languages	11	6.3	S-Cr. *kiša* (neutral) *dažd* (poetic), Pol. *deszcz*, Rus. *дождь* 'rain'
	175	100.0	

Table 6.17 *Russian-to-Polish lexical development in Swadesh (2017)*

		Polish	d	i	r	s	Total
Russian	d	Count	19	18	0	0	37
		% within Russian	51.4	48.6	0.0	0.0	100.0
	i	Count	0	114	5	0	119
		% within Russian	0.0	95.8	4.2	0.0	100.0
	r	Count	0	3	8	0	11
		% within Russian	0.0	27.3	72.7	0.0	100.0
	s	Count	0	7	0	1	8
		% within Russian	0.0	87.5	0.0	12.5	100.0

d – semantic differentiation, i – inheritance, r – replacement, s – stylistic differentiation

explore. The argument made here is that they have to be integrated into a wider and more complex network of data, gathered and analyzed using consistent methodological apparatus.

I have already noted in Chapter 3 that the deep layer of lexical identity can be used for the study of dialects, not only standard languages, as demonstrated in the present chapter. Two lines of research are possible: building a cultural lexical profile of one dialect by contrasting it with the others and building a cultural lexical profile of a dialect or any other colloquial variety by contrasting it with the standard language. Slavic languages offer abundant material for both these lines of research. Thus, Slovenian features seven

Table 6.18 *Russian-to-Serbo-Croatian lexical development in Swadesh (2017)*

		Serbo-Croatian	d	i	R	s	Total
Russian	d	Count	11	26	0	0	37
		% within Russian	29.7	70.3	0.0	0.0	100.0
	i	Count	3	102	11	3	119
		% within Russian	2.5	85.7	9.2	2.5	100.0
	r	Count	0	8	3	0	11
		% within Russian	0.0	72.7	27.3	0.0	100.0
	s	Count	0	8	0	0	8
		% within Russian	0.0	100.0	0.0	0.0	100.0

d – semantic differentiation, i – inheritance, r – replacement, s – stylistic differentiation

Table 6.19 *Polish-to-Russian lexical development in Swadesh (2017)*

		Russian	d	i	r	s	Total
Polish	d	Count	19	0	0	0	19
		% within Polish	100.0	0.0	0.0	0.0	100.0
	i	Count	18	114	3	7	142
		% within Polish	12.7	80.3	2.1	4.9	100.0
	r	Count	0	5	8	0	13
		% within Polish	0.0	38.5	61.5	0.0	100.0
	s	Count	0	0	0	1	1
		% within Polish	0.0	0.0	0.0	100.0%	100.0%

d – semantic differentiation, i – inheritance, r – replacement, s – stylistic differentiation

dialectal groups distributed in strongly diversified geological environments (littoral – *Primorska narečna skupina*, highlands – *Gorenjska narečna skupina*, flatlands – *Prekmurska narečna skupina*, and five others; for more information, see Priestly, 1993; Logar, 1983/1984; and Logar and Rigler, 2016). Given the differences in the geographical setting, it would be logical to test the hypothesis that the dialects spoken in the littoral differ from those spoken in the highlands in the lexical profile of the field of geographical nomenclature (and possibly others: e.g., agriculture, weather). Similarly, rich material for the second line of research is offered in the so-called common Czech, widespread colloquial vernacular, which can be lexically contrasted with standard Czech (for more see Daneš, 2003; Čermák, 2006; Cvrček, 2006; and Short, 1993a).

Table 6.20 *Polish-to-Serbo-Croatian lexical development in Swadesh (2017)*

		Serbo-Croatian	d	i	r	s	Total
Polish	d	Count	4	15	0	0	19
		% within Polish	21.1	78.9	0.0	0.0	100.0
	i	Count	10	116	13	3	142
		% within Polish	7.0	81.7	9.2	2.1	100.0
	r	Count	0	12	1	0	13
		% within Polish	0.0	92.3	7.7	0.0	100.0
	s	Count	0	1	0	0	1
		% within Polish	0.0	100.0	0.0	0.0	100.0

d – semantic differentiation, i – inheritance, r – replacement, s – stylistic differentiation

Table 6.21 *Serbo-Croatian-to-Russian lexical development in Swadesh (2017)*

		Russian	d	i	r	s	Total
Serbo-	d	Count	11	3	0	0	14
Croatian		% within Serbo-Croatian	78.6	21.4	0.0	0.0	100.0
	i	Count	26	102	8	8	144
		% within Serbo-Croatian	18.1	70.8	5.6	5.6	100.0
	r	Count	0	11	3	0	14
		% within Serbo-Croatian	0.0	78.6	21.4	0.0	100.0
	s	Count	0	3	0	0	3
		% within Serbo-Croatian	0.0	100.0	0.0	0.0	100.0

d – semantic differentiation, i – inheritance, r – replacement, s – stylistic differentiation

It is important to understand that lexical divergence tracking is not just a way to diachronically establish the lines of development that have led to the present-day lexical differences. This kind of tracking also shows the levels at which the speakers of various languages are still determined by the common lexical heritage – how much common Slavic heritage still remains in present-day Slavic languages and in what form.

As previously noted, the deep layer that was discussed in the present part of this monograph is about words, their inheritance, modification or replacement, their internal semantic structure (e.g., the metaphors that guide the development of that structure), their links to other words through subject-matter fields, word formation, and associative networks. The units of the deep lexical layer

Table 6.22 *Serbo-Croatian-to-Polish lexical development in Swadesh (2017)*

		Polish	d	i	r	s	Total
Serbo-	d	Count	4	10	0	0	14
Croatian		% within Serbo-Croatian	28.6	71.4	0.0	0.0	100.0
	i	Count	15	116	12	1	144
		% within Serbo-Croatian	10.4	80.6	8.3	0.7	100.0
	r	Count	0	13	1	0	14
		% within Serbo-Croatian	0.0	92.9	7.1	0.0	100.0
	s	Count	0	3	0	0	3
		% within Serbo-Croatian	0.0	100.0	0.0	0.0	100.0

d – semantic differentiation, i – inheritance, r – replacement, s – stylistic differentiation

are organized in a core of the most common lexical items (most examples used in this part were dealt with the lexicon from that sphere, using frequency lists as criteria) and the periphery of a less-used lexicon. No matter how specific a word or concept may be to any given culture, if it belongs to the lexical periphery, it is going to shape the identity of the speakers less than the units from the lexical core. For that reason, the previously discussed examples included the units from the core. The changes in this layer are generally glacial. They encompass semantic shifts and word replacements that, as a rule, take an extended period of time to take effect. The speakers' control over these processes is negligible and so is the presence of the elites. Indeed the processes are ultimately carried by the speakers and their elites, but that happens spontaneously rather than by planned intervention. Even the most unreasonable lexical planners would not embark on enforcing the obligatory difference between *hand* and *arm* in Slavic languages or any similar type of intervention. For that precise reason, if any interventions are present, they can only be remote when a certain maneuver from the surface layer becomes stabilized in the deep layer with the flow of time.

To conclude this part of the book on the deep lexical layer of cultural identity, I would like to point out once again that the goal of this book is to propose possible directions for consistent research rather than to offer definitive answers to the observed linguistic aspects of cultural identity. In the next part, I will turn to the exchange lexical layer of cultural identity.

Part III

The Exchange Layer

7 Cultural Influences

Part III of this book concerns the exchange layer of cultural identity. Factors of different historical development have clearly divided Slavic languages and often the territories within the same language (compare, for example, five centuries of Ottoman Turkish rule in the Balkans versus a century and a half of the partition of the Polish language space between Prussia, Russia, and Austria-Hungary). These differences are mirrored in the external linguistic history, most notably in the structure of the respective lexicons of Slavic languages.

As already noted in Chapter 3, research on the exchange layer focuses on the features of words and phrases. The principal feature is the origin of a word or phrase and the pivotal division is between inherited and borrowed lexical items. This will be the topic of the present chapter. There are two additional important components of the exchange language profile. First, languages differ in the ratio of cultural versus geographical contact borrowing. The latter category comprises the following: horizontal geographical contact (i.e., lexical exchange with neighboring languages, for example between Serbian and Romanian), concurrent vertical geographical contact (of a dominant national language with a local language, e.g., Russian and Evenki, which is native to Russia and China), and subsequent vertical geographical contact (of a dominant language with a substrate language, e.g., Illyrian for Serbo-Croatian and Macedonian). This will be discussed in Chapter 8. Second, the direction of lexical transfer is also important for the cultural identity of investigated languages. Practically all languages are both donors and recipients, but the ratio of inbound and outgoing transfer varies from language to language, and it can shift like a pendulum with time. The most notable example is English with mostly inbound transfer after the Norman Conquest to the dominance of the outbound transfer in the twentieth and twenty-first centuries. Lexicons and their speakers are also profiled by the ratio of outbound and inbound lexical transfer. The direction of transfer will be explored in Chapter 9.

In this chapter, I will present two examples of accounting for cultural influences in the lexical layer. The first will consist of the synchronic contrastive analysis between two Slavic languages, the second will concern the development of an important segment of the exchange layer in one of them.

7.1   Synchronic Contrasting

Given the rich tradition of research on lexical exchange in Slavic languages, mostly borrowing from the languages of cultural influence, and strong normativist traditions in the surface layer, all Slavic languages feature numerous dictionaries of lexical borrowings (most commonly called: foreign word dictionaries). To illustrate this, Šipka (2000a), a bibliography of Serbo-Croatian dictionaries, attests 68 dictionaries of lexical borrowings for Serbo-Croatian in the time span from 1830 to 2000. Numerous dictionaries have multiple editions, and numerous new dictionaries of lexical borrowings were published since the publication of this bibliography.

It seems that the material from these dictionaries of lexical borrowings can be used to contrast the exchange layers of Slavic lexicons. Assuming that we are contrasting two Slavic languages, interesting questions here are the following: first, how much is the same and how much is different in the structure of the borrowed lexicon? In other words, is lexical borrowing something that contributes more to the general Slavic cultural identity or more to the identity of each particular Slavic language? Second, what is the ratio of the sources of borrowing in the two observed Slavic languages? A follow-up question can be formulated here in respect of which sociocultural and historical circumstances shaped the ratio of the sources of borrowing. Third, what is the distribution of borrowing in the general lexicon, relative to that in specialized fields? Finally, for each of the specialized fields, how much does each source of borrowing shape it? The last two questions expand on the previous two, giving a more detailed picture of the differences and similarities between the exchange lexical layers of the two observed Slavic languages.

In the next section I will outline the methodological challenges of using contrastive data from Slavic loanword dictionaries to answer the aforementioned questions and suggest the solutions intended to mitigate some of these problems.

Answering these four questions (the general differences, the differences in the sources of borrowing, the differences in the structure of the sources, the differences in the participation of the loanwords in the general lexicon versus specialized fields of usage, and the differences in how the sources of borrowing profile specialized fields) assumes a *tertium comparationis* in contrasting the two Slavic languages in question. In Chapter 3, I identified the problems stemming from the usage of the loanword dictionaries, namely sampling bias, language labeling bias, and field labeling bias. I have also identified the solutions intended to mitigate these problems. There is little that can be done about the sampling bias if one works with existing dictionary datasets. One natural solution is to acknowledge this research limitation. Furthermore, comparing percentages rather than numbers is an obvious solution to account for a different number of loanwords in the two contrasted dictionaries.

The language labeling bias can be mitigated in several ways. First, taking into consideration just the last link in the borrowing chain makes the situation somewhat less complicated and mitigates some of the language labeling bias. As a result, the differences between the two languages are reduced to the difference in that language, as opposed to the differences in establishing or not establishing the chain, differences in the ordering of the links in the chain, etc. More importantly, establishing a taxonomy of language groups, which enables contrasting at a macrolanguage level, significantly mitigates language labeling bias.

The principal problem of the field labeling bias is that the two observed dictionaries may feature a different ratio of general versus specialized vocabulary, which stems from the authors' strategies (more versus less labeling) rather than from objective circumstances in the two observed languages. Nothing can be done about this in the research of existing datasets, and this kind of contrasting should not be made. Nevertheless, some solutions may be implemented at the level of particular languages and language groups by using a macrolanguage generality index, which would measure the level of generality (and, by the same token, specificity) of a language relative to generality in the entire body of loanwords. This index is computed in the following manner: the percentage of unlabeled words in that language minus the average percentage of unlabeled words in the dataset. The same index can be tabulated for each of the fields as follows: field prominence index is equal to the percentage of the field in question minus the average percentage for all fields in that dataset. A similar index can be tabulated for the degree to which a language profiles a particular field. This field profiling index can be computed by taking the percentage of a language in a given field minus the percentage of the language in the entire dataset. This index is also not dependent on the authors' strategies. Another problem with the fields is that the same entry can be labeled differently in two dictionaries. Here too, creating a hierarchy of macrofields (e.g., bringing psychology, sociology, anthropology, under the macrolabel of social sciences) eliminates labeling bias to some extent.

As a result, the following strategies of contrasting will be deployed here:
- All limitations (e.g., the discrepancy between the language dataset and the dictionary dataset) should be clearly stated.
- Contrasting the percentages of language and field macrocategories should be used to eliminate some of the existing labeling bias.
- Using the indexes of generality, presence, and profiling further mitigates some of the existing challenges.

I will now proceed with exemplifying this by contrasting a Serbian (de facto Serbo-Croatian) and a Russian loanwords dictionary. I will demonstrate the deployment of the four indices in contrasting two Slavic loanwords dictionaries: Egorova (2014), a Russian dictionary, and Klajn and Šipka (2006), Serbian in name but Serbo-Croatian in spirit, given that the materials from the entire area of this language are included in the dictionary. The two dictionaries appeared in approximately the same time period (published only nine years apart). The two dictionaries differ in size, with the Serbian dictionary being more than double in size. Once all cross-referenced entries and the loanwords of uncertain origin and those stemming from the names of people, companies, products, etc. were eliminated, the number of extracted entries (those that featured the label of the language of origin) was 26,643 for Klajn and Šipka (2006) and 9,426 for Egorova (2014). These numbers are somewhat higher than the numbers of labeled entries, given that each meaning with a field label was included as a separate entry. Thus, for example, if a word of Greek origin has one meaning labeled as physics and another labeled as medicine, there would be two entries in the database: Greek – physics and Greek – medicine. The entries that did not feature a field label were counted only once. Given that the same procedure was deployed for both dictionaries, for all involved languages and fields, its limitations are minimal. Only subject-matter labels that refer to concrete fields were extracted, while all others (such as humorous, colloquial, outdated, specialized) were disregarded, i.e., counted as non-labeled entries, given the absence of a subject-matter label.

Following the idea of simplification in contrasting, stated in the previous section, only the first stated language of origin was recorded. Again, given that the same procedure was deployed in both dictionaries and for all languages, its limitations are minimal. The initial data from both dictionaries contained two variables, with the language of origin, as stated in the dictionary, in one column, and the field label or zero (for unlabeled cases) in the second. This was then recoded into two new variables with macrolanguage and macrofield values (see Figure 7.1).

The two recoded variables were used to contrast the Serbian and the Russian datasets. Macrolanguage categories were distinguished based on the principal sources of cultural influences. There were three groups of European languages,

	Initial Variables		⟶	Recoded Variables
	Language	Field	Macrolanguage	Macrofield
Example	*Greek*	*Physics*	*European–classical*	*Sciences–natural*

Figure 7.1 Initial and recoded variables

Classical (Greek and Latin), Germanic (e.g., German, English), and Romance (e.g., French, Italian); Near Eastern Languages (Turkic, Arabic, Persian); other languages (which included both contact languages such as Hungarian for Serbian and Finnish for Russian, and far-away languages such as Chinese and Japanese); and Slavic languages. The fields were generalized into the categories of arts (e.g., music, fine arts), beliefs systems (e.g., religion, astrology), natural, engineering, and mathematical sciences (e.g., physics, geography, computing), social sciences and humanities (e.g., psychology, linguistics), sports, and two categories of vocational terms, including production (e.g., plumbing or car mechanics nomenclature), and services (e.g., culinary or administrative). Each of these fields represents a different environment for cultural influences, e.g., popular culture in arts and sports, older cultural influences in vocational terminology, and belief systems. Just as the macrolanguage categories are established based on the sources of cultural influences, the fields are generalized based on their potential to receive cultural influences. The entire research scheme was organized with a view to answering the questions about the exchange layer of Slavic cultural identities while minimizing the challenges discussed in the previous section.

I will now discuss the data based on the four indices: the macrolanguage generality index, the macrolanguage prominence index, the macrofield prominence index, and the macrofield profiling index. The discussion of each index will be preceded by a description of their tabulations and followed by additional data about concrete languages and fields as featured in the two-dictionary dataset. "S" in the tables stands for the Serbian dictionary dataset, "R" for the Russian.

The index of generality was calculated in the following manner. An average percentage for all six macrolanguage groups, in the entries that were not field-labeled, was first calculated. Then, the index of generality was computed in the following manner: macrolanguage generality index = macrolanguage presence in the general lexicon minus average presence in the general lexicon. The positive value of this index shows that the macrolanguage group is used in the general lexicon more than average, i.e., that the level of generality of that macrolanguage group is higher than average. The negative value means that the level of generality is lower than average, i.e., that the macrolanguage group tends to get more use in the sphere of specialized vocabulary. Table 7.1 shows the results.

From the data in Table 7.1 we can see that European sources consistently have negative generality index values and that their average generality index is identical in the two observed dictionaries. This means that the main European sources of influence contribute to the specialized vocabulary much more than Near Eastern, Slavic, and other sources. Another interesting fact is that Near Eastern terms show a higher degree of generality in Russian than in Serbian.

Table 7.1 *Language generality indices*

Source	S	R
European – Classical	−8.9	−13.1
European – Germanic	−8.5	−6.7
European – Romance	−2.8	−0.3
Average for European sources	−6.7	−6.7
Near Eastern	6.5	16.2
Other	10.6	5.3
Slavic	3.17	−1.4

The status of other sources is opposite. All this mirrors the cultural history of the two languages, primarily the fact that Turkish played a more important role in the development of some terminologies in Serbian, mostly those of traditional crafts.

The macrolanguage prominence index was tabulated as a percentage of the macrolanguage in question minus the average macrolanguage percentage. Its positive value means that the macrolanguage in question has a higher-than-average presence and, conversely, its negative value means a lower-than-average presence of the macrolanguage. Table 7.2 shows the values obtained.

The results from Table 7.2 first show that the exchange lexical layer of both languages is shaped primarily by the three primary European sources of influence (robustly positive average indices in both Serbian and Russian). The structure of the borrowed lexicon is similar in the two languages, and the differences between classical and living European languages stem from the tendency of the Serbian authors to label Greek or Latin as the last link in borrowing rather than German or French, as is the case in the Russian dictionary. In reality, in Serbian and Russian alike, originally Greek or Latin words have been introduced through German or French influences. Another interesting fact is that there is a higher presence of the Near Eastern macrolanguage category in Serbian, which is another consequence of different historical circumstances. Ottoman Turkish presence in the Balkans lasted five centuries and ended in the nineteenth century. In contrast, the Golden Horde, Mongol-Tatar rule of Russia was limited to the second half of the thirteenth and the whole of the fourteenth century, and Turkic Tatars were just one segment of the ruling elite. The high prominence of Near Eastern words can also be seen in the research tradition of Serbo-Croatian. Thus, Čaušević (2016) reports that the first dictionary of Turkish loanwords in the history of Turkology was published by Miloš Mandić, a Serb from Bosnia.

If we look at the ratio of the languages in the two groups, the most frequent classical language in Serbian is Latin with 58.2% of all entries from classical

Table 7.2 *Macrolanguage presence indices*

Source	S	R
European – Classical	35.2	17.5
European – Germanic	1.6	15.9
European – Romance	−0.3	12.4
Average for European sources	*12.2*	*15.3*
Near Eastern	−6.0	−15.1
Other	−15.0	−15.6
Slavic	−15.6	−15.1

languages and in the Russian dictionary it is Greek with 52.8%. This may partially be a consequence of assigning ultimately Latin words German or French etymology in the Russian dictionary as opposed to treating them as Latin in the Serbian. In the Serbian dictionary the most common Germanic language is German with 56.8% of all Germanic languages followed by English with 39.3%. This ratio is very similar to the one in the Russian dictionary with 57.7% of German and 37.3% for English. The most common Romance language in the Serbian dictionary is French (63.6% of all Romance languages) followed by Italian (29%). The dominance of French is even more pronounced in the Russian dictionary (85.5% for French and 10.3% for Italian). This may be a consequence of contact borrowing from Italian in Serbo-Croatian. The structure of the Near Eastern borrowings is another consequence of different historical circumstances. The most common Near Eastern language in the Serbian dictionary is Turkish with an overwhelming 91.1%, while in the Russian dictionary the Arabic sources are first (32.2%), followed closely by Turkic languages (29.1%). This again is a clear consequence of different historical circumstances. In the "other" category, the dominant language in the Serbian dictionary is Hungarian with 43.9% (a clear consequence of contact borrowing), while in the Russian dictionary Sanskrit is first, with 23.4%. In general, there is a higher number of languages of this category in the Russian dictionary, including, for example, a visible presence of contact borrowing languages such as Finnish and Chinese (7.5% each) and Mongolian (4.7%). Finally, the most dominant Slavic language in the Serbian dictionary is Russian with 84.3% (a clear consequence of cultural influence through religious, historical, and ideological ties), and the Russian dictionary has Polish in the top spot with 95.4% of this macrolanguage category. In general, we can see that the big picture of the spheres of cultural influences is very similar to the one in the two observed datasets, while at a lower level there are differences stemming from sociohistorical circumstances.

Table 7.3 *Macrofield presence indices*

Field	S	R
Arts	-2.9	-1.5
Belief systems	-3.8	-2.5
Sciences – natural	14.0	6.8
Sciences – social	6.0	1.7
Sports	-4.9	-2.4
Vocational – production	-5.1	-1.3
Vocational – services	-3.1	-1.0

The macrofield prominence index is tabulated as a percentage of the field in question minus the average percentage of all fields. A positive value means a higher-than-average presence of the field, and a negative value a lower-than-average presence of the field. Given that the two observed dictionaries may feature different strategies of labeling, this and the next index should be approached with much more caution than the previous two, and the results should be interpreted with a much higher level of limitations. Table 7.3 shows the values found.

Despite all the differences, which most probably stem from different labeling strategies that could not be completely eliminated with the deployment of macrofields, we can still see that sciences (primarily natural, engineering, and mathematical) are the main field of cultural influence. This is a direct consequence of sociohistorical circumstances where, in both languages, scientific terminology came from somewhere else and, consequently, features numerous borrowed words, much more than terminology and nomenclature in other fields. Obviously, this does not change the fact that in both languages there may be domestic equivalents of these borrowed terms. This reveals only a relative presence of the science macrofields in the group of fields where borrowed words are found.

Finally, the macrofield profiling index for each macrolanguage group was tabulated as follows: the percentage of that particular macrolanguage in the macrofield minus the average percentage for all macrolanguage categories in the macrofield. A positive value of the index means a higher-than-average presence in the macrofield, and a negative value means a lower-than-average presence. From this index, we can see how any given macrolanguage group contributes to profiling any given macrofield. Here again, one should be aware of the limitations stemming from different labeling strategies. Table 7.4 shows the results obtained.

From Table 7.4 we can see that European languages play a strong role in profiling natural, engineering, and mathematical sciences, that Slavic languages are important in profiling the terminology of social sciences, that Romance languages are important in arts (more in Serbian than in Russian), and that

Table 7.4 *Macrofield profiling indices*

	Arts		Belief systems		Sciences – natural		Sciences – social		Sports		Vocational – production		Vocational – services	
	S	R	S	R	S	R	S	R	S	R	S	R	S	R
European – Classical	-1.9	0.3	0.7	-0.1	15.0	8.5	2.3	1.6	-1.1	-0.7	0.3	-0.1	-2.3	-0.6
European – Germanic	0.1	0.6	-0.8	-0.3	6.5	2.5	-3.3	0.8	2.0	0.7	1.2	1.6	1.1	2.7
European – Romance	4.7	1.1	-1.0	-0.3	-2.3	1.1	-4.6	0.1	0.4	-0.6	0.1	0.7	3.0	0.7
European – Average	*1.0*	*0.7*	*-0.3*	*-0.3*	*6.4*	*4.0*	*-1.9*	*0.8*	*0.5*	*-0.2*	*0.5*	*0.8*	*0.6*	*1.0*
Near Eastern	-2.9	-0.9	-0.7	1.3	-8.0	-3.4	-1.1	-1.3	-1.2	-0.8	-0.8	-0.3	-1.6	-1.2
Other	0.3	-0.9	-0.4	0.2	-6.0	-6.0	0.9	-3.9	0.0	2.1	-0.2	-1.0	0.1	-1.2
Slavic	-0.3	-0.2	2.1	-0.7	-5.3	-2.7	5.8	2.7	-0.2	-0.8	-0.6	-1.0	-0.3	-0.5

Romance and Germanic languages are important in vocational terminology. With some minor exceptions (e.g., other languages in sports or Near Eastern languages in belief systems in the Russian dictionary), in all other cases macrolanguage groups make a lower-than-average contribution to profiling the fields. These main trends are again consequences of sociohistorical circumstances. The data from this table show that Western languages overwhelmingly profile the most dominant field of natural, engineering, and mathematical terminology.

The present investigation points to the challenges of using loanword dictionaries to contrast exchange lexical layers of cultural identity in Slavic languages. These challenges stem primarily from different dictionary compilation strategies. There are only a limited number of ways to provide the answers to these challenges if we work with existing data. Four indices were proposed to provide partial answers to the challenges of working with the existing datasets of Slavic loanword dictionaries. These include the generality index, the macrolanguage prominence index, the macrofield prominence index, and the macrofield profiling index. Their deployment was demonstrated in contrasting a Serbian (de facto Serbo-Croatian) and a Russian dictionary. The analysis has revealed similarities in the main trends of development of the exchange lexical layer and some minor differences stemming from different sociocultural circumstances. Needless to say, a durable solution to the challenges of comparisons of this kind (and many others) would be the development of dictionary compilation guidelines for Slavic dictionaries, which would eventually overcome the shortcomings of this kind of contrasts.

What is also interesting to see is that, in both languages and for all macrolanguages and macrofields of borrowing (which also includes general borrowings as the largest category), there exists a high level of concentration and hence a low number of effective components. This means that a low number of key components contributes to the lexical profiling of cultural identity in this segment. Using generally available free software (Wessa, 2016), the values shown in Table 7.5 were obtained for Herfindahl–Hirschman's Index (HHI),[1] the concentration Index, and the effective number of components.

We can see that the effective number of components for both macrolanguages and macrofields is only somewhat above 1 and that it never reaches 2 components. At the same time, there are no conspicuous differences between the two languages under comparison.

7.2   The Dynamics of the Exchange Layer

I will now demonstrate the dynamics of the exchange layer [of identity] using the example of Near Eastern loanwords in Serbo-Croatian. Near Eastern

---

[1] For an accessible explanation of the measure, see Taagapera and Goffman (1981).

Table 7.5 *Fragmentation and concentration indices for*
Serbian and Russian macrolanguages and macrofields

Macrolanguages	S	R
HHI	0.33	0.30
Normalized HHI	0.20	0.17
Concentration	0.60	0.56
Effective number of components	1.67	1.78
Macrofields	S	R
HHI	0.41	0.63
Normalized HHI	0.34	0.59
Concentration	0.77	0.86
Effective number of components	1.30	1.16

loanwords (words from Turkish and those from Arabic and Persian that were mostly borrowed through Turkish) are a clear marker of identity that separate Slavic languages with a longer exposure to the Ottoman Turkish rule from those with limited exposure to Turkish or any other Turkic language. For example, contrastive analysis of loanwords in Russian and Serbo-Croatian presented in section 7.1 has revealed significant differences in the proportion of Near Eastern loanwords between these two languages (1.6% for Russian versus 10.7% for Serbo-Croatian).

Similarly, Near Eastern loanwords are used as a means of identification and distancing in nationalist discourses and practices of some South Slavic linguists. The identification role can be seen in Kadić (2014:158) "To što su srbsko-hrvatski normativci vršili izgon orijentalnih riječi iz zajedničkog književnog jezika nije imalo ama baš nikakve lingvističke razloge i opravdanje, nego je podrazumivalo političku pozadinu hegemonističko-asimilatorske aspiracije prema Bošnjacima." (The fact that Serbo-Croatian normativists have conducted an expulsion of Near Eastern words from the common literary language did not have any linguistic reason and justification whatsoever. Rather, it was assuming a political background of hegemonist-assimilatory aspirations toward Bosniaks.) We can see that Near Eastern loanwords are seen as critical for Bosniak linguistic identity.[2] One should note that high praises of this text were sung by leading Bosniak intellectuals, such as Dževad Jahić (a linguist) and Abdulah Sidran

---

[2] Bosniak is the designation for one of three major ethnic groups in Bosnia (the other two being Serb and Croat). The standard language variety common for nearly all Bosniaks (but not for Serbs and Croats in Bosnia) is called Bosnian by Bosniaks, and Bosniak by Serbs and Croats. Given that Bosniaks are the primary speakers of that particular variant of Serbo-Croatian, I am using the form Bosnian for the language standard, as the name the primary speakers of that variant have chosen to identify with. The term Bosniak for the ethnic group is undisputed.

(a writer), as well as their Norwegian supporter, linguist Svein Mønnesland.[3] Views of this kind are nothing new given that the whole recent Bosniak linguistic nationalist campaign commenced with the efforts by Alija Isaković, whose dictionary (Isaković, 1995) uses Near Eastern loanwords as a key argument to declare a separate Bosnian language. The distancing is seen in the projects of Croatian-Serbian differential dictionaries published by Croatian authors, from Brodnjak (1991) to Samardžija (2015), where Near Eastern words (that are actually not used in the present-day Serbian variant) are contrasted with non-Near Eastern words in Croatian, just to distance Croatian from this lexical stock. In the Croatian case, in sharp contrast with Bosniaks, it is the deficit of Near Eastern loanwords that allegedly makes Croatian separate from Serbian. These strategies are a part of broader linguistic nationalist maneuvers in the Balkans, discussed at length and in depth in Kordić (2010).

In light of the discussion hitherto, it is interesting to see what the real extent of the differences is, based on Near Eastern loanwords – how important they are in separating Serbo-Croatian from Slavic languages with a lower level of exposure to Turkic languages, and how significant they are in separating the variants of Serbo-Croatian. Primarily, the question is how critical they are in profiling the Bosnian variant. In the following section I will sketch the general approach of this research to then discuss its methodology and results in the next two sections.

In this research, I took a sample of letters *D*, *Dž*, and *Đ* (approximately 10 percent of all entries in the dictionary) from Škaljić (1966), a classic dictionary of Near Eastern loanwords in Serbo-Croatian. I then checked their status in the current standard variants of Serbo-Croatian. Needless to say, the ideas of what constitutes the standard language vary quite considerably, as demonstrated by the aforementioned Smakman (2012), who surveyed over one thousand non-linguists from England, Flanders, Japan, the Netherlands, New Zealand, Poland, and the United States and concluded that although the ideas about the standard language have very little in common, one can recognize a socially distinctive (exclusive) notion of the standard language and a socially cohesive (integrative) one. Here I am following Smakman's (2012) socially distinctive (exclusive) notion of the standard language, as this variety needs to be edited (using dictionaries as reference). This would include administrative, legal, scholarly language, news, etc. and exclude informal colloquial and literary language (which are typically not the target of normative interventions). This understanding of standard language is the best platform for the study of the status of Near Eastern loanwords, as it is most closely tied to the surface layer of cultural identity and its interplay with the exchange layer.

---

[3] See the following media report: http://coolin.ba/promocija-knjige-safeta-kadica-bosanski-jezik-izmedu-lingvocida-i-lingvosuicida-inserti/, accessed on December 15, 2017.

I first determined the status of these loanwords myself and then had it verified with two educated native speakers of each of the ethnic variants in question: Bosnian, Croatian, and Serbian variants (a total of six informants). I excluded from the sample the entries that were just cross-referenced rather than fully treated (e.g., *džigit* versus *jigit*) and all proper names (e.g., personal, geographical). The sample then comprised the entries of general words that were provided with a full definition in this dictionary.

The following values were assigned to the status of these entries in the present-day variants of standard Serbo-Croatian.

a. The word is used, it is not restricted, and it is the only word that covers that particular meaning or meanings in question (short description: retained exclusively).

b. The word is used, it is not restricted, but there is also another word of Slavic or other non-Near-Eastern origin that covers that particular meaning or meanings in question (short description: retained non-exclusively).

c. The word is used, it is restricted (e.g., used only in the sphere of religion), and it is the only word that covers that particular meaning or meanings in question (short description: retained restricted exclusively).

d. The word is used, it is restricted, but there is also another word of Slavic or other non-Near-Eastern origin that covers that particular meaning or meanings in question (short description: retained restricted non-exclusively).

e. The word is not used, another word of Slavic or other non-Near-Eastern origin covers that particular meaning or meanings in question (short description: replaced).

f. The word is not used because the entity to which it refers is not used anymore (short description: phased out).

The status was assigned to the entry based on the fact that it is used in at least one of the three observed variants of Serbo-Croatian. An ensuing qualitative analysis then revealed if differences between the variants can be ascertained, and it identified the semantic fields of the words involved.

One should keep in mind the following limitations. First, a sample was used, not the whole population of the entries in this dictionary. Second, there may be disagreement about the classification of some cases. Table 7.6 shows the general results obtained.

We can see that only 18.3% of this sample is retained in any of the three observed Serbo-Croatian variants. Moreover, only 2.3% of the sample is used exclusively, and it is not restricted. This points to the fact that the aforementioned seemingly large differences between Russian and Serbo-Croatian are, in fact, much less pronounced. As anybody in the field of lexicography knows, unabridged dictionaries and specialized dictionaries of lexical borrowings are graveyards of unused words. An overwhelming majority of the entries in this

Table 7.6 *The current standard language status of a sample of Near Eastern loanwords from Škaljić (1966)*

		Frequency	Percent	Example
1	retained exclusively	13	2.3	*dušek* 'comforter', *džep* 'pocket', *džeparac* 'pocket money'
2	retained non-exclusively	13	2.3	*deva* 'camel', *dželat* 'executioner', *div* 'giant'
3	retained restricted exclusively	28	5	*džemat* 'jama'ah', *dženet* 'jannah', *džuz* 'juz''
4	retained restricted non-exclusively	49	8.7	*dohakati* 'prevail', *dova* 'dawah', *dućan* 'store'
5	replaced	348	61.9	*džahil* 'ignorant', *deniz* 'sea', *džam* 'glass'
6	phased out	111	19.8	*džaili* 'respected elders', *džilit* 'thin and long spear', *džanfez* 'formerly used reflecting silk fabric'
	Total	*562*	*100*	

sample, comprising 61.9%, are in fact replaced by other words, almost invariably of Slavic origin. This may suggest that the ongoing lexical conversion of Slavic languages (in addition to the incorporation of Western loanwords of Greco-Latin origin, mostly through German and French) has been driven, among other things, by the reestablishment of the words of Slavic origins.

Moving on to the variants of Serbo-Croatian, in the first category, there are no lexical differences between the variants. Some differences do exist in categories 2 and 4 and they are as follows: *deva* is used in the Croatian and Bosnian standard but not in Serbian; *dud* is used everywhere, but Croatian also has *murva*, which is not common in Bosnian and Serbian; *dernek, dernečiti*, and *deverati* are used primarily in Bosnian and so are *daidža, daidžinica, daidžić*, and *dedo*. Finally, *dućan* is used primarily in Croatian. There is thus a handful of examples which contribute to the differences between the variants in a disregardable manner, and only in underlining the cultural identity of the Bosnian variant. Interestingly enough, in this sample the Croatian variant had two Near Eastern loanwords more than its Serbian counterpart.

A vast majority of restricted vocabulary (13.7 percent of this sample) is restricted to the field of Islam. These are terms like *džemat, dženet, džunup, džehenem, dženaza, džuma*, etc. One should note that these terms do not contribute to the lexical differences between the three variants given that the same terms will be used to refer to the phenomena from the field of Islam in all three of them. Obviously, Bosniaks, and even Serbs and Croats from Bosnia, may be more familiar with them than Serbs from Serbia and Croats from Croatia, but that does not change the general parameters of this lexical stock. Furthermore, textually these differences may be somewhat more pronounced, given that some of them are quite naturally more frequent in the Bosnian variant where the majority of speakers are (at least by declaration) followers of Islam; however, that too is not a structural lexical difference.

Near Eastern loanwords appear to underline the Central and East South Slavic cultural identity in the exchange layer of cultural identity, when compared with Slavic languages with a limited exposure to Turkic languages. There are solid empirical figures demonstrating those differences based on dictionaries of loanwords. At the same time, in clearly political maneuvers in the surface layer of lexical identity, they have been purported to be a major factor in making the variants of Serbo-Croatian separate standard languages, which is not supported by the data.

The data from this research point to the fact that both aforementioned claims (about the differences between the languages based on the exposure to the Ottoman Turkish rule and about these words as profilers of Serbo-Croatian variants) need to be revised. Near Eastern words are much less important in defining cultural identity, of those Slavic languages with prolonged exposure to the Ottoman Turkish rule, than the raw figures from the dictionaries would suggest. As already noted, dictionaries of loanwords, just like large monolingual dictionaries are for the most part graveyards of unused words, which makes the picture somewhat skewed. It seems that there is a clear movement in the exchange lexical layer of cultural identity in which Near Eastern loanwords are replaced by inherited words. Some of them become phased out given that they refer to the concepts of the Ottoman Turkish administration, military, old crafts, ethnic garbs, meals not prepared anymore, etc. All this then leads to the convergence of Slavic lexical identities.

At the same time, the figures obtained here clearly refute linguistic nationalist rhetoric about the role of Near Eastern words at the standard language level. Certainly, in non-standard colloquial language forms as well as the language of literature and dialects, numerous differences do exist based on ethnic, territorial, socioeconomic, and many other criteria. However, that does not mean that they can be transplanted to the standard language field (in its exclusive sense). The differences in that linguistic form are practically insignificant. The limitations of the present research (e.g., that it uses a sample, not the population, that there may be disagreement about classifying certain cases) do not in any way change this big picture.

It has been shown in this chapter that broad cultural categories of loanwords encapsulate cultural influences and clearly contribute to the exchange layer of lexical identity. They give testimony to different sociohistorical backgrounds of particular Slavic languages. Even more than that, they are, as we have seen in the second section of this chapter, involved in the dynamics of underlining ethnic identities. The systematic analysis that is advocated throughout this book not only reveals the role of the exchange layer in shaping cultural identity in the lexicon but can also provide a realistic account of the status of culturally relevant loanwords that goes beyond unfounded and politically motivated nationalist discourse about them. The next important segment of the exchange layer are the loanwords stemming from geographical contact, and I will consequently turn to them in the next chapter.

8   Geographical Contact

While it makes perfect methodological sense to distinguish between cultural influences and geographical contact, the following caveat should be inserted. First, there is an area of overlap between the two. For example, German is a language of cultural influence for all Slavic languages, but it is also a language of geographical contact for some of them. Second, the status of a language can change over time. Thus, for most South Slavic languages, Turkish used to be the language of geographical contact and cultural influence, but then it changed its status to only the language of cultural influence. Vlajić-Popović (2015) has clearly demonstrated, using the example of Serbian and Greek, how complex lexical exchange can be and how many changes in status can happen over time. However, for practical purposes, to be able to build a contrastive profile, one needs to segregate languages into definite categories. The fact that the borders between them may be fuzzy should certainly be acknowledged as a limitation. In this chapter contact borrowing will be analyzed from two different perspectives – synchronic, involving those languages that presently maintain contact with the language for which the profile is being built, and diachronic, encompassing the lexicon stemming from contact borrowing over time.

8.1   Synchronic Study of Contact Borrowing

The following categories of lexical transfer relevant in this field were identified in Chapter 3: horizontal geographical contact (i.e., lexical exchange with neighboring languages, for example between Serbian and Romanian), concurrent vertical geographical contact (of a dominant national language with a local language, e.g., Russian and Evenki, which is native to Russia and China), and subsequent vertical geographical contact (of a dominant language with a substrate language). As in the case of cultural borrowing, I am using the language prominence index here. The analysis uses data from Egorova (2014) for Russian and Klajn and Šipka (2006) for Serbo-Croatian.

The first element of the contrastive lexical profile of each of these two languages is the ratio of cultural and contact exchange. The second is the ratio of different forms of contact transfer, and the third the structure and relative prominence of different languages in contact exchange. Given that

Table 8.1 *Types of borrowing in Egorova (2014) and Klajn and Šipka (2006)*

Type/Language	Russian	Serbo-Croatian
Cultural borrowing	97.7%	99%
Contact borrowing	2.3%	1%
	(2.1% horizontal, 0.2% vertical)	(1% horizontal, 0.04% vertical)

subsequent vertical transfer is not consistently noted in the dictionaries of foreign words, that kind of borrowing will be excluded from the analysis.

The ratio of cultural and contact borrowing in both languages is presented in Table 8.1.

As can be seen, the difference is overwhelming. Any limitations of this data cannot change the fact that the exchange lexical layer of both of these languages has been shaped primarily through cultural borrowing and that contact borrowing plays only a very limited role in lexical exchange. This is consistent with studies like Capuz (1997:92–93), who notes the influence of English on Romance languages: "Although dealing with a situation of cultural borrowing (indirect, impersonal, without large bilingual groups), English models pervade all the linguistic levels, in addition to the lexical one, where English pressure is, as expected, far stronger than in any other." One should repeatedly note that these results pertain to the languages having or not having current geographical contact with Russian and Serbo-Croatian, respectively. Historically, as will be seen in the next section of this chapter, a broader circle of languages was involved in lexical contacts, but these languages were at the same time languages of cultural influence. Thus, the border between these two categories is somewhat fuzzy, and, in historical perspective, the dominance of cultural borrowing is not so overwhelming. I will elaborate on this in the second part of this chapter.

The two languages differ in the repertoire of the languages involved in the contact transfer. As can be expected, Russian includes more languages in both categories. The similarity lies in the fact that for both Russian and Serbo-Croatian lexicons there is one language that sticks out with a considerably higher prominence index. The distribution of languages is presented in Tables 8.2 and 8.3.

In both investigated languages, there is one dominant language in horizontal contact (Polish for Russian and Hungarian for Serbo-Croatian), and for borrowing in Russian, Tatar dominates vertical transfer. A qualitative look at the contact borrowings in both languages shows that 98% of borrowings in Russian and 86% in Serbo-Croatian belong to the general vocabulary. This is considerably higher than for the entire borrowed lexicon, which is 56.4% for Serbo-Croatian, and 78.7% for Russian, which gives a positive value of 19.3 in the generality index for the Russian and 19.6 for the Serbo-Croatian contact

Table 8.2 *Contact borrowing languages in Egorova (2014)*

Language	Prominence index
Polish	72.56
Chinese	−3.56
Finnish	−3.56
Mongolian	−5.22
Norwegian	−5.22
Georgian	−6.89
Kazakh	−6.89
Azeri	−7.44
Lithuanian	−7.44
Uzbek	−7.44
Ukrainian	−7.44
Estonian	−7.44
Tatar	33.15
Evenki	−5.31
Kalmyk	−5.31
Komi	−5.31
Udmurt	−5.31
Crimean Tatar	−5.31
Nanai	−5.31
Sami	−5.31

Table 8.3 *Contact borrowing languages in Klajn and Šipka (2006)*

Language	Prominence index
Hungarian	47.29
Venetian	3.35
Romanian	−14.08
Albanian	−15.21
North Italian	−17.11
Bulgarian	−18.62
Macedonian	−18.62
Romani	0

lexicon. This means that the contact lexicons in both languages feature approximately the same level of generality, which is significantly higher than among the borrowings from cultural exchange. The factors of higher generality of contact borrowings mitigates the dominance of the cultural borrowings in some way, given that the sphere of usage of a small number of contact borrowings features a broader range of use.

The data presented in this chapter hitherto look into present-day contact languages, which does not offer a full picture of contact borrowings. We can certainly see the dominance of cultural over contact borrowing and the dominance of particular languages in contact borrowing. However, contact between languages changes over time, and the full picture of contact borrowings is there to be had in a diachronic approach to this phenomenon. This kind of research will be presented in the second section of the chapter.

8.2   The Dynamics of Contact Borrowing

The dynamics of contact borrowing involves numerous intricacies. One should keep in mind that classic views about gradual incorporation of borrowings have recently been challenged by Poplack and Dion (2012), who used English borrowings in Quebec French to show that they are adapted abruptly. It is also important to note that the lexical borrowing comprises various types. Thus Capuz (1997) distinguishes importation, loan blends or hybrids, and substitution or loan translation. Romanova (1985) has shown with the examples from Russian, Ukrainian, and Polish that the effects of contact are pertinent not only in outright lexical borrowing but also in word formation. The problem is also to determine the historical depth of borrowing, as pointed out by Walczak (1997). A further problem are the so-called migratory loanwords, as pointed out using the material of Slavic languages by Thomas (1985). Vlajić-Popović (2015) clearly showed that a chain of languages is often involved in lexical transfer. All this should be kept in mind in the qualitative analysis of contact borrowing.

The importance of contact for the development of Slavic languages was reviewed and abundantly exemplified by Grenoble (2012), who concluded:

It is fair to say that there is no Slavic language which has been unaffected by contact. In fact, many of the contact effects date to prehistoric times and the structure of modern Slavic languages can only be understood with some understanding of earlier and current contact. (Grenoble, 2012:595)

Slavic languages abound in studies devoted to their lexicons. These studies include an overwhelming number of monographs about borrowings from various languages and general vocabulary reviews. In order to demonstrate how a qualitative diachronic contact exchange profile can be built, I used general reviews of Serbo-Croatian vocabulary (Popović, 1955; Brozović and Ivić, 1988; Šipka, 2005; Dragićević, 2010a, and Dragićević, 2018) to come up with a list of languages and fields which have historically shaped the contact segment of the exchange layer of that language (see Table 8.4). The findings were then supported by monographs devoted to the lexical influences of historical contact languages on Serbo-Croatian.

Table 8.4 *Serbo-Croatian diachronic contact languages*

Source of contact	Field(s)	Examples
Late Latin	Flora, fauna, household	*bosiljak* 'basil', *jegulja* 'eel', *vrt* 'garden'
Balkan substrate	Animal husbandry, mountainous terrain	*balega* 'dung', *ćuka* 'hill'
Byzantine Greek	Administration, the Orthodox Church, daily life	*despot* 'despot', *spanać* 'spinach', *anđeo* 'angel'
Dalmatian and Italian dialects, esp. Venetian	Administration, daily life, fishing	*blitva* 'chard', *jarbol* 'mast', *mankati* 'miss'
Hungarian	Daily life	*varoš* 'town', *ašov* 'shovel', *lopov* 'thief'
Medieval German	Daily life, mining	*ceh* 'guild', *škare* 'scissors', *kuhinja* 'kitchen'
Ottoman Turkish	Administration, religion, daily life	*kadija* 'kadi', *hodža* 'khoja, imam', *alat* 'tools'
Austrian German	Administration, military, technology, daily life	*princ* 'prinz', *general* 'general', *šina* 'rail', *knedla* 'dumpling'

Most languages that are identified as major lexical influences in Table 8.4 are concurrently the languages of cultural influence (Latin, Greek, Italian, German, and Turkish). It is therefore rather difficult to assess how much is contact borrowing and how much cultural influence (for example, some florae and faunae may be a result of late Latin contact borrowing, but most of them are definitely a result of cultural influence through modern-era scientific Latin).

Including the diachronic dimension of and using the data from Klajn and Šipka (2006) and consulting relevant monographs and papers (most notably Škaljić, 1966; Hadrovics, 1985; Vajzović, 1999; Sočanac, 2002; Golubović, 2007; Radić, 2015; Vlajić-Popović, 2015), one can estimate the percentage of contact borrowing to be between 15 and 20 percent with approximately one half of this number being borrowings from Turkish. In addition, these figures are for standard language in its entirety – colloquial forms and dialects offer a different picture. For example, Jurančič (1982) establishes four regional lexical zones – Alpine, Pannonic, Mediterranean, and Eastern – each with distinct contact influences: German in the first, Hungarian in the second, Italian in the third, and Turkish in the fourth. Most of these lexical items either are obsolete or have a clear regional feel, and they are used mostly in literature (i.e., in both cases they are used in standard language only in the wider sense of that term but not in the narrower sense).

In summary, cultural influences remain dominant while contact borrowing, seen from a diachronic perspective, has a much more prominent role than at present (but still remains dwarfed by cultural influences in vocabulary).

A separate issue is the speakers' awareness of word origins. For example, a vast majority of speakers in Bosnia (where Turkish loanwords are colloquially most pronounced of all Serbo-Croatian speaking regions) consider *astal* 'table, desk' a Turkish borrowing rather than Hungarian (out of fifty-six people I interviewed, fifty had that opinion, five were not sure, and only one correctly identified it as Hungarianism). This is much more pronounced with calques. For example, I asked the speakers about the word *nastavnik* 'teacher' and offered the following possibilities:

a. *nastav(iti)* 'to continue' + -*nik* 'agentive suffix, akin to -er in English';
b. *nad-* 'above' + *stav(iti)* 'put' + -*nik* 'agentive suffix' (this was the correct answer, a calque from Greek, as attested by Vlajić-Popović, 2015);
c. not sure.

The first option was chosen by twenty-nine people, the second, the correct one, by only seven, and the "not sure" option by twenty-four. This lack of awareness about the origins of some lexical items (which is particularly pronounced with the calques) should be kept in mind as one of the limitations of the present research. However, in most instances, with straightforward vocabulary borrowings, the speakers will have a feeling if the word is borrowed or not and also an idea about the language of borrowing. In many cases their opinion will be correct. Speakers are far less aware of the calques, and they certainly do not shape their cultural identity the way borrowed words do. The fact that it is much more difficult to establish that something is a calque than it is to prove that a word is a borrowing compounds the problem. For example, Serbo-Croatian features the word *viljuškar* 'forklift', literally: 'fork vehicle'. On the one hand, one can claim that this is a lexical calque from the English *forklift*. On the other hand, one can equally convincingly claim that this is an indigenous metaphor (the carrying element of the vehicle indeed looks like a fork) and that similarity with English is just incidental. For all these reasons, calques are not prominent in this monograph. The same is true about lexical influences in affixes. For example, Macedonian features a well-known example where the traditional suffixes *-ачница* and *-арница* are replaced by *-apa* in consequence of Serbo-Croatian lexical influence, most of them meaning roughly 'the place of' (e.g., *пиварница/пивара* 'brewery'). Thus, Veleva (2006:115) writes: "Именките добиени на овој начин брзо ги заменуваат постојните зборови со слично значење, а на тој начин се предвидува и архаизирање на традиционалните зборообразувачки модели (*книжара:книжарница / килимара:килимарница / месара:месарница / жичара:жичарница: жичница*)." (The nouns formed in this manner /with the suffix -apa, D.Š/ are quickly replacing the existing words with similar meaning, which is a predictor of the archaization of traditional word-formation models [*bookstore / carpet factory / butcher's / cable car*].) All this being the case, examples of this kind are rather rare and the speakers are generally not aware that they stem from lexical influences. Hence, they remain beyond the scope of the present monograph.

It is important here that cultural influences in the exchange layer contribute to one's linguistic identity. For example, speakers of Serbo-Croatian, Macedonian, and Bulgarian will be acutely aware of Turkish lexical heritage in their language (and they will purposefully use them to signal the informal character of their discourse in some cases), which will be absent from the speakers of Czech or Sorbian. Even in those Slavic areas where this lexical heritage commands some attention of researchers (as evidenced for Polish by Stachowski, 2014), speakers generally do not pay attention to it but, rather, focus on German and other similar influences. Furthermore, contact borrowings are instrumental in shaping regional identities. Thus, contact borrowings from Italian dialects, most notably Venetian, clearly shape the regional linguistic identities of coastal Croatia and Montenegro. Obviously, unlike cultural borrowings, these contact borrowings that shape regional linguistic identities are only a part of a broadly understood standard language rather than its narrowly understood core. The intricate relationships of these lexical strata in the surface layer will be discussed in Chapters 10–12.

Languages not only borrow words but also lend them (hence the use of the term exchange throughout this book). The ratio between lexical borrowing and lending represents another parameter of linguistic identity, which will be discussed in the next chapter.

9   Inbound and Outbound Exchange

In the previous two chapters I discussed inbound lexical exchange. However, the exchange layer of lexical identity is also shaped by the outbound lexical transfer. To use a well-known example, the exchange layer of the English language is, among others, shaped by numerous Norman borrowings. However, it is also determined by the fact that countless words from that language have been incorporated in innumerable other languages all around the globe. Not only is this fact relevant in an abstract construal of spontaneous international cultural exchange, but it also involves concrete speakers, who will have an idea of the status of their language in lexical exchange and be able to recognize words from their own language in the languages that feature such borrowings (e.g., the speakers of English will easily recognize English words for *milk, cheese, ticket, television, radio,* (i.e., ミルク [miruku]、チーズ [chīzu]、チケット [chiketto]、テレビ [terebi]、ラジオ [rajio]), and many others that have been incorporated into Japanese). That global or regional presence of the lexicon of one's own language or lack of such presence will contribute to the cultural identities of their speakers. They are also a consequence of a language functioning as a global or regional lingua franca. In that sense, outbound lexical transfer and, more specifically, the balance between the inbound and outbound lexical profile also shapes speakers' cultural identity.

Among Slavic languages, Russian is a well-known example of a donor language for the languages of Russia and the Russian near abroad, in other words, for the russophone cultural sphere. It also features clear positive lexical transfer balance with all other Slavic languages. One can see in the previous chapter that lexical influences of the indigenous languages of Russia on the Russian language remain marginal (with Tatar being the only noticeable source of influence). In sharp contrast, the lexical influence of the Russian language to all these languages is overwhelming. This is well documented in a series of publications by the Institute of the Russian Language of the Russian Academy of Sciences about the languages of the peoples of Russia. Thus, Alekseev and Shihalieva (2003), discussing Russian borrowings in Tasabarian (just to exemplify Russian lexical influences), state 62 words for professions, 79 words for sociopolitical phenomena, 130 words for scientific and technological terminology, and 116 words used in daily life. Most words are very common, such as *author, student, army, organization, motor, radio, necktie, coffee,* etc. Similar data is provided, among many others, by Alekseev and Ataev (1998) for Avarian and by Alekseev and Šejkhov (1997) for Lezgian. A clear picture of an extreme imbalance in lexical transfer of these languages emerges, with Russian being dominant in this relationship. Speakers of both languages in any given pair of indigenous languages of Russia, on one side, and the speakers of Russian, on the other, are acutely aware of the status of their respective language, which in turn is a part of their linguistic identity.

A similar interaction can happen between standard Slavic languages and non-standard non-Slavic forms, as demonstrated by the case of Romani in many Slavic countries. In all these contexts Slavic languages are dominant. While part of the lexical transfer from Slavic languages into Romani comes from the dialects, general media and the school systems definitely cause transfer from the standard-language lexical stock. Thus, for example, Ćirković and Mirić (2017), a Romani Gurbet–Serbian dictionary of the city of Knjaževac, Serbia, discuss, in the foreword to their dictionary, Serbian loanwords that were omitted from the dictionary as their meaning is transparent to the speakers of Serbian. Among those words, one can find 87 nouns, 10 adjectives, and 104 verbs. These lists include very common items such as *bolnica* 'hospital', *koža* 'skin, leather', *sijalica* 'lightbulb', *reka* 'river', *okruglo* 'round', *dugo* 'long', *isplatil* 'pay off', *osetil* 'feel', *učil* 'learn', and *pušil* 'smoke' (Ćirković and Mirić, 2017:10–11). One should add to this count all those Serbian borrowings that are attested in the dictionary and hence not included in this list because they are not transparent, or they have a specific terminological or an additional meaning. This case clearly shows the relationship between the two languages in question.

As already noted in Chapter 3, several measures to account for the ratio of lending and borrowing in the exchange layer are proposed here. The *lexical transfer index* for language A is the percentage of words in the total of lexical exchange that are lent to language B in the general lexicon of language B, minus the percentage of words borrowed from language B in the general lexicon of language A (i.e., lexical transfer index = language A general lexical borrowings from language B – language B general lexical borrowings from language A). Positive values of the index (for language A) mean transfer surplus, whereas its negative values mean that a deficit is present. The range of this index goes from 100 (language A would have that value if the entirety of the lexical transfer consists of borrowings in language B from language A) to the negative value -100 (that would be the value of the index for language B in the previously described situation). In addition, two macrofield indices

Table 9.1 *Field prominence index in*
Serbian–Albanian lexical exchange

Field	Prominence index
Farming	−4.49
Nature and geography	−4.49
Household	−9.62
Material culture and spiritual life	18.59

(the macrofield prominence index and the macrofield profiling index) that were used in the exchange profile are also proposed for the study of the direction of lexical transfer.

I will exemplify this by Serbian–Albanian lexical transfer, using the data from Stanišić (1995). Out of the five subject-matter areas Stanišić treats in this monograph, I selected four, given that the field of social terminology, the fifth subject-matter area, is not provided with a consistent list of lexical transfer items, as was the case with the other four fields. In other words, social terminology was excluded from the analysis given that the author offers a discursive account of the processes in borrowing with only some examples of concrete vocabulary. In addition to the inclusion of social terminology, those words which were previously considered Albanian borrowings in Serbian, but which Stanišić claims have been refuted as such, were not included in the analysis. In the lexicon that was subjected to the analysis, Serbian had a positive transfer index of 18. The only exception was the field of material culture and spiritual life, where the index for Serbian was negative (−10).

We can see that the field in which Albanian has a positive lexical transfer index has the highest prominence index. That means that in the other three fields with a negative prominence index, Serbian has a higher positive transfer index than the average 18. All in all, the exchange is somewhat stronger going from Serbian to Albanian than into the opposite direction, but there are also lexical fields where this relationship is reversed.

Two other interesting pairs are Serbo-Croatian versus Romanian and Serbo-Croatian versus Hungarian. Both Romanian and Hungarian are often cited as featuring a sizable number of Slavic borrowings in their lexicons. Obviously, Serbo-Croatian borrowings are just a part of that material, others being Old Church Slavonic, Russian, Ukrainian, and Slovak. However, even if we assume a very conservative estimate of the number of Serbo-Croatian words in the mass of Slavic borrowings in these two languages, there is no doubt that with both languages, and especially with Romanian, the balance is shifted heavily to the Serbo-Croatian side, with the transfer index being strongly positive for the latter language. Here are some figures that may point to this kind of balance. Vesku (1973) presents a small number of Romanian borrowings into Serbo-Croatian, mostly shepherding terms. He presents only twelve examples. Similarly, Klajn and Šipka (2006) attest 15 Romanian borrowings into Serbo-Croatian. The situation with Slavic borrowings in Romanian is drastically different. Vojvodić (2002) attests around 9,000 such borrowings. During the period of the fifteenth and sixteenth centuries alone, Oczko (2014) attests 1,530 basic terms and 1,064 derivates. If we assume very conservatively that only 10 percent of the Slavic mass in Romanian comes from Serbo-Croatian and base our calculation on Vojvodić (2002), and Klajn and Šipka (2006), that would give us the positive transfer balance index for Serbo-Croatian of 96.72.

The imbalance is considerably less drastic in the case of Hungarian. Hadrovics (1985) includes around 800 Hungarian lexical elements in Serbo-Croatian (which also includes those cases where Hungarian was just one of the segments in the borrowing chain), while Klajn and Šipka (2006) attest 152 direct Hungarian loanwords in Serbo-Croatian. Kniezsa (1955), a study of Slavic elements in Hungarian, attests 4,167 such borrowings. If one conservatively estimates the number of Serbo-Croatian borrowings at around 2,000 (in Hungarian there are no significant Church Slavonic and Bulgarian borrowings which are essential in Romanian), Serbo-Croatian has a positive lexical transfer index of 43.

When we compare the balance of lexical transfer between Slavic languages, it is quite clear (even if we have in mind all intricacies of establishing lexical influences rightly pointed out by Lilič 1973) that Russian features exceptionally high positive values of the index toward all other Slavic languages (with Polish being the only one with some very limited reciprocity). The numbers of Russian borrowings in eight Slavic languages attested by Ajduković (2004b:26) prove this point. The author included in his dictionary 1,225 Serbian, 496 Croatian, 437 Slovenian, 1,415 Macedonian, 3,802 Bulgarian, 504 Czech, 513 Slovak, and 505 Polish borrowings from Russian. Except for Polish, the number of the borrowings from these languages into Russian is marginal. Studies like Čundeva (2017), a monograph devoted to Russian borrowings in standard Macedonian, show that Russian lexical influence has a long history and that it affects various lexical fields.

The dominance of one language is an objective fact in lexical transfer, but one should also be aware of the fact that even marginal transfer can be felt as an identity profiler by some speakers. A case in point are statements like "The Italians, the Slavs, and above all, the Russian Jews, make steady contributions to the American vocabulary and idiom" (Mencken, 1921:ch. 4, s.v.), where de facto insignificant Slavic lexical borrowings in English are seen as a contribution to American English lexical identity. These maneuvers, which build identity by interpretations and interventions, will be front and center in the next three chapters devoted to the surface layer of lexical identity.

Summarizing the part of the present monograph devoted to the exchange layer, its focus is on the features rather than the words in their entirety. In this particular case, the distinction between the inherited Slavic lexicon on the one hand and borrowed lexical items on the other is the primary feature that contributes to the cultural identity profile. Speakers will make lexical choices partially based on this distinction. They will also have opinions, and they will attach value judgment to either side of this distinction. At a lower level, the cultural circle of the source language of cultural or contact exchange represents an important profile builder. Again, speakers will be aware of these cultural circles (e.g., Western European versus Near Eastern, classical versus living Western European languages) and potentially attach value judgment to the words from these circles. Finally, the subject-matter feature is an additional profiling element, e.g., operatic terminology in many languages features noticeable Italian lexical influences, automotive terminology is in German, and computing terminology in English. The speakers will be aware of this distribution in subject-matter fields and find certain lexical influences natural and normal in certain fields. How the fields are matched with source languages for borrowing is either common for all Slavic languages (as in the case of operatic, automotive, and computing terms in general usage) and sometimes they will be specific to one language or group of Slavic languages (e.g., administrative terms in Polish with strong German influences: *ratusz* < *Rathaus* 'city hall', *burmistrz* < *Bürgermeister* 'mayor', etc. or tools of Turkish provenance in Serbo-Croatian: *čekić* < *çekiç, turpija* < *törpü*). The features that profile lexical cultural identity in this layer are thus thematically organized, first in the general thematic categories of the donor languages (e.g., Western European, Middle Eastern) and then in the subject-matter fields such as technology, arts, and so on. While cross-language lexical exchange happens in consequence of broader sociohistorical and technological processes, speakers can potentially modify the exchange by accepting or rejecting inbound lexical transfer. However, this happens rarely given that most of the exchange happens spontaneously and speakers are using borrowed words, most of which cannot be replaced. Similarly, there is a limited role of the elites in this layer. Some maneuvers in surface layer may end up changing some proportions in the exchange layer. However, the general structure of the layer is mostly influenced by spontaneous processes. The change in the balance between inherited and borrowed words or between any categories of borrowings is generally a consequence of spontaneous processes, for example, that the lexemes from some cultural circles, say Near Eastern, are becoming obsolete and others, such as those from English, are becoming more common. It goes without saying that the changes in this layer are slow. There may be situations where a single loanword or cohorts of them are accepted abruptly, but generally it takes a considerable amount of time to shape the general features of this lexical layer. The way in which it shapes cultural identity is based on the sources of cultural influence and contact and the balance of exchange with other languages, and that is not something that changes overnight. The intervention type here is indirect, given that the intervention-induced changes in this layer may only happen in consequence of a maneuver from the surface layer.

Part IV

The Surface Layer

10   Lexical Planning

Based on Ferguson's model (see Ferguson 1996:277–294), lexical planning is seen as a process triggered by sociohistorical environments. The results of this process are confronted with the attitudes of the speakers (to be situated on a scale from full acceptance to rejection). These planned lexical items along with the attitudes toward various lexical items (in particular those from the exchange layer contrasted with the engineered ones or those that are considered "proper" by the elites versus those that are not) reflect cultural identity in the surface layer. The phenomena of *lexical engineering* and *lexical refereeing* are seen as key strategies of planned interventions in the lexicon, as opposed to its spontaneous development. The term *lexical engineering* is used in reference to a conscious introduction of new lexemes, while *lexical refereeing* encompasses the practice of segregating words into normative categories (standard–non-standard, correct–incorrect, etc.). It is very often so that concrete maneuvers in the surface layer include both engineering and refereeing. For example, when a field of borrowed words is targeted for replacement as "not consistent with the spirit of the language" (which is an often-heard normative disqualification of such lexical items), the first step is lexical refereeing that results in a negative evaluation of these words (other common normative statements may be that these words may lead to a loss of ethnic or national identity or that they are superfluous given that better domestic solutions are available). This is then followed by lexical engineering, that is, the introduction of the replacements that the elites prefer. This practice can be seen in numerous Slavic normative language publications which offer advice for correct use, including lexical use (e.g., Hamm et al., 2014 for Croatian).

Given the common inextricability of the two elements of lexical planning, in this chapter I will talk about maneuvers without differentiating between engineering and refereeing. As I noted before, these maneuvers generally have different motivations in terminological planning and in general language planning. In terminologies, the need to introduce a new word is most commonly a necessity as new concepts emerge on a daily basis. At the same time, the move to give preference to just one of several full synonyms is more commonly justified by the need for unimpeded communication in the field. General language planning, on the other hand, typically encompasses more diversified strategies and less straightforward motivation. As such, general lexical planning is considerably more relevant for building the surface layer of cultural identity. It is also important to note at the very outset that not all kinds of maneuvers are equally present in all Slavic languages. For example, while the maneuver of establishing normative authority in lexical refereeing (labeling words as appropriate or inappropriate) seems to be omnipresent, introducing lexical replacements is restricted to certain regions and historical periods.

Several parameters of lexical engineering and refereeing are important, most notably their prominence and scope. I have discussed in Chapter 2 Huemer's (2013) review of the notion of authority (primarily political) in various authors and intellectual traditions, most of them penned after Weber's seminal essay on three types of authority. The picture that emerges is that a multitude of justifications have been used and a variety of sources have been introduced. In the particular context of this monograph, it is important to realize that establishment of normative linguistic authority can take various forms and resort to various justifications. Obviously, normative linguists will always make claims that the source of their authority is rational, but in reality the decisions may have various other motivating factors behind them (e.g., nationalism, *amour-propre*, etc.). This particular idea of normative linguistic authority is widespread in all Slavic cultures, where normative linguists play a significantly more prominent role than in English-speaking and numerous other cultures.

I have also mentioned the line of research going from Gellner (1983), who emphasized the constructivist nature of nationalism, to Brubaker (2002, 2004, 2009) who understands ethnicity not as a state but rather as a process. It is already noted in the literature (see Kordić, 2010) that nationalism plays an important role in lexical planning. The relation between the standard form of the language and its rural and urban dialects is front and center in the practice of lexical refereeing. The linguistic interventionism is definitely in connection with sociohistorical categories, such as the notion of being cultured and the concept of the intelligentsia (the general body of speakers of the standard language is expected to be linguistically cultured and follow the advice of language planners, a group within the intelligentsia). Even the source concepts that define planning in Slavic languages remain sidelined in English. Neither *cultured* nor *intelligentsia* belong to the most common words in English, the latter is a borrowing from Russian (see *OED*, s.v.) and for the former (where only one of its meanings has to do with people, others with plants and such), there is an even more obscure English synonym *kulturny* (see *OED*, s.v.), again, borrowed from the Russian language.

The identity aspects of this layer are in part determined by the delineation of the lexicon in the standard language in respect of non-standard varieties or other languages. While each language is defined by its dialectal base and surrounding languages, some cases in the Slavic world are highly prominent. Thus, the profile of standard Slovenian is in part determined by its relationship to a most diversified dialectal base (see Logar, 1983/1984; Priestly, 1993; Logar and Rigler, 2016). Standard Czech is determined by its relation to common Czech, the widespread colloquial vernacular; for more see Short (1993a), Daneš (2003), Čermák (2006), and Cvrček (2006). Belarussian is determined by its relation with *trasyanka* (a mixed form of Belarussian and Russian dialect), as it is by its general diglossia with Russian (for more see Mayo, 1993 and Liskovec, 2002) and just as Ukrainian is in part determined by the existence of *surzhyk* (a Ukrainian–Russian language mixture), and again its diglossia with Russian (see Shevelev, 1993; Flier, 1998; and Bernsand, 2001). Both Ukrainian and Belarussian are in part defined by their relationship with Polessian (see Duličenko, 1995 and Arkušin, 2014). Macedonian and Bulgarian are determined by its mutual relationship (for more see Lunt, 1984; Friedman, 1993, 1996/1997; and Scatton, 1993). Similarly, both Upper and Lower Sorbian are determined by one another (see Stone, 1993b). Kashubian is determined by its relationship with Polish (see Stone, 1993a; Popowska-Taborska and Boryś, 1996; and Popowska-Taborska, 1998). Standard languages can also be defined by their polycentric nature (i.e., their ethnic or geographical variants), and the best-known case of that kind is Serbo-Croatian (see Brozović and Ivić, 1988; Browne, 1993; and Kordić, 2010 for scholarly treatment, and for reviews for a general readership focusing mostly on political issues, see Thomas, 1998; Okuka, 1998; and Greenberg, 2004). The nature of the complex relationship between standard Slavic languages and their substandard equivalents is discussed by Lehman (1988a and 1988b). All these relationships are to a great extent profiled by lexical similarities and lexical delineations.

The aforementioned examples create a general language profile of each involved language. What is common to practically all Slavic languages is the prominent role that normative linguists play in public discourse. It is they, along with other members of the elite, to be more precise, the intelligentsia (writers, journalists, politicians, and even performing artists), who engage in lexical planning and refereeing through series of macro maneuvers, from bringing about specialized publications such as normative dictionaries, manuals of orthography, etc. (with ensuing perpetuation of lexical recommendations by teachers and language editors) to general appearances in the media. The macro maneuvers are generally geared toward establishing linguistic authority and commonly also national/ethnic unity. Macro maneuvers include series of micro maneuvers in which concrete operations are conducted on words and their features. Thus, for example, publishing a normative dictionary is a part of a prescriptivist macro maneuver, while the practice of assigning normative labels to the words in that dictionary represents a micro maneuver. Similarly, a teacher's normative feedback to their students is another micro maneuver and so are a language editor's concrete interventions (e.g., suggesting a replacement of a non-standard word with its standard-language equivalent). This chapter is devoted to macro maneuvers, and Chapter 12 to the micro maneuvers in lexicography.

Numerous examples in the present and the previous parts of this monograph are taken from Serbo-Croatian. Calling it a standard language is, politically, as controversial as calling it two, three, or four separate standard languages. While full scholarly elaboration supporting my decision to consider it a pluricentric standard language can be found in Kordić (2010), my personal decision was primarily influenced by the following simple reasons.

First, lexical differences between the ethnic variants are extremely limited, even when compared with those between closely related Slavic languages (such as standard Czech and Slovak, Bulgarian and Macedonian), and grammatical differences are even less pronounced. More importantly, complete understanding between the ethnic variants of the standard language makes translation and second language teaching impossible. For example, while it is possible to hear a Serb complaining that he/she cannot understand a Slovenian movie because it is not subtitled (Slovenian is the closest relative of Serbo-Croatian), that would be an absurd statement with a movie in standard Croatian. Similarly, a Bosnian guest worker going to Slovenia may be motivated to take a course in Slovenian, while taking a course in Croatian would be unimaginable. Translation and second language acquisition are what greatly generates the need to talk about separate standard languages. It is obvious that other scholars may have a different opinion on this score. All this being said, the issue of one or several separate standard languages remains marginal in the present monograph given that the proposed areas and techniques for the study of the lexical layers of cultural identity would not have changed an iota had I assumed a different stance on Serbo-Croatian (I would have just used different terminology when talking about this concrete language case).

As already noted in Chapter 3, I propose two measures for the prominence of macro maneuvers. Both of them are burdened with methodological challenges which need to be taken into account when interpreting the results. The first one, the *macro maneuver prominence indicator*, shows the percentage of the normative lexical content toward descriptive lexical content. For example, if one is to analyze published non-subject-matter monolingual dictionaries, the following question can be asked. What percentage of those dictionaries (e.g., orthographic dictionaries, loanword dictionaries, normative monolingual dictionaries) are published with an eye to lexical planning as compared to general monolingual dictionaries (e.g., general language dictionaries, historical dictionaries)? Depending on the maneuver and the time period, we can speak about broad and narrow maneuvers. The second proposed measure is the *macro maneuver lexical volume indicator*, which shows the proportion of the lexicon affected by lexical planning. There are deeper maneuvers that affect more lexical mass, and shallow ones, which affect relatively narrow lexical strata. It is furthermore proposed that these values be brought into connection with anthropological dimensions discussed in Chapter 2 (see Hall 1959, 1966; Hofstede and Hofstede, 1994). Thus, for example, broader and deeper maneuvers may indicate that the power distance dimension and the uncertainty avoidance dimension have higher values in those cultures than in the cultures with languages where these maneuvers are not so prominent.

I will exemplify the first indicator by looking into normative versus non-normative content in a bibliography of lexicography, a bibliography of lexicology, and a language column in a newspaper.

The first example uses a bibliography of Serbo-Croatian dictionaries (Šipka, 2000) to tabulate the macro maneuver prominence indicator for non-subject-matter monolingual dictionaries. Only monolingual dictionaries were taken into consideration and then subject-matter dictionaries, e.g., mathematics, law, religion, were excluded (given my interest in general-language lexical planning). The remaining dictionaries were devoted to the general language, treating it either in its entirety or from some angle (e.g., language use in a dialect, correct usage). The dictionaries that had a prominent normative component were the following: standard language dictionaries, dictionaries of foreign words, dictionaries of orthography and correct usage, and dictionaries of the differences between the variants of Serbo-Croatian. The dictionaries that did not feature a prominent normative component were general monolingual dictionaries, encyclopedic dictionaries, historic dictionaries, etymological dictionaries, frequency dictionaries, dialectal dictionaries, and dictionaries of slang and colloquialisms. When the results were tabulated, it turned out that the dictionaries with a normative component had a positive macro maneuver prominence indicator of 0.35 (which means that there is slightly over one-half of normative dictionaries in the mix). Most common non-normative dictionaries are those treating dialects (nearly one-half), while among normative dictionaries, those devoted to foreign words and those that advocate correct usage (especially in orthography) are most common with 47% and 44% respectively. Having slightly over one-half of monolingual non-subject-matter dictionaries being prescriptive is significantly high, especially when we compare this situation with English-language dictionaries, where descriptive dictionaries dominate the market.

The next study was devoted to the presence of the normative content in the papers devoted to the lexicology of Serbo-Croatian. The material from Šipka (2007b), a bibliography of such papers from the early nineteenth century until the year 1988, was used. Bibliographic units devoted to metalexicography and terminology were excluded and only those that treated lexicological problems remained. The results showed the positive index value for normative-minded papers of 30. The main contributions to the volume of this particular maneuver in lexical prescriptivism are papers devoted to individual words or groups of words (where the use of a domestic word is advocated over a commonly used borrowed word, and where the authors claim that common use of a word or its sense is inappropriate, etc.). Here again, one can see an exceptionally high level of lexical prescriptivism.

Finally, I took one year of articles with the tag "Serbian language" from *Politika*, the most prestigious Serbian daily newspaper and one of the oldest newspapers in that part of the world. I selected the window from December 10, 2016 to December 9, 2017.[1] This newspaper does not have a permanent language columnist, so the content of the articles devoted to language is not defined by the orientation of the columnist (as is the case with the prestigious Serbian weekly *NIN*, where nearly all articles about language are normative in their nature, given that its permanent columnist Ivan Klajn follows that orientation). The tabulation of the results reveals the positive value of the prominence indicator for normative articles of 18.

The prominence of the normative linguistic content in the elites can also be seen beyond the circle of linguists. Thus, in April of 2017, a group of over 200 intellectuals (mostly writers, actors, but also numerous linguists) published a declaration on the common language, which, among others, claimed that Serbian, Croatian, Bosnian, and Montenegrin are not separate languages but rather variants of the common language.[2] This particular move was against the dominant surface-layer normative maneuver among Croats, which strives to prove that Croatian is a standard language separate from Serbian and other variants of Serbo-Croatian. The declaration triggered an avalanche of criticism (in all Serbo-Croatian speaking areas but most resolutely in Croatia), among others from the Croatian president[3] and the prime minister of Croatia.[4] Needless to say, in most other countries such political figures busy themselves with issues more pressing than the purely academic status of their standard language. This too shows a high prominence of the surface-layer macro maneuvers in the circle of social and political elites that is considerably wider than the environment of normative linguists. A similar example of lexical norming that exceeds the circle of normative linguists can be seen in a recent

---

[1] Summaries are available at www.politika.rs/sr/tags/articles/2106/srpski-jezik/ (accessed on December 11, 2017).
[2] See http://jezicinacionalizmi.com/deklaracija/ (accessed on December 11, 2017).
[3] See www.vecernji.hr/vijesti/grabar-kitarovic-deklaracija-o-zajednickom-jeziku-je-sasvim-mar ginalna-stvar-o-kojoj-se-ne-treba-raspravljati-1159853 (accessed on December 11, 2017).
[4] www.vecernji.hr/vijesti/kako-bih-to-podrzavao-tko-to-moze-podrzati-u-hrvatskoj-1159464 (accessed on December 11, 2017).

Polish government move to outlaw the phrase *polski obóz zagłady* 'Polish death camp'. [5]

While the provenance of the examples used in the present monograph has to do with my primary scholarly interests, the maneuvers of establishing authority and ethnic/national unity are by no means restricted to the South Slavic realm. I have already mentioned the concept of the *culture of language* or *culture of speech* and this is how these concepts are used on the Internet: *культура речи* 1,250,000 Google[6] hits or *культура языка* 683,000 hits in Russian, *kultura języka* in Polish 37,200 hits, *jezička kultura* 24,900 hits, and *jezična kultura* 11,600 hits in Serbo-Croatian. This notion is practically unknown in English and many other languages. Even more so, there are more specialized concepts of the same ilk, such as the Polish word *poprawnościowy* 'pertaining to linguistic correctness' with 21,700 Google hits. One productive line of research in all Slavic languages may be to calculate the prominence of the maneuver of establishing normative lexical use in school textbooks (e.g., enforcing the appropriate word and rejecting its possible contenders) intented for native-speaker language classes (e.g., Russian in Russia, Polish in Poland). That kind of textbook content would be measured up toward the non-normative lexico-logical content, for example, explaining what a synonym is. The same can be done with the instructors' feedback to their learners (a micro maneuver stem-ming from the normative macro maneuver), for example, in corrected students' essays. One could calculate how many of those are normatively motivated (e.g., replacing a non-standard word with its standard equivalent) and the extent to which they are geared toward general lexical precision or richness (e.g., proposing a more specific word). Based on all hitherto presented cases, I would hypothesize that the prominence index of these macro- and micro maneuvers may be considerable higher in Slavic cultures than in many others, including the cultures of the English language.

Another important parameter of the impact a maneuver may have is its lexical volume indicator, namely what percentage of the vocabulary is affected by the maneuver. The prominence and the lexical volume do not always go hand in hand. For example, in the 1990s, during the bloody disintegration of Yugoslavia, the maneuver of introducing new words or their forms in the Croatian and Bosnian variant (aimed at giving them a status of a separate standard language) was very prominent in linguistic circles and public dis-course alike. However, the lexical volume of this maneuver was extremely limited. My own investigation of the database used for Šipka (2002) shows that out of nearly 45,000 new words from the 1990s only 1.86% were marked as

---

[5] See www.politico.eu/article/poland-to-ban-phrase-polish-death-camps-nazi-germany/ (accessed on January 29, 2018).
[6] All Google counts were performed on January 25, 2018 with quotation marks around the search term.

specifically Croatian (and that includes 0.45% of those words that were not used in mainstream media but only in mostly radical nationalistic political media outlets). For Bosnian, this percentage was even lower: a total of 0.69% (which includes 0.15% of words used in radical nationalistic media outlets only).

While nationalistic agendas may be specific to just some areas in the Slavic world, the idea of normative prescriptivism is present in practically all Slavic languages. An interesting question in this regard is what percentage of the lexicon is potentially affected by such interventions. While it is extremely difficult to make any reliable estimates, let alone come to firm figures, some data may be indicative in this regard. The "holy trinity" of prescriptivism in Slavic cultures are a manual of orthography (typically accompanied by an orthographic dictionary), a standard-language dictionary, and a normative grammar. These three are typically available for various Slavic languages or their ethnic variants. Of these, grammars are of no relevance to this monograph, and the micro maneuvers in the dictionaries will be discussed in Chapter 12. Orthographic dictionaries, a regular accompaniment to the manuals of orthography (or manuals of style, as they are called in English), may be a good indicator of the size of the lexicon affected by prescriptive macro maneuvers. Thus, for example, Šipka (2011), a Serbian orthographic dictionary (de facto, orthographic, orthoepic, and partially, grammatical dictionary), attests over 60,000 entries. This dictionary includes only those words which have written or pronounced forms or grammatical features that may be problematic in the standard language. In addition to the words listed in the dictionary, there are others that require normative intervention because they tend to be used in the meanings that are not prescribed by the normativists. The words that have usage features which are problematic from the standpoint of normativist maneuvers (they are obsolete, colloquial, dialectal, they belong to a different ethnic variant) should also be included. Finally, there are words of foreign origin where the lexical norm leans toward an already existing word of the inherited Slavic stock. If all this is taken into consideration, it is clear that the estimated figure grows to include a half million words that the unabridged dictionary of the Serbian Academy of Sciences and Arts is projected to comprise once it is finished at some point in this century. This is definitely not the case in languages such as English, where prescriptivist tendencies are considerably lower, which also yields a lower estimated lexical volume indicator for this macro maneuver.

It is obvious that the macro maneuver lexical volume indicator depends on the breadth of the maneuver. The maneuver that separates Croatian lexical items from Serbian ones is considerably narrower than the maneuver that separates the standard use of the lexicon from the non-standard one. Inside this broad maneuver, it is possible to distinguish its narrower components. One example would be the drive to suppress the "unnecessary" foreign words which already have established synonyms in the inherited Slavic stock. Such an example would be disqualifying *rentati* 'to rent', a borrowing from English in Serbo-Croatian, given that the verb *iznajmiti/iznajmljivati* 'to rent' already exists in the inherited Slavic lexical stock. This particular macro maneuver features a considerably lower lexical volume index than the general prescriptivist drive.

If we connect these findings with the dimensions established in cross-cultural psychology and cultural anthropology (discussed in Chapter 2, see Hofstede and Hofstede, 1994), the following hypothesis can be formulated. The heightened tendency to establish linguistic authority in the lexicon is connected to collectivism (everybody should be encompassed by normative rules) and uncertainty avoidance (there should always be a rule that is followed to avoid uncertainty). A common complaint from normative linguists is the refusal of the general body of speakers to follow normative rules, and a common complaint from speakers interested in standard language is about those situations where there is no straightforward rule to follow, which leaves them disoriented.

A range of maneuvers in the surface layer operate on the material of the deep and exchange layers. The Serbo-Croatian language has provided two real-life laboratories of lexical changes, one in the nineteenth century, the other in the 1990s. The abrupt technological, political, and social changes in both these periods called for new words to be introduced and also for some old words to be replaced. In both instances, it was possible to conduct this introduction of new words and possibly replacement of an old one by taking a borrowed word (which includes the exchange layer) or making an innovation using inherited material and patterns (which includes the deep layer) or a combination of both (with both the deep and the exchange layer involved). These two situations will be discussed in Chapter 13 given that the dynamics of the dialog between the elites and the majority of speakers greatly determined their final outcome.

As previously noted, macro maneuvers encompass micro maneuvers, i.e., concrete normative operations on words. While dictionaries are not the only ground of such micro maneuvers (these are also conducted on a daily basis by, for example, language editors, teachers), they are surely the most common and the most prominent of such venues. Additionally, the datasets of dictionary micro maneuvers are readily available. The next chapter will be devoted to the dictionary micro maneuvers in the surface layer.

11   Lexicographic Traditions

Lexicographic traditions of Slavic languages in general and South Slavic languages in particular have been commanding considerable attention for quite some time, as demonstrated by Plotnikova (2000), who probed various Slavic dictionaries and traditions, Lučić (2002) where South Slavic traditions were discussed, and Bockholt (1990) devoted to Serbo-Croatian dictionaries. In this chapter I am continuing that research tradition, incorporating it into the proposed model for the study of micro maneuvers in the surface lexical layer of identity.

The nexus between macro maneuvers and micro maneuvers will be discussed in the first section of this chapter. Dictionaries are a part of macro maneuvers given that they are embedded into a broader social environment. They are also a ground for identity-based micro maneuvers. I will use a triangular model, based in communicative lexicography, to demonstrate how the two types of maneuvers interact. The second section of this chapter will then be devoted to a cross-Slavic contrasting of micro maneuvers in the field of usage labels. The final section will provide an example of diachronic lexicographic macro- and micro maneuvers.

11.1   The Nexus of Maneuvers

The nexus of macro- and micro maneuvers will be explored using a triangular model informed by cognitive sociolinguistics and communicative metalexicography (see Yong and Peng, 2007 and Geeraerts et al. 2010). If we apply the two aforementioned approaches to study the sociolinguistic factors in South Slavic lexicographic traditions, dictionaries are construed as socially embedded. They represent systems of intercultural communication between the compiler and the user, where both involved parties have certain attitudes and belief systems about linguistic variation. However, the situation is more complex than that. Dictionaries have often been the ferment of change, and, even more frequently – they mirrored or incorporated social changes.

The relation between the three key components of the process (factors, elements, and strategies) is represented in Figure 11.1. As can be seen, the

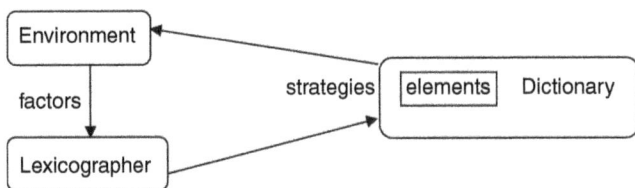

Figure 11.1 Sociolinguistic aspects of lexicography

factors influence lexicographic strategies, which shape the elements but at the same time provide feedback to the environment for the dictionary. As such, they represent the nexus of macro maneuvers and micro maneuvers. The research presented in this section is based on the material of Serbo-Croatian dictionaries attested in Šipka (2000). Additionally, a Macedonian dictionary will be used. A bottom-up approach was espoused in that concrete empirical material and used to extract generalizations in answering the following three broad questions:

a. Which macro maneuvers and, more broadly, sociocultural, political, and historical factors have influenced lexicographic production?
b. Which dictionary components have been subjected to and formed by the aforementioned extralinguistic factors?
c. Which lexicographic micro maneuvers have been adopted to negotiate various sociolinguistic factors in the dictionary compilation process?

The material from one or more dictionaries exemplifies each particular factor, component, and strategy. The next step was the establishment of broader patterns in all three segments. In addition to using the data from the aforementioned dictionaries, I have also used various material related to the dictionaries, including debates, interviews, and media appearances, by the lexicographers and other linguists.

The general methodological approach is thus bottom-up, a feature that is shared with some recent lexicological contributions such as Hanks (2013). The analysis of the aforementioned dictionaries suggests the establishment of the following factors of influence, i.e., the elements of the social environment that shaped the dictionary compilation process at one juncture or another.

a. Ideology and religion
b. Economy
c. Politics and geopolitics
d. In-group vs. out-group dynamics
e. Modernization
f. Cultural influences.

I will discuss each of the factors in turn.

Ideology and Religion

The first Croatian dictionary, Verantius (1595), which was a direct product of the Renaissance mores and conducts, can illustrate the influences of ideology. The entire Renaissance mindset made it possible to establish the status of (as the author calls them in the title of the dictionary) "the five noblest languages" for Italian, German, Hungarian, and Čakavian Croatian, along with Latin, which had attained that status before the Renaissance, and have their words appear in the dictionary. Similarly, the advent of the Islamic religion in the Balkans enabled a lexicon with the macrostructure that follows the conventions of that cultural sphere, namely Uskufi (1631). In this Bosnian–Turkish dictionary in rhymed verses, the very form of dictionary presentation (its versed structure) is something that was quite common in Islamic cultures of the time. Ideology has also shaped South Slavic lexicographical landscape at a lower level. Thus, for example, two Counter-Reformation Croatian–Latin dictionaries (Habdelić, 1670 and Bellosztenecs, 1740) are largely a product of the ideological cleavage between Jesuits and the order of St. Paul, where the dictionaries served as the tools of attracting the youth into their respective high schools. Ideological considerations have also shaped microstructural lexicographic treatment. A very interesting example of micro-ideological influence is offered by a monolingual Serbo-Croatian dictionary authored by Miloš Moskovljević (1966). The neutral rather than negative treatment of the entry *četnik* (royalist World War II guerrilla fighter), which in and of itself was an ideological maneuver (as the author refused to follow condemnation of these anticommunist royalist forces, condemnation that was expected in the Communist period, when the dictionary was compiled), led to the ban of this dictionary, which was finally lifted after the fall of Communism.

Economic factors vary significantly in terms of the level at which they exert influence. On the one hand, there are cases such as Karadžić (1818), a Serbian language dictionary based on the spoken dialect of the author's region, which eventually dethroned literary Church Slavonic tradition. This dictionary is a direct result of the emergence of a new economic class, the bourgeoisie, and its power struggle with the representatives of the traditional feudal system (more on this conflict in the content of Karadžić's dictionary can be found in Popović, 1981). On the other hand, there are dictionaries such as Grujić (1959) that have had countless further editions, and which were designed as cheap low-quality lexicographic projects where the target language equivalents are just listed after the source language word. As can be seen from Šipka (2000), the same author appears as the sole author or co-author in various other Serbo-Croatian bilingual dictionaries: Spanish, Italian, German, French, Chinese, Russian, Slovenian, and Macedonian. In this particular case, the economic factor at stake is the desire for quick profit, regardless of the quality of the product.

In politics and geopolitics, the dictionaries show the influence of local and global geopolitics, as well as a range of political issue dimensions, from the issue of centralization versus (con)federalization to the issue of political correctness and cultural appropriateness. The issue dimension of centralization versus (con)federalization is most prominently illustrated by Jonke and Stevanović (1967–1976). This six-volume dictionary was published jointly by Matica srpska, a major Serbian cultural association, and Matica hrvatska, a major Croatian cultural association. Following massive Croatian accusations of the Serbian part of the team for unitarism (see, e.g., Brozović, 1969) the Croatian association (Matica hrvatska) withdrew from the project and the remaining four volumes were authored by the Serbian institution (Matica srpska) without Croatian collaboration. The discussion as to how the variants of Serbo-Croatian are going to be represented in the dictionary (less prominently, as Serbs would have liked it, or more prominently, as was desired by Croats) mirrored the preferences about the political organization of Yugoslavia, the country where the dictionary was compiled. In general, Serbs were unitarists, Croatians were separatists. Similar geopolitical games are reflected in Dimitrovski et al. (1961–1966), a Macedonian dictionary, where the authors chose to include Serbo-Croatian explanatory glosses. This was a direct consequence of Macedonia being a part of Yugoslavia, attempting to deflect any historical Bulgarian claims on Macedonia being Western Bulgaria and the Macedonian language being Western Bulgarian. Finally, the aforementioned ban of Moskovljević's dictionary (1966) shows the consequences of not following what was political correctness of the day. More recently, there are strong voices, such as Savić (2009), demanding a gender-sensitive language in the dictionaries.

Ethnic identity is certainly the most prominent generator of in-group versus out-group dynamics. The aforementioned dictionary edited by Jonke and Stevanović (1967–1976) is an example of ethnic cohesion, primarily defining Croatian linguistic and ethnic identity in contrast to Serbian. Ethnic cohesion resulted, at a later point in time, in dictionaries such as Brodnjak (1991), which lists lexical differences between Croatian and Serbian. Particularly interesting this regard is the case of the Bosnian standard. Commencing with the publication of Isaković (1995), and followed later by several other dictionaries (see the review of the most recent ones in Mešanović-Meša, 2012), Bosnian was established as the third Serbo-Croatian standard, seeking to emphasize its peculiarities and create equidistance from the remaining two, Serbian and Croatian, which had served as principal tools in the process. However, in-group vs. out-group dynamics was also created by other factors, as the aforementioned example of the competition between the Jesuit and order of St. Paul dictionaries shows.

Modernization can be seen in a range of dictionaries. On the one hand, there is the practice adopted in Ristić and Kangrga (1936), which, in the spirit of Constructivism, replaced verbal usage labels with icons (e.g., cogwheels for a machine engineering term, a note sign for a musical term, two crossed swords for a military term, etc.). On the other hand, there are the much more profound influences of modernization. Most notably, older lexicographic tradition (from the fifteenth to the early nineteenth century) remains intertwined with literary production. For example, a dictionary can be seen as a work of literature (as is the case with the aforementioned rhymed Uskufi, 1631), or dictionary entries may contain various short literary forms such as stories and verses (which are attested in practically every dictionary of that period, and very prominently in Karadžić, 1818). As societies modernized in the late nineteenth and early twentieth century, these literary elements disappeared.

Cultural influence, the final societal factor that I was able to identify, influences primarily bilingual dictionaries. On the one hand, there are purely mechanical elements influenced by this factor, such as the fact that in fifteenth- to nineteenth-century Croatian lexicography, dictionaries published in the north (closer to Hungary) used the Hungarian system of noting the characters [that were]not present in the basic Latin script, while those published in the south (closer to Italy) followed the Italian system. Thus, what is *lj* (as in *ljubav* 'love', IPA symbol: ʎ) in contemporary Croatian orthography was rendered as *ly* in the north (e.g., in Habdelić, 1670) and *gli* in the south (e.g., in Della Bella, 1785). On the other hand, the number of bilingual dictionaries for any particular language is directly proportionate to the cultural influence of that language. Thus Šipka (2000) shows that English, German, Russian, and French were the primary sources of cultural influence on the entire region in various historical periods, as reflected in the high number of Serbo-Croatian bilingual dictionaries: English (330), German (270), Russian (120), and French (102). One can also see a sharp increase in the number of English bilingual dictionaries (compared to German and French) after World War II, which shows the shifting tides of cultural influence.

Needless to say, one can see a combination of two or more factors in one dictionary, as already noted for the dictionary by Jonke and Stevanović (1967–1976), which features political and ethnic factors. I have also already noted that practically every dictionary, and this is very prominent in the dictionaries with direct normative intent, is part of a macro maneuver to establish linguistic authority in the field of the lexicon.

The following dictionary components are shaped by the aforementioned factors of influence:

a. language choice
b. dictionary naming
c. choice of the graphic system

d. front and back matter
e. macrostructure, and so:
  i. vocabulary selection
  ii. ordering
f. microstructure, and so:
  i. entry word
  ii. grammatical treatment
  iii. definitions
  iv. usage labels
  v. cross-referencing.

Language choice covers both the choice of including Serbo-Croatian in its entirety or just one of its ethnic variants (the former was preferred during the existence of Yugoslavia and the latter after its breakup in the early 1990s) and the choice of languages for bilingual and multilingual dictionaries. The aforementioned choice of languages in Verantius (1595) or the twentieth-century explosion of bilingual Serbo-Croatian–English dictionaries clearly shows how this element is affected by societal factors.

Dictionary naming is another affected component. For example, many Croatian dictionaries published between 1945 and 1990 (attested in Šipka, 2000), would name the language Croatian or Serbian (in line with the general separatist attitude), while Serbian dictionaries used the designation Serbo-Croatian (again reflecting the general unitarist attitude). Historically, a number of different names were used, e.g., Illyrian, Slovine, Dalmatian, depending on the authors' ethnogenetic theories.

Front and back matter have often been the place where various political language-related attitudes had been laid out, from Micaglia (1649–1651), who states in the Foreword that among various forms of the Illyrian language (his term for Central South Slavic), the language spoken in Bosnia is, by general consent, the most beautiful ("Ogn'un dice che la lingua Bosnese sia la piu bella"). The author compares this to the Italian situation and the prestigious status of some dialects. Interestingly enough, this statement, completely devoid of its context, is commonly quoted as an argument for the establishment of the Bosnian standard, i.e. as a supporting argument in that macro maneuver. In that campaign to establish Bosnian as a separate standard language, which commenced in the early 1990s, the dictionary front matter (e.g., in Isaković, 1995) was a platform for the expression of various language-related political attitudes.

Affected macrostructural elements include vocabulary selection and ordering. For example, one additional reason why Moskovljević (1966) was problematic lay in the fact that it included just Serbian rather than broader Serbo-Croatian vocabulary (as was expected in the times of linguistic unitarism in Serbia). Similarly, the rhyming structure, i.e., the lack of alphabetic ordering in Uskufi (1631), is a direct consequence of the fact that it belongs to a particular Islamic lexicographic tradition, in which dictionaries of that type were common.

Finally, practically any element of the microstructure can be affected. Which words assume the position of the headword is influenced by vocabulary selection, and the cases vary from, say Voltiggi (1803), who is extremely inclusive, so as to incorporate not only the words from all Serbo-Croatian dialects but also other Slavic languages, to Brodnjak (1991), who is extremely exclusive, including only those headwords that are supposedly exclusively Croatian or exclusively Serbian. Grammatical treatment is another microstructural segment affected by the sociopolitical environment. Thus, in early Croatian dictionaries, verbs were listed in the first-person present tense, just as in Latin dictionaries. As the influence of the Latin language subsided, dictionaries switched to listing verbs in the infinitive (which is the practice that survives to the present day). Thus, for example, Habdelić (1670) lists verbs in the Latin language manner and Della Bella (1785) in the modern, infinitive form. That definitions can be affected is shown by the aforementioned Moskovljević (1966), which was problematic because of the neutral rather than negative definition of the entry for *četnik*, a World War II royalist guerrilla fighter (negativity was expected in the communist society of that time). Another obvious element is usage labels, especially normative ones. For example, many Bosniak words and forms like *babo* 'father', *lahko* 'easily', which were considered non-standard dialectal or colloquial in pre-1900s dictionaries, were elevated to the level of the standard language (and accordingly lost dialectal or colloquial usage labels) in Isaković (1995) and subsequent Bosnian dictionaries. Finally, cross-referencing can also be affected. A major bone of contention in Jonke and Stevanović (1967–1976) was the cross-referencing of ethnic variants. One major objection of the Croatians was the excessive practice of treating Serbian word forms and then just cross-referencing their Croatian counterparts (which was, in their view, a practice motivated by unitarism and favoritism of the majority ethnic variant).

The dataset of this project allows the differentiation of the following lexicographic strategies:

a. enforcement
b. submission
c. avoidance
d. masking.

The strategy of *enforcement* is the most straightforward and the most proactive of the four strategies. The lexicographer uses the dictionary to enforce a certain idea. Thus, for example, practically all general monolingual Bosnian dictionaries, Isaković (1995), Jahić (1999), Halilović et al. (2010) and others, represent attempts to enforce the idea of a separate Bosnian standard language.

The idea is political in its nature: politics shape society, which in turn influences the dictionary (what will be included and what its purpose is) so that the dictionary ultimately becomes a tool of political activism. Similar is the situation of the aforementioned Macedonian dictionary (Dimitrovski et al., 1961–1966), which establishes standard Macedonian within Yugoslavia (hence explanations are in Serbo-Croatian).

Submission, the second established strategy, can be seen in subsequent dictionaries by the Croatian author Bratoljub Klajić. At the time of the Independent State of Croatia, a Croatian Nazi statellite entity, during World War II, this linguist co-authored a manual and dictionary of Croatian orthography, which very aggressively advanced the idea that Croatian is a language separate from Serbian (Cipra and Klaić, 1944). Only seven years later, in socialist Yugoslavia, this author penned a dictionary of loanwords, which assumed Serbo-Croatian linguistic unity (Klaić, 1951). The author's strategy is thus submission to the new political circumstances.

Avoidance, the third strategy, can be seen from Benson (1998). This dictionary bears the following name: *Standard English–SerboCroatian, SerboCroatian–English Dictionary: A Dictionary of Bosnian, Croatian, and Serbian Standards* in a clear attempt to avoid non-productive political discussions as to Serbian, Croatian, and Bosnian being separate languages or just variants of a polycentric standard language called Serbo-Croatian (for more about this discussion, see Kordić, 2010).

Masking is the final strategy found in the observed dataset, which can be seen in the argumentation of the Serbian participants in Jonke and Stevanović (1967–1976). Namely, unitarist drives were presented as the desire to make the dictionary more functional (for example in cross-referencing from Croatian to Serbian forms). Thus, one political agenda is pursued under the guise of another purely lexicographic strategy.

Going back to questions posed at the beginning of this section, the following can be stated. A rich network of factors from society influences the observed dictionaries. Practically all dictionary components can be affected by these factors. Finally, the lexicographers of this tradition have been deploying various micro maneuvers in both reacting to the societal factors and trying to actively shape society (most notably by the strategy of enforcement). All this shows that the dictionary-making process remains deeply embedded in the fiber of society and its changes over the centuries. This, in turn, shows inextricable links between macro- and micro maneuvers.

To sum up, dictionaries are commonly seen as dull lists of words, even by lexicographers themselves as in the famous definition by Samuel Johnson, where a lexicographer is defined as: "a writer of dictionaries; a harmless drudge, that busies himself in tracing the original, and detailing the signification of words" (Johnson, 1755, Foreword). In contrast to this image of drudgery, the analysis in this section clearly demonstrates that dictionaries should be seen as rich depositories of social practices. In keeping with this notion, the work of the lexicographer should be viewed as being in constant dialog with the prevailing cultural, social, and ideological context.

11.2   The Micro Maneuvers

In this section, I will address a concrete lexicographic micro maneuver – the deployment of exclusion usage labels in the construal of non-standardness.

The term *exclusion labels*, as used here, is a subset of usage labels. I will hence commence with defining usage labels. In its broader sense, *usage* refers to any kind of relationship of words or their features (their meanings or their forms) and their language production/reception context. This ranges from the required morphosyntactic form of that particular context to semantic links the word may have, and the effects the word creates in that context. In its narrower sense, *usage* excludes any phonetic, phonological, prosodic, morphosyntactic, and core semantic parameters. In that sense, this term refers to a higher, lower, or absolute valence of the word or its feature toward certain contexts (e.g., toward one period in time or region but not toward another) or a certain contextual effect (e.g., offensiveness, facetiousness). I will employ *usage* in this narrower sense and the concrete scope of the phenomena covered with it will be outlined later in this section based on the review of the practice in lexicography and metalexicography. *Label* is any succinct, customary and, as a rule, repeatedly deployed reference to the usage parameters. In a typical case, such customary and repeated references are either listed in the front matter, e.g., *obs.(olete), Am.(erican), off.(ensive)*, or established in linguistic and/or lexico-graphic practice of the language in question (e.g., grammatical labels showing the inflection of the word, such as *gave, given* under *give*). Not every reference to usage is a label – there are also glosses, which refer to usage, such as *used only in Shakespeare's works* for the word *honorificabilitudinitatibus*. *Usage labels*, given that the narrower meaning of usage is employed here, refer to succinct customary references to the valence of the words or their features toward certain contexts or contextual effects. This precise usage of the term can be found in Béjoint (2010:12): "A usage label is a noun or adjective indicating the kind of context in which the word is normally used: *slang, literary, American, Medicine*, etc. Usage labels are usually abbreviated (*sl, lit, US, med*, etc.). They are of different kinds: social, geographical, stylistic, etc. corresponding to different varieties of language."

By *exclusion labels* I refer to a kind of usage labels which have the potential to exclude a labeled item from a contemporary standard language or at least its core. The idea of standard and non-standardness will be discussed first and then the labels themselves will be addressed.

When applying the proposed model to the study of the dictionary labels in their role of excluding words and their forms from the standard language, one first needs to address the idea of non-standardness followed by the role of dictionary labels in the context of declaring a lexical item, its form or meaning, substandard.

The idea of non-standardness assumes the existence of a standard language variety. In defining what that standard language variety is, I will start with the social dynamic field of a standard variety (Ammon, 1995:80, summarized in English in Takahashi, 2004:177–178). This field, as defined by Ammon, includes five key elements: majority population (i.e., the members of the community of speakers), norm authorities, in charge of language corrections, codifiers, who create language codex (such as orthographic dictionaries), linguistic experts, who issue their expert opinions, and model speakers/writers, whose linguistic performance serves as the basis for norm codification. A majority population creates primary rules, which are uncodified, while four other aforementioned factors of the process (norm authorities, codifiers, linguistic experts, and model speakers/writers) create secondary norms, which are codified.

Ammon (2004) elaborates on this process and goes on to note that "the categorization (delimitation) of standard from non-standard forms is not always a simple yes–no decision, though there are unquestionable standard forms and unquestionable non-standard forms, namely those for which all the above mentioned forces agree" (Ammon 2004:278; reference is made here to the five stakeholders – majority population, codifiers, linguistic experts, norm authorities, and model speakers/writers – mentioned above).

Monolingual dictionaries of standard Slavic languages typically involve all four factors identified by Ammon: they attract considerable interest in the majority of population, lexicographers are seen as codifiers, linguistic experts are present and so are norm authorities, and finally dictionary examples typically involve model writers. Despite the fact that dictionary compilers may state that their dictionary is descriptive rather than normative, dictionary users (Ammon's majority population) perceive such dictionaries as a source of authority. As Milroy and Milroy (2012:4) aptly state: "The attitudes of linguists (professional scholars of language) have little or no effect on the general public, who continue to look to dictionaries, grammars and handbooks as authorities on 'correct' usage. If, for example, lexicographers (dictionary-makers) attempt to remove all traces of value-judgment from their work and refuse to label particular usages (such as ain't) as 'colloquial' and others as slang, there is likely to be a public outcry." Similar thoughts can be found in Ammon (2004: 276–277) in his discussion of "social forces establishing and controlling standard varieties." Needless to say, ideas of what constitutes the standard language vary quite considerably, as demonstrated by Smakman (2012) in his aforementioned study where he concluded that one can recognize the socially distinctive (exclusive) notion of the standard language and the socially cohesive (integrative) one.

The role of monolingual dictionaries in standardization can be seen in (mostly political) attempts to form new Slavic standard languages. Thus, Dževad Jahić, a standardizer of Bosnian, states the following in a TV interview: "In order for a language to be normed, it has to have an international language code . . . as well as a grammar, a dictionary, and a manual of orthography, in that order."[1] Similarly, a recent manual of Montenegrin orthography features the following passage: "the secretary of education and science . . . asked the Council [on Montenegrin language] to . . . form a task force charged with preparing a final version of a proposal for a manual of orthography, grammar, and dictionary of the Montenegrin language."[2]

Dittmar (2004) discusses the idea of non-standard language forms in German-, English-, and French-speaking cultures. German tradition is definitely closest to the Slavic language traditions, in particular in its establishment of the colloquial language (Umgangssprache), which serves somewhat like a buffer zone between standard and substandard. Ammon (2004:278) notes: "*colloquial* (or German *umgangssprachlich*) . . . can be taken to mean (1) 'colloquial standard', i.e., a stylistic level within the standard norm or (2) 'non-standard'."

The idea of standardness and hence non-standardness is rather problematic. Ammon (2004) offers an elaborate account of the level of ambiguity and category overlapping in this sphere. For our purposes here, I will understand standard language in its narrower sense, as those language varieties subject to standardizing efforts by codifiers, linguistic experts, and norm authorities. I am thus following Smakman's (2012) socially distinctive (exclusive) notion of the standard language, as this variety needs to be edited (using dictionaries as reference). This would include administrative, legal, scholarly language, and news and exclude informal colloquial and literary language (which are typically not the target of normative interventions). This understanding of standard language is the best platform for the study of exclusion labels, as it is uncontroversial that a kind of lexical norm can be enforced in such varieties by excluding certain words from the norm. Needless to say, an operational definition of standard deployed here does not attempt to establish a new understanding of the standard language – it is merely striving to simplify matters and make them analyzable.

In this view, non-standard vocabulary would include items that are inappropriate in standard language varieties. Thus, for example, excretion or sex-

---

[1] www.youtube.com/watch?v=LXV9cRTMvjU (accessed on June 29, 2015)
[2] www.gov.me/files/1248442673.pdf (accessed on June 30, 2015).

Table 11.1 *Types of usage labels (Svensén, 2009:316)*

Criterion	Type of marking	Unmarked centre	Marked periphery	Examples of labels
Time	diachronic	contemporary language	archaism – neologism	arch, dated, old use
Place	diatopic	standard language	regionalism, dialect word	AmE, Scott, dial.
Nationality	diaintegrative	native word	foreign word	Lat., Fr.
Medium	diamedial	neutral	spoken – written	colloq., spoken
Sociocultural	diastratic	neutral	sociolects	pop., slang, vulgar
Formality	diaphasic	neutral	formal – informal	fml, infml
Text type	diatextual	neutral	poetic, literary	journalese, poet, lit.
Technicality	diatechnical	general language	technical language	Geogr., Mil., Biol., Mus.
Frequency	diafrequential	common	rare	rare, occas.
Attitude	diaevaluative	neutral	connoted	derog., iron., euphem.
Normativity	dianormative	correct	incorrect	non-standard

related obscenity would be non-standard, given that it cannot be freely used in the standard language varieties (unlike in colloquial and literary genres). Dictionaries would hence typically mark such word accordingly.

What I named *exclusion labels* represents a subset of lexicographic usage labels. Svensén (2009:316) provides a very comprehensive account of usage labels types in Table 11.1.

One should note that Table 11.1 represents a handy English-language version of the categories found in Hausmann (1989:651) with another version found in Hartmann and James (2001:151). In this approach, subject-matter labels are called diatechnical; they are restricted to a specific technical language and defined in contrast to general language. It is noteworthy that this classification remains strongly Eurocentric. For example, it does not contain gender (words used exclusively by males or females, i.e., in thus marked texts), age (items used by younger or older people, etc.), and other similar categories, as these are not so frequent in European languages and are rather rare in European dictionaries. (On a side note, even European dictionaries use labels such as "youth language".) The very idea of something being technical presumes a kind of society we know from European countries. In contrast, the idea of subject matter would be much more appropriate for other cultural settings, given that it does not presume any kind of advanced technology.

A majority of established types of labels may serve as exclusion labels. The most direct labels of this kind are dianormative ones. Exclusion can also, rather straightforwardly, be achieved by diachronic, diatopic, and diastratic labels. All those labels exclude words from a contemporary standard language. A part of diaphrasic labels (e.g., informal) as well as diaevaluative labels certainly have an indirect exclusion potential. In other words, while their primary role is to mark the attitude, they carry a certain potential of being understood by the users as exclusion labels (see section 11.2 on the discrepancy between the compilers' intentions and users' understanding of the text). Other labels are just marking an area or a feature within the standard language.

Monolingual Slavic general dictionaries have a two-way communication with society. On the one hand, they are at the receiving end of normative authorities (i.e., they are expected to follow general delimitations of the standard and substandard sphere). On the other hand, lexicographic strategies, in particular the use of exclusion labels, are an agent of normative enforcement.

Almost all Slavic languages have a tradition of considering literary languages as standard. Most common reference to the standard language implies literature. *Литературный язык* in Russian, *język literacki* in Polish, *литературен јазик* in Macedonian, *книжовен език, литературен език* in Bulgarian, *knjižni jezik* in Slovenian, and *književni jezik* in Serbo-Croatian all mean 'literary language'. Attitudes toward standard language are perhaps best reflected in Ščerba (1957), where he states that the most basic function of literary language is to be generally accepted and generally understandable: "основную функцию, которую должен выполнять литературный язык и которая в сущности только и делает его литературным, т.е. **общепринятым**, а потому и **общепонятным**" (Ščerba, 1957:114). It is of particular importance that Ščerba offers linguistic arguments for a campaign initiated by Maxim Gorky to protect the Russian literary language from being dirtied by dialectisms and vulgarisms: "беречь русский литературный язык от засорения его диалектизмами и вульгаризмами" (Ščerba, 1957:128). One can clearly see the idea of non-standardness, and the macro maneuver to exclude certain lexical items from the standard.

Practically all Slavic lexicographic traditions follow this literary language agenda and have the need to define it by excluding certain items, which belong to the forms of language that are not generally accepted and/or generally understandable. I will now look into such lexical strata and their corresponding usage labels.

In practically all contemporary monolingual Slavic dictionaries (and four of them will be analyzed here), one can find the following two ideal types of exclusion labels:

a. Primary exclusion labels, i.e., such labels as *slang*, where the dictionary compiler's intention was to clearly exclude certain words, their meanings, or forms from the standard language;

b. Secondary exclusion labels, e.g., *vulgar*, where the label was used to signal something else (in this case the attitude), but its effect in users can be that of exclusion.

In their real-life application, these ideal types blend into one another and there in fact exists a continuum of exclusiveness from strong and clear exclusion from the standard language to weak and borderline exclusion effect.

To test the effect of exclusion, a list of labels was presented to the users of Serbian dictionaries (the labels were taken from Vujanić et al., 2011, a Serbian monolingual dictionary). Those labels that were considered potentially excluding from the standard language were included in this list. The participants were asked to determine if the word marked by such a label would be appropriate for the use in the standard language (e.g., in the evening news on national TV). Most participants were recruited from the Facebook list "Naš jezik," which includes persons interested in the Serbian language, most of them users of Serbian monolingual dictionaries. The first nine labels were primary exclusion labels, as they mark the word as belonging to a lexical subfield which is predominantly non-standard, or at least it does not belong to the core standard-language lexicon. The remaining six labels refer to the attitude associated with the word or its feature, so their primary role is not exclusion. The survey data were collected in June 2017. Table 11.2 shows the results obtained.

As can be seen, all labels listed in this survey have the potential to exclude a lexeme or its feature from standard Serbian. While the effect of exclusion

Table 11.2 *Users' judgments about acceptability of labels in the standard language*

	Yes	No
slang (шатровачки)	78.26% (54)	21.74% (15)
jargon (жаргонски)	68.12% (47)	31.88% (22)
regional (регионално)	57.97% (40)	42.03% (29)
vulgar (вулгарно)	56.52% (39)	43.48% (30)
old literary style (старокњижевно)	56.52% (39)	43.48% (30)
archaic (архаично)	55.88% (38)	44.12% (30)
folksy (народски)	54.41% (37)	45.59% (31)
school student speech (ђачки)	51.47% (35)	48.53% (33)
colloquial (разговорно)	49.28% (34)	50.72% (35)
familial/homely (фамилијарно)	47.06% (32)	52.94% (36)
pejorative (пејоративно)	45.59% (31)	54.41% (37)
derisive (подругљиво)	34.78% (24)	65.22% (45)
contemptuous (презриво)	30.43% (21)	69.57% (48)
ironic (иронично)	27.54% (19)	72.46% (50)
facetious (шаљиво)	27.94% (19)	72.06% (49)

Table 11.3 *Users' judgments about acceptability of labeled words in the standard language*

Word (label in Vujanić et al., 2011)	Yes	No
говнарија (vulgar)	0.00% (0)	100.00% (40)
окинути на годину (school students' speech)	0.00% (0)	100.00% (40)
жаца (ironic)	0.00% (0)	100.00% (40)
аратосиљати се (folksy)	2.50% (1)	97.50% (39)
бос по глави (facetious)	2.50% (1)	97.50% (39)
цвикераш (derisive)	2.50% (1)	97.50% (39)
гологуз (pejorative)	2.50% (1)	97.50% (39)
ачити се (colloquial)	5.00% (2)	95.00% (38)
брајкан (folksy and familial/homely)	5.00% (2)	95.00% (38)
гладибрк (facetious)	5.00% (2)	95.00% (38)
безец (jargon)	7.50% (3)	92.50% (37)
лацман (folksy)	10.00% (4)	90.00% (36)
наровашен (regional)	12.50% (5)	87.50% (35)
дажд (archaic)	20.51% (8)	79.49% (31)

is indeed somewhat lower in attitude labels, there is a solid number of users (on average well over one-third for these labels) who perceive them as having an excluding function. There are also such users whose definition of the standard language is so broad as to include in it all spheres of the lexicon, so that nothing will be excluded.

To eliminate the factor of different definitions of the standard language and give the decision about non-standardness a concrete touch and feel, another survey was conducted (also in June 2017), asking if concrete words, labeled in Vujanić et al. (2011) with one of the aforementioned labels, would be acceptable in the speech of an evening news anchor. Table 11.3 shows the results obtained.

As can be seen very clearly, concrete words in a concrete setting are seen as generally unacceptable in the standard language in its narrower sense. It is also worth noting that there is no difference between primary and secondary exclusion labels. I will now proceed with the four dictionary case studies.

The following four case studies of contemporary Slavic monolingual dictionaries will be discussed: Russian (Ožegov and Švedova, 1992), Polish (Żmigródzki et al., 2012), Serbian (Vujanić et al., 2011), and Slovenian (Bajec et al., 2000). These four observed dictionaries share a general approach to standardness and non-standardness, but they differ substantially in lexicographic deployment of primary and secondary exclusion labels. These differences are seen even in the front matter, where there exists considerable variation in the space devoted to explaining the set labels (from the extremely elaborate Polish case to the laconic Serbian). Then, each dictionary deploys a slightly different set of labels and labels its entries differently.

Each of the four observed dictionaries will be analyzed first, which will be followed by a comparison of their particular approaches. For each of the four dictionaries, I will first discuss the set of relevant labels and their descriptions, and then turn to their count.

In the front matter of their Russian monolingual dictionary, Ožegov and Švedova (1992) provide a 612-word-long text about usage characteristics of the words and their marking in the dictionary. These authors divide usage labels (they call them notes, "пометы") into three categories: (a) stylistic, i.e., labels expressing style characteristics of the word ("пометы, указывающие на стилистическую характеристику слова"); (b) specialized, i.e., technical use ("специальное"); and (c) temporal labels, i.e., those that point to the historic perspective of the word ("пометы, указывающие на историческую перспективу слова"). This approach is quite interesting in that most primary and secondary exclusion labels belong to the same category, i.e., to stylistic labels.

The following repertoire of relevant exclusion labels is deployed in this dictionary:

a. Stylistic labels: non-literary colloquial ("просторечное"), regional ("областное"), contemptuous ("презрительное"), disapprobatory ("неодобрительное"), disparaging ("пренебрежительное"), facetious ("шутливое"), ironic ("ироническое"), vituperative ("бранное"), and rude ("грубое");

b. Temporal labels: old ("старое") and obsolete ("устаревшее").

It is interesting to note that there is also the category colloquial ("разговорное"), which is defined as being a part of the standard language, just more informal ("оно не выходит из норм литературного словоупотребления, но сообщает речи непринуждённость" ['it does not go beyond the norms of the standard-language word-use, but rather state the informal character of the discourse']). Also, although primary and secondary exclusion labels are featured in the same category of stylistic labels, secondary labels are still characterized as signaling devices, stating that the words contain emotional, expressive characterization ("в слове содержится соответствующая эмоциональная, выразительная оценка обозначаемого явления"). In addition, the vast majority of the labels used in this dictionary are potentially excluding. Those that are not excluding are the following: literary ("книжное"), high register ("высокое"), official/ formal ("официальное"), and specialized/technical ("специальное"). In addition, there is the aforementioned colloquial category, which is declaratively non-excluding.

The distribution of the relevant labels in this dictionary is presented in Table 11.4.

Table 11.4 *Exclusion and non-exclusion labels in Ožegov and Švedova (1992)*

Primary exclusion labels

English	Russian	Number
regional	обл. – областное	222
non-standard colloquial	прост. – просторечие, просторечное	3230
old	стар. – старое	225
obsolete	устар. – устаревшее	2604
Total		6281

Secondary exclusion labels

English	Russian	Number
vituperative	бран. – бранное	52
rude	груб. – грубое	12
ironic	ирон. – ироническое	412
disapprobatory	неодобр. – неодобрительное	784
contemptuous	презр. – презрительное	128
disparaging	пренебр. – пренебрежительное	114
facetious	шутл. – шутливое	652
Total		2154

Non-exclusion labels

English	Russian	Number
high register	высок. – высокое	766
literary	книжн. – книжное	1961
official/formal	офиц. – официальное	267
colloquial	разг. – разговорное	960
specialized/technical	спец. – специальное	3636
Total		7590

This dictionary contains 40,229 entries. The total number of labels used is 16,025 (40% of the number of entries), with exclusion labels constituting 21% (primary exclusion 16%, secondary exclusion 5%) while non-exclusion labels account for 19% of all instances of labeling. Given that some entries contain more than one label, the proportion of labeled entries is somewhat smaller than 40%. These numbers are more interesting in that they show the relationship between exclusion and non-exclusion labels (their distribution is approximately the same) as well as between primary and secondary exclusion labels (the former are used four times more frequently than the latter). To demonstrate the use of the index proposed here, the maneuver of assigning exclusion labels has the micro maneuver prominence indicator of positive five, while assigning primary exclusion labels over secondary has the positive micro maneuver prominence index of 52.

Table 11.5 *Exclusion labels in Żmigródzki et al. (2012)*

Primary exclusion labels

English	Polish	Category	Number
former	dawne	temporal	98
colloquial	potoczne	stylistic	2698
Varsovian	Warszawskie	geographic	2
Cracovian	Krakowskie	geographic	15
Posnanian	Poznańskie	geographic	1
Silesian	Śląskie	geographic	1
Lvovian	Lwowski	geographic	0
Vilniusian	Wileńskie	geographic	1
youth	młodzieżowe	societal	23
criminal	przestępcze	societal	8
social environment	środowiskowe	societal	49
Total			2896

Secondary exclusion labels

English	Polish	Category	Number
pejorative	pejoratywne	expressive	300
scornful	pogardliwe	expressive	63
vulgar	wulgarne	expressive	99
facetious	żartobliwe	expressive	223
Total			685

Żmigródzki et al. (2012), a Polish monolingual dictionary, devote a whopping 1,520 words to discussing usage labels (which they call qualifiers, "kwalifikatory"). They also provide a very elaborate classification of these labels. The following types are distinguished: chronological "chronologiczne," frequency "frekwencyjne," stylistic "stylistyczne," geographic scope related "dotyczące zasięgu geograficznego," societal scope related "dotyczące zasięgu środowiskowego," specialized "specjalistyczne," and expressive "ekspresywne." Only the category of frequency labels does not contain any exclusion labels. The category "specialized" contains mostly non-excluded items, but it also contains excluded professional colloquial lingo.

The labels used in this dictionary and their frequency are presented in Table 11.5. Here again one can see that primary exclusion labels are used much more frequently than their secondary counterparts (nearly five times more). Given that this dictionary deploys an array of specialized labels, it would be difficult to count all non-exclusion labels. However, the fact that the label "literary" (*książkowe*) in Żmigródzki et al. (2012) has the count of 2,111 and "administrative" (*urzędowe*) has the count of 206 may indicate that this dictionary uses exclusion and non-exclusion labels, just as I found in the Russian dictionary. It is important to note that this Polish monolingual dictionary is still a work in progress (it currently contains around 12,000 entries), which may change the ratio of the labels once the project is completed. One noticeable difference in relation to the Russian dictionary is the fact that there is no division between the standard colloquial and the non-standard colloquial. The label "colloquial" is defined here to pertain to the units used in informal situations, which are impossible to use in formal situations ("jednostki używane w sytuacjach nieoficjalnych, niemożliwe do użycia w sytuacji oficjalnej").

Vujanić et al. (2011), a Serbian monolingual dictionary with approximately 80,000 entries, devotes a laconic 43-word note stating that some words contain etymological, sphere-of-usage, and subjective-evaluation labels. One can thus see which labels are used from their concrete use and the list of abbreviations. It is obvious that the authors are aware of the different nature of the primary exclusion labels (they are called sphere-of-usage labels, which also includes non-exclusion labels) and secondary exclusion labels (called subjective-evaluation labels, which can also contain some non-exclusion labels). Relevant labels are presented in Table 11.6, along with their frequency.

It is interesting to note here that the ratio between primary and secondary exclusion labels is quite different from that of the previous two analyzed dictionaries. Primary exclusion labels are used in Vujanić et al. (2011) just over twice as much as secondary exclusion labels. Just as in the case of the Polish dictionary, it would be close to impossible to count all non-exclusion labels, but the fact that of the labels that are a part of the standard language the label "administrative" (административно) has only 38 uses and "literary" (књижевно) just 120, most of which are actually literary criticism terms, points to the fact that this dictionary uses non-exclusion labels much less than the previous two dictionaries.

Bajec et al. (2000), a Slovenian monolingual dictionary of 97,669 entries, devotes 774 words in the front matter to discussing relevant types of labels. The authors of this dictionary divide the labels into the following categories: (a) terminological, (b) stylistic-stratal, (c) expressive, (d) temporal-frequency, and (e) special normative labels. The last four types of labels are relevant in the process of excluding words and their features from standard Slovenian.

Stylistic-stratal labels comprise some non-exclusion labels (biblical, literary, poetic, administrative journalistic, elevated) but also exclusion labels (dialectal, child-language, colloquial, lower colloquial, slang). Bajec et al. divide those into two clear groups listing the first group of labels under (a) and the second under (b).

Expressive labels include the following: expressive, euphemistic, ironic, hypocoristic, low, contemptuous, facetious, and vulgar. Although all of them can potentially be exclusive, that role is reserved primarily for negatively connoted labels.

Table 11.6 *Exclusion labels in Vujanić et al. (2011)*

Primary exclusion labels		
English	Serbian	Number
archaic	архаично	199
old literary style	старокњижевно	11
colloquial	разговорно	961
regional	регионално	181
folksy	народски	708
slang	шатровачки	23
jargon	жаргонски	218
school student speech	ђачки	24
Total		2325

Secondary exclusion labels		
English	Serbian	Number
vulgar	вулгарно	70
expressive	експресивно	83
familial/homely	фамилијарно	51
pejorative	пејоративно	518
derisive	подругљиво	22
contemptuous	презриво	12
ironic	иронично	240
facetious	шаљиво	62
Total		1058

Temporal-frequency labels encompass the following items: increasing use, diminishing use, rare, old, and obsolete. The final two are primary exclusion labels, while the first three remain non-exclusion.

Finally, a remarkable characteristic of this dictionary, when we compare it with the three other Slavic monolingual dictionaries, is the fact that it contains prescriptive labels, i.e., the most direct form of exclusion from standard Slovenian. There are two items of this kind: incorrect and unestablished.

Exclusion labels, along with their frequency, are presented in Table 11.7.

As can be seen, owing to the profuse use of the label "expressive," the number of primary and secondary labels is approximately the same.

Again, given that there is no unified "specialized/technical" label, it would be difficult to point out how many non-exclusion labels are used, but the fact that "literary" (*knjižno*) has 9,809 uses and journalistic (*publicistično*) 2,356, one could conjecture that non-exclusion labels are used in a similar magnitude as their exclusion counterparts.

Here, I defined the standard language in its narrower sense, as those language varieties that are subject to standardizing efforts by codifiers, linguistic experts,

Table 11.7 *Exclusion labels in Bajec et al. (2000)*

Primary exclusion labels

English	Slovenian	Number
incorrect	nepravilno	24
unestablished	neustaljeno	92
lower colloquial	nižje pogovorno	503
colloquial	pogovorno	2133
dialectal	narečno	1958
slang	žargonsko	512
child-language	otroško	111
old	starinsko	4793
obsolete	zastarelo	3893
Total		14019

Secondary exclusion labels

English	Slovenian	Number
expressive	ekspresivno	12355
low	nizko	217
contemptive	slabšalno	1447
facetious	Šaljivo	254
ironic	ironično	178
vulgar	vulgarno	123
Total		14574

and norm authorities. This would include administrative, legal, scholarly language, news, and so on but exclude informal colloquial and literary language (which is typically not the target of normative interventions). The question ensuing from the review of the four Slavic monolingual dictionaries is what strategies the authors of these dictionaries deploy in excluding lexical items or their features from the standard language in its narrower sense? In other words, the question is how do these dictionaries serve their users (e.g., language editors) who need to verify if the word or its feature is acceptable in an edited standard language text?

What follows from the review presented here is that there is a variety of means by which the exclusion from the standard language is achieved. The range of strategies goes from a very rare direct prohibition (the Slovenian label "incorrect" and the Russian "non-standard colloquial") to pointing to the fields traditionally considered non-standard (e.g., dialect and slang) to pointing to the features incompatible with the standard language, as defined here (e.g., vulgar). We saw that all analyzed dictionaries use primary exclusion labels, pointing to non-standard fields of usage, and secondary exclusion labels, pointing to their non-standard features. Primary exclusion labels are generally more frequent, but the number of secondary exclusion labels is also substantial. Both categories of labels, primary and secondary, have fuzzy edges. With the exception of the Russian dictionary, where the category of "non-standard colloquial" is clearly established, in three other analyzed dictionaries, "colloquial" actually means "informal" and the judgments of the acceptability in the standard language (as defined here) may vary. To a lesser degree this is true for the labels "old" and "archaic" too. In secondary exclusion labels, the categories like "familial" or "facetious" bring about the same kind of uncertainty with regard to acceptability. It was already demonstrated in the case of the Russian dictionary and conjectured in another three dictionaries that the compilers of these dictionaries are equally concerned with marking certain fields within the standard language (e.g., technical use) as they are with excluding items from the standard. The use of exclusion and non-exclusion labels is equally substantive.

A part of the problem with fuzzy edges of primary and secondary exclusion labels is that, through a historic association of the standard with literary language (in spirit and often in name too), Slavic cultures maintain mostly the broader (cohesive) notion of the standard language. While the distinctive idea remains to be enforced in publications, such as manuals of orthography, and grammatical and stylistic reference works, dictionaries seem to largely neglect the narrower (distinctive) notion of the standard language. In order to eliminate or at least to reduce users' uncertainty about the acceptability of some items in the standard language, one would need to define the range of the standard language in its narrower sense and deploy the labels accordingly, by determining the cohort of primary and secondary labels not compatible with standard language texts.

11.3   The Dynamics of Maneuvering

In this section I will provide a more detailed diachronic view of macro- and micro maneuvers in a highly influential Serbian dictionary by Vuk Stefanović Karadžić (1818 and 1852) using the same methodology discussed in sections 11.1 and 11.3. This dictionary was a pivotal stepping stone in establishing standard Serbo-Croatian. It has been repeatedly ascertained (most notably in Popović, 1964 and Ivić, 1987), that in the early nineteenth century, when Karadžić was writing and subsequently publishing the first edition of his dictionary, there had been an ongoing ideological, and partially religious, conflict between the dominant traditional clergy from the northern Serbian lands (a part of the Austro-Hungarian empire) and insurgent bourgeois and populist elements from the south (which was at the time a part of the Ottoman Turkish Empire). Karadžić was a prominent representative of the latter group, which was glorified as ideologically correct throughout the final part of the nineteenth and the whole of the twentieth century (with minor exceptions, such as Selimović, 1967, who pointed out negative consequences of the break with the previous tradition of the northern Serbian lands). It is important to consider how the elements of the dictionary were influenced by this ideological conflict less in its second edition than in its first. An additional ideological conflict, concurrently a battlefield of geopolitical influences, was the geopolitical orientation of the two sides in this conflict (the clergy was supported by the Russian Empire and the bourgeois populists were backed by the Austro-Hungarian Empire). All other environmental factors follow this basic ideological cleavage: a different economic base (feudal vs. bourgeois), different political programs (conservative vs. liberal), and a different stance toward modernization (preservation vs. modernization). Economically, Karadžić was a member of the new bourgeois class (opposed to the established feudal-clerical elites), and this belonging was not merely academic. His status is also visible in the practical problems of gathering the funds for the publishing of the dictionary. Popović (1964:107) writes: "Međutim, da bi se 'Srpski rječnik' najzad pojavio, valjalo je otkloniti i druge smetnje, materijalne, koje takođe nisu bile male. Vuk se nadao da će nešto novca za izdavanje dela dobiti od samih pretplatnika. Međutim, oni su se slabo odazivali." (However, in order for the Serbian Dictionary to be finally published, other hurdles, the not insignificant financial ones, needed to be overcome. Karadžić hoped that he would get some funds to publish his work from his subscribers. However, their response was poor.) The politics and geopolitics of Austroslavism also influenced Karadžić through his mentor, Austrian censor Jernej Kopitar. Popović (1964:70) writes: "Kopitar je voleo i ovu postojeću – Meternihovu Austriju. Ne samo kao činovnik no i iz ličnog patriotizma i građanskog uverenja, on se borio za njen kulturni procvat i hteo je da proširi njen duhovni i politički uticaj na južnoslovensko stanovništvo na Balkanu." (Kopitar also loved this existing country – Meternich's Austria. Not only as its servant but also out of his personal patriotism and civic persuasion, he fought for its cultural advancement, and he wanted to extend its spiritual and political clout to the Slavic population in the Balkans.) Finally, his program made him a modernizer who was confronted by the established clergy-dominated elites who were preservation oriented. All these factors form a clear in-group cohesion on both sides. The differences and the cohesion were somewhat weaker in the second edition, but they were still present. If we take a look at Karadžić's dictionaries in the context of South Slavic lexicographic traditions (discussed in section 11.1 and in Šipka, 2000 and 2016), a remarkable fact was that this kind of in-group cohesion was not based on geography (as was common in the previous period) or ethnic background (which was common in the twentieth century), but based in ideology. In the previous lexicographic tradition, this split was noted in a considerably weaker measure and without the geopolitical component in the competition of the orders of St. Paul and St. Francis in northwest Croatia (see the Foreword to Šipka, 2000 for more).

Of the four lexicographical strategies discussed in section 11.1 (enforcement, submission, avoidance, and masking), enforcement is absolutely dominant in Karadžić's work. His lexicographic work is a part of a macro maneuver intended to enforce a modernist bourgeois populist program by equating the lexicon of the literary language with that of its dialectal base. Numerous micro maneuvers, from naming the dictionary to the use of the alphabet to vocabulary selection, and various microstructural elements of the dictionary, are a direct consequence of such macro maneuver. At the same time, the existence of the dictionary in its sociocultural surroundings is an attempt to execute an ideological project. Other strategies (submitting to pressures from society, avoiding addressing an issue, or masking the treatment by appearing to doing something else) are only marginally present in the first edition and only slightly more pronounced in the second.

I will now look into concrete micro maneuvers resulting from the enforcement of the aforementioned ideological macro maneuver. The choice of the dialectal base for the literary language (to replace the dominant Serbo-Slavic, "slavjano-serbski," a mixture of the Russian and Serbian reduction of Church Slavonic) and the ensuing lexical selection for the dictionary was the first micro maneuver alligned with the ideological program. This micro maneuver was radical in the first edition, as the author tried to enforce the dialect of his local village as the new literary language. This radical strategy was somewhat corrected in the second edition, when the author realized, while translating the New Testament into Serbian, that the lexicon of this dialect remained insufficient to express many abstract concepts. The naming of the dictionary as Serbian (rather than Slavic-Serbian) and using a version of the Cyrillic script that was different from the dominant one – simplified in comparison with the existing Russian-based one – were all additional micro maneuvers along the same ideological lines. In the dictionary macrostructure, the Foreword, especially its beginning (Karadžić, 1818:iii–viii), was an outright micro maneuver to enforce the new program. The very first sentence attests to that: "Ima već blizu iljada godina kako Srblji imaju svoja slova i pismo, a do danas još ni u kakvoj knjizi nemaju pravoga svog jezika!" (There has been nearly one thousand years since Serbs have their letters and script but up to this day there had been no book in which they have their real language.) Some minor elements of submission can be seen in the dictionary microstructure, in its purely technical part. First, numerous microstructural elements follow the existing South Slavic lexicographic tradition, initiated by Della Bella (1785) – for more information see Šipka (1991). Second, one can see submission to Kopitar's influence, who advocated some solutions from a Modern Greek dictionary. Popović (1964:103) writes about Kopitar: "tražio je da se 'Srpski rječnik' u svemu ugleda na rečnik novogrčkog jezika, koji je bio počeo da izlazi u Carigradu 1815." (He insisted that the Serbian

Dictionary follow in all aspects the Modern Greek Dictionary that started to appear in Constantinople in 1815.) Finally, the presence of various folk tales, riddles, etc. is a sign of following the predominant Romanticist philological tradition (although that tradition was also a part of the ideology in the new burgerois circles, so this micro maneuver is partially an expression of enforcement).

What is interesting about the two editions of the Serbian dictionary, in the light of the dynamics of micro- and macro maneuvers, are the changes in the general orientation between the first and the second edition. While the overarching macro maneuver of the second edition remains the enforcement of the new philological program, some micro maneuvers were dramatically changed. Lexical selection in general and the inclusion of obscene words in particular attest to this. The first edition of the dictionary encompassed 26,000 entries and its second edition 47,000. There are two principal reasons for this discrepancy. First, by visiting other regions, Karadžić extended the dialectal base of his dictionary, moving away from just the dialect of his native village (Popović, 1964:409–416 discusses the sources of this new lexicon). While this change contributes to the qualitative differences between the two editions, it is still a micro maneuver, along the line of the enforcement of the new philological project. The second source of the new lexicon are borrowings and calques from Serbo-Slavic. This micro maneuver has its prehistory in Karadžić's translation of the New Testament (see Popović, 1964:369–372). The radical program of equating the literary language form with the dialect that was present in the first edition was moderated in the second edition, as the dialectal lexicon was insufficient for the intricacies of translating literary texts in the New Testament. The introduction of this new abstract lexicon is partly an expression of submission and partly a consequence of the need to solve a concrete problem of translation. The second clear area of submission was the treatment of obscene words. As I showed in Šipka (1987), the first edition of the dictionary contains digestive obscene words (e.g., *govno* 'shit'), and also sexual ones (e.g., *kurac* 'cock, prick'), which is consistent with the program of enforcement, as these words were used abundantly in the author's dialect. This micro maneuver changes in the second edition to exclude sexual obscene words, which is a clear expression of submission to the dominant mores and pressures from the conservative clergy.

The two editions also feature some minor differences in the microstructure that show the strategy of modernization (e.g., more elaborate grammatical and accentual information, more elaborate usage labels). However, the dictionary still contains elements of intertextuality and represents a philological rather than linguistic work. It suffices to consult Karadžić (1852:275), where the entry *klinčorba* contains a folk tale and the entry *klis* a detailed ethonographic description of that folk game.

What follows from the present case study of the dynamics of macro- and micro maneuvers is that the intricate relationship between macro maneuvers and their execution in dictionary micro maneuvers varies over time and gets corrected based on the feedback from the sociocultural environment in which the dictionary functions. The changes in vocabulary selection in the second edition are a clear case in point. However, the ultimate outcome of any maneuvers of the elites, lexicographers, or any others is the acceptance or rejection by the general population. Karadžić's modified program, conducted in the second edition, was eventually accepted by and large. Lexical identity in the surface layer is equally defined by the macro- and micro maneuvers of the elites and the attitudes of the general population of speakers toward these maneuvers. I will turn to these attitudes in Chapter 12.

12   Attitudes

The ultimate measure of the speaker feedback is the percentage of the words affected by lexical planning that is accepted by speakers. In Chapter 3, I proposed that the *lexical maneuver acceptance indicator* be used, a scale ranging from the negative value of −100 (complete rejection of planned intervention) to 0 (the balance of the intervention with the status quo ante) to 100 (full acceptance of the intervention). This measure operates on the dataset of all lexical materials affected by the maneuver. At a point in time that is reasonably distant from the maneuver for the usage to stabilize (e.g., ten years), the ratio of the lexical material introduced in the maneuver and the status quo material is tabulated. The value of −100 means that no lexical material from the maneuver is in use at that point in time, that is, everything found in the corpora belongs to the status quo lexical material that the maneuver strives to replace. This represents full rejection of the maneuver in question. The value of 100 means that there is no status quo material – in other words, the maneuver is fully accepted. The value of 0 means an equal size of lexical material stemming from the maneuver and that which the maneuver intends to replace, i.e., the point of equilibrium between acceptance and rejection. The index is calculated as the percentage of the lexicon from the lexical intervention that is accepted minus the status quo lexicon that survives after a certain period of time. Real-life values fall on both sides of zero (the point of equilibrium), which enables comparison of the maneuvers across time and languages. Given that this measure requires longitudinal studies, another indicator, measuring speaker attitudes at one moment of time is proposed, namely the *speaker attitude direction indicator*. This indicator is calculated in the following manner. Using a representative sample of texts which advocate lexical changes, and which enable comments (e.g., on Facebook or from online newspapers), one tabulates the ratio of positive and negative comments. The value of 100 is assigned if all comments are positive, the value of −100 is assigned if all of them are negative and zero means the balance of positive and negative comments. This index can operate on datasets of like versus dislike user's comments, and on more sophisticated raw data, such as those stemming from the deployment of the Likert scale (in which case one would assign −2 to "strongly disagree," −1 to "disagree," 0 to "no opinion," 1 to "agree," and 2 to "strongly agree"). Again, the index is calculated as the difference between positive and negative comments. This indicator can point to the prospects of a maneuver being eventually accepted or rejected. Attitudes from the speaker side can point to anthropological dimensions. For example, a high rate of the lexical maneuver acceptance indicator can point to a high level of the uncertainty avoidance dimension and of collectivism.

It is also important to note that only the attitudes of the users of the standard language form to which the maneuvers pertain are relevant in this regard (i.e., not those of dialect users that do not use the standard language form). In earlier historical periods, they may be users of a literary language or some other pre-standard language form, but the body of speakers was dominated by those who exclusively used the dialect form. It goes without saying that the number of speakers of the standard language form grew with the democratization of literacy.

Another important note that should be made here is that attitudes represent a rather intricate conceptual construct (for more, see Fazio and Olson, 2003). In addition to the intensity and direction (that have already been discussed) attitudes also feature centrality. Thus, a person can exhibit strong attitudes for or against a lexical engineering or refereeing maneuver, yet the whole issue may be peripheral in that person's system of beliefs and attitudes. Needless to say, those speakers to which these attitudes are more central, play a more prominent role in the process. Similarly, the classical three-part attitude model assumes that attitudes feature affective, cognitive, and behavioral components. In this particular context and with a certain degree of simplification, somebody may love or hate a newly introduced word or the fact that a word is refereed as non-standard (the affective component), or they may consider its introduction or refereeing wrong or right (the cognitive component, in this case evaluative), and some may even actively support it or fight it (the behavioral component). Obviously, those with a strong behavioral component of the attitude in question play a more prominent role in the process. The concrete research problem with these finer aspects of the attitude lies in the fact that they cannot be reliably retrieved from existing datasets. They would require rather intricate, time-consuming, and costly surveys. Hence my concentration on those components that are readily available in the existing datasets.

As previously noted, the lexical history of Serbo-Croatian includes two significant periods of intensive lexical interventions (along with other such periods): nineteenth-century national revival movements, and lexical changes during the wars of 1990s.

The first period has been partially discussed using the example of the two editions of Karadžić's dictionaries. While it would be very difficult to come up with a precise value of the indicator for his lexical reforms, it can be estimated with confidence that it is very high in the positive territory – only a very limited number of the status quo words are still used today and most of their replacements are still in use.

Thomas (1988:141–147) offers a narrower consistent sample of the words introduced by the members of the Illyrian movement, the Croatian nineteenth-century counterparts of the Serbian language reformer by the name of Vuk Karadžić. Thomas analyzed 155 words of the Slavic inherited stock that were meant to be replacements for internationalisms borrowed from German. Thomas (1988) found that, out of 155 words, 87 were still in use in the late twentieth century, and 18 of them were eventually replaced by internationalisms (which is de facto retention of the status quo). Thus, 105 words still in use represent either the acceptance of the lexical introduction maneuver or its rejection by accepting the status quo. The remaining 39 were replaced by new Slavic coinings or competing Illyrian terms, and they were excluded from my calculation. The indicator shows that the lexical intervention during the Illyrian movement was highly successful, with the indicator value of positive 64. Obviously, this kind of research has numerous limitations (most notably, as Thomas himself recognized, it is based on the dictionary data, which does not necessarily reflect the usage data), but from this high value of the indicator, it is possible to get a general feel for the acceptance of the maneuver.

Langston and Peti-Stantić (2014:269) provide data for the second interesting period in the Croatian standard, the 1990s. Although their sample is extremely limited (comprising only 13 words), it can provide some mechanisms behind lexical planning. In this sample, they looked into pairs of words that coexisted before the lexical interventions of the 1990s and where the goal of the intervention (mostly refereeing and less engineering) was to select only one of them as a correct Croatian word and reject the other. In the pre-1990s Croatian corpus the words intended to be selected by the interventions were less prominent than those that were destined to be rejected by the index value of −33.77, which is the baseline acceptance for the words subjected to the maneuver. The authors then created three post-intervention corpora: a corpus of blogs, a corpus of a newspaper with a cosmopolitan orientation and of a newspaper with a nationalist orientation. The prominence value changed to −10.72 in the blog corpus, − 5.29 in the cosmopolitan newspaper, and a staggering positive value of 58.25 in the nationalist newspaper. One can see that the post-interventionist values show only a very moderate acceptance of the maneuver in the blogs and the cosmopolitan newspaper (a move upwards of 22.98 and 28.48 points, respectively, with the value still in the negative range) and resounding acceptance of the maneuver in the nationalist newspaper (a jump of 93.03 points with the value firmly in the positive territory). This points to an interesting fact that acceptance can vary from one context to another and that the intervention may bring the results that are contrary to the initial intention of the elites. In this case the intention was to create Croatian unity in language use and distancing toward Serbian, but the maneuver de facto divides Croatians into the cosmopolitan and the nationalist camp. We will see this in more detail in a Bosnian case study further in this chapter. Further qualitative data about the background of language policy in Croatia at that time can be found in Czerwiński (2005).

Langston and Peti-Stantić (2014:243–244) have also provided data that exemplify the speaker attitude direction indicator. They present survey results (on a small and non-representative sample of several hundred respondents), where one of the questions is about purism, which was a formidable force in the Croatian lexical interventions of the 1990s. Each of the questions was used in the 2000 and 2004 survey. For the statement "I believe that all internationalisms should be replaced with the words of Croatian origin," the following values emerged from each of the two surveys: 2000 – 58.4% disagrees, 13.5% neutral, 30.7% agrees; 2004 – 49.1% disagrees, 13.8% neutral, 37.29% agrees. If we exclude neutral responses, the speaker attitude intensity value was −27.7 in 2000 and −11.9 in 2004. This difference may simply be a consequence of a small and non-representative sample. However, if we stipulate that the sample did not play a role, we can see how the indicator shows that the rather mild negative attitude toward this statement in 2000 became even milder in 2004.

To use another example on a very limited dataset, the news that the Montenegrin language (one of the four ethnic variants of Serbo-Croatian) was given its ISO code, was published by the most prestigious Serbian daily *Politika* on December 13, 2017.[1] Only 24 hours after the publication, the news gathered 26 main comments, 21 were negative toward the recognition of Montenegrin as a separate language, 4 were positive, and one was neutral. The negative comments gathered 546 "recommendations" (one would click on that button as a signal of supporting the comment), and there were only 17 positive ones. When we calculate the indicator, the maneuver had a very strong negative direction among the readers of *Politika* amounting to −97.

The next example of the attitudes toward lexical engineering also concerns the changes of the 1990s in Serbo-Croatian. The final decade of the twentieth century in the territory of that language was marked by abrupt, fundamental, and far-reaching technological, economic, political, and lifestyle changes. On the one hand, global technological changes, such as rapid growth of information technologies, gene manipulation techniques, and so on have permeated all regions of the former Yugoslavia. The same is true of the global emergence of new ideologies (such as postmodernism) and artistic movements. On the other hand, the democratic revolutions of 1989 in Eastern Europe and

---

[1] www.politika.rs/sr/clanak/394398/Region/Amerikanci-priznali-crnogorski-jezik-a-svoj-jos-nisu (accessed on December 14, 2017).

the resulting termination of a bipolar world order have triggered a series of profound changes specific to the region. The following post-1989 sociopolitical changes need to be mentioned here:

1. Wars in Croatia, Bosnia-Herzegovina, and Kosovo 1991–1999;
2. Disintegration of the former Yugoslavia into the Republic of Slovenia, Bosnia, and Herzegovina, the Former Yugoslav Republic of Macedonia, and the Federal Republic of Yugoslavia (with the split of the latter into Serbia and Montenegro at a later point in time);
3. Transition to a multi-party and eventually democratic political system;
4. Transition to market economy;
5. Increased nationalism in all spheres of public life;
6. Revival of religious practices;
7. Lifestyle changes.

Data from my own database of Bosnian, Croatian, and Serbian words introduced in the 1990s were analyzed to determine the extent of ethnically motivated lexical changes. This database was used as a knowledge base for Šipka (2002). The database was created using textual corpora and existing new words dictionaries. Principal textual corpora encompassed major media outlets, i.e., Serbian daily *Politika* (www.politika.org.yu, 3.8 million tokens from the second half of 1999), Croatian daily *Vjesnik* (www.vjesnik.hr, 1.8 million tokens from 1999), Bosniak weekly *BH Dani* (www.bhdani.com, 1.6 million entries from 1998 and 1999), Croatian *Narodne novine* (www.nn.hr, 600 000 tokens from 1992–1999). Several other specialized corpora, such as the *Hrvatski vojnik* (Croation Soldier; www.hrvatski-vojnik.hr) were also used. The database also included words from two previously published dictionaries of new words (Klajn, 1992; Brozović-Rončević, 1996), lists extracted from various movies, TV programs, linguistic discussions, and so on. Last not least, Otašević (2001), a list of new words made available by Otašević, was also included.

All lexemes gathered from the aforementioned sources were filtered against two of the most reliable Serbo-Croatian–English dictionaries, Benson (1992) and Drvodelić (1989). If words or their meanings were not attested in these two dictionaries, they were included in the database. This procedure yielded 44,879 entries.

In the aforementioned database, ethnically marked items have the frequency as shown in Table 12.1.

One should add that the lexemes are marked according to their systemic features. Radical Bosnian, Radical Croatian, and Radical Serbian are the lexemes which cannot be found in major media but rather in marginal sources, such as extremist media. For example, the Croatian word *munjkovni* 'electrical' is used in extremist media such as *Nezavisna Država Hrvatska* (www.hop.hr) but not in the Croatian national TV or major newspapers.

Table 12.1 *Ethnically marked items in the 1990s database for Šipka (2002)*

Group	Examples	Number	Percent
Serbian Ekavian	*međususedski* 'neighboring', *mega-uspeh* 'mega success', *proterivač* 'one who expels'	1880	4.19
Croatian	*bojišnica* 'battlefield', *božićnica* 'Xmas bonus', *uradak* 'paper, article'	632	1.41
Radical Croatian	*datkovni obradnik* 'data processor', *munjkovni* 'electronic', *rednik* 'compter'	203	0.45
Bosnian	*lahko* 'easily', *mehko* 'softly', *poselamiti* 'greet', *šehid* 'fallen hero'	243	0.54
Radical Bosnian	*dekika* 'minute', *greb* 'grave', *hudovica* 'widow', *krhat* 'frail', *zijehati* 'yawn'	68	0.15
Serbian	*instalisati* 'install', *naduvan* 'bloated, inflated', *pasuljast* 'bean-like'	61	0.14
Radical Serbian	*đeneral* 'general', *sohran* 'stash', *toržestven* 'festive', *vaznositi* 'ascend'	20	0.04
Marked, Total		3107	6.92
Unmarked		41772	93.08
Total		44879	100.00

The data presented in the previous table does not support a popular perception of broad ethnically motivated lexical changes, often expressed in the internet sources, such as news groups *soc.culture.croatia* and *soc.culture. yugoslavia* throughout the 1990s. The actual number of these ethnically marked words is, in fact, limited (7 percent). It seems that the popular perception is based on confusing prominence with frequency. From this we can see that, primarily, the cognitive component of the attitude toward lexical planning includes not only the overall evaluation of the macro maneuver in question but also a perception about its prominence (in this case rather inconsistently with objective data).

A particularly interesting interplay of language and identity (see Riley, 2007 for a general discussion, and Fishman, 1999 with regard to language and ethnic identity) can be observed in Bosnian, the language of the Bosniaks (Bosnian Muslims), where an attempt has been made to transform the situation in which the Bosnian form was lexically closer to the Serbian than to the Croatian variant and in which Bosniak identity was not emphasized strongly enough. The intended transformation relied on introducing words in the Croatian form (e.g., *juče* 'yesterday' instead of *juče*, *definirati* 'define' instead of *definisati*) as well as elevating previously non-standard Bosnian lexical items to the level of standard (e.g., *babo* 'father' instead of *otac*, *lahko* 'easy' instead of *lako*). The intended result of the changes was creating equidistance from Serbs and Croats as well as emphasizing a Bosniak identity (more in Maglajlić, 2002).

Table 12.2 *Pilot study data for new Bosnian words*

	Start BiH	Novi horizonti
Total	28,0721	34,0070
Bosnian (B)	176	5,527
	0.063%	1.625%
Bosnian, e.g.: *lah(a)*k*	6	67
non-Bosnian, e.g.: *lak**	63	1
Bosnian, e.g.: *amidž/da{j\i}dž**	10	44
non-Bosnian, e.g.: *uj/tet/stri**	10	4

In reality, as it will be demonstrated, these ideological maneuvers had a considerably limited reach. In order to get insight into the proportion of Bosnian words recently introduced from the non-standard forms into the standard language, two newspaper corpora were analyzed in a pilot study of 2006. The magazine titled *Start BiH* (www.startbih.info) represents a general, secular, European-oriented newspaper source, while *Novi horizonti* (www.novihorizonti.com) represents an Islamic media outlet. The results presented in Table 12.2 show that the percentage of formerly non-standard Bosnian words is practically infinitesimal in both newspapers. This is true for both those lexical items, which represent formerly non-standard phonetic features, e.g., *lahak* 'light, easy', formerly non-standard, versus *lak* 'light, easy', and those which were formerly non-standard as lexemes, e.g., *amidža* 'maternal uncle', formerly non-standard, versus *ujak*, *tetak* 'maternal uncle', or *daidža* 'paternal uncle' versus *stric* 'paternal uncle'.

While these new formerly non-standard Bosnian lexemes are characterized by a very low frequency and play a very limited role in differentiating Bosniaks from Serbs and Croats, they have some role as differentiating factors between Islamic media outlets (which have been embracing them fully and unreservedly) and the secular ones (which are by and large hesitant to accept them). This then represents an interesting case where the original political intervention in the language substance yields a result quite different from the envisaged one. Obviously, two newspaper texts do not constitute a representative sample of Bosniak media outlets, which is why these results were not tested statistically. Rather than that, this investigation generated the following two hypotheses.

1. The corpus distribution of new Bosnian words is very limited and they are hence not a significant marker of Bosniak identity.
2. New Bosnian words are more likely to be found in conservative texts, which makes them an indicator of conservatism within the Bosniak ethnic group.

In order to test these hypotheses, the following two corpora were used in a 2010 study, encompassing the following major Bosniak media sources, based on their self-expressed Islamic orientation (Islamic media, number 2 below) or the lack of such proclamation (general media, number 1 below).

1. General media corpus (less conservative) BHDani www.bhdani.com, Bosna ekspres www.bosniaexpress.com, Bošnjaciwww.bosnjaci.net, Bošnjački topraci www.bosnjacki-topraci.net, Kitabhana www.kitabhana.net, Walter www.walter.ba, Nova Grapska www.novagrapska.com, OHR www.ohr.int, ONASA www.onasa.com.ba, Oslobodjenje www.oslobodjenje.com.ba, Sabah www.sabah-ba.com, SlobodnaBosna www.slobodna-bosna.ba, Superbosna www.superbosna.com, StartBih www.startbih.info

2. Islamic media corpus (more conservative) Bošnjakinja www.bosnjakinja.net, Džemat www.dzemat.org, ElKalem www.elkalem.com, Islam www.islam.co .ba, Muslimanski glas www.muslimanskiglas.com, Nahla www.nahla.com, Novi horizonti www.novihorizonti.com, Preporod www.preporod.com, Rijaset IZ www.rijaset.net, Saff www.saffbih.com

The following procedure was deployed:

1. An undergraduate research assistant was given two lists of Bosniak electronic newspapers and magazines (general and Islamic) and instructed to compile two corpora of approximately the same size and number of sources. She remained uninformed about the purpose of this research, which separated data collection from its analysis and hence made the procedure more objective.

2. I consequently used PERL scripts and SPSS 14 to analyze the two corpora, tabulating percentual distribution, and X^2.

As can be seen in Table 12.3, this research confirmed the two hypotheses and the results were very similar to those in the aforementioned investigation of two Bosniak magazines.

The data was recoded to test the statistical significance of the results using Pearson's chi-square test for association. The first variable was the level of conservatism (Islamic texts were coded as (1), non-Islamic texts as (0), the second variable was the presence of Bosniak lexemes (1 – a specific

Table 12.3 *General Bosniak Corpus versus the Islamic Bosniak Corpus data*

Tokens	General Corpus	Islamic Corpus
Total	997149	997861
Bosniak	754	17555
Percent	0.076%	1.759%

Table 12.4 *The number and percentage of Bosnian word forms*

Category	Number	Percent
Bosnian word forms total	2,824	100%
Bosnian word forms in Islamic outlets	373	13.21%
Bosnian word forms in general outlets	177	6.27%

Bosniak lexeme, 0 – a general lexeme). The analysis shows a statistically significant association (x^2 (2, n=1995371) = 2010986.44, p= 0.00)[2] between the type of text (general vs. Islamic) and the use of new Bosniak lexemes.

Finally, the percentage of the recorded new words, which are actually used in real-life texts, was tested. When fully inflected, new Bosnian words comprise 2,824 word forms. As can be seen from Table 12.4, only a small portion of them is actually used and that percentage is twice as high in Islamic media outlets.

It is clear from the above data that, despite all efforts to introduce new Bosniak words, their appearance in media outlets remains limited (i.e., most of these lexemes are not used at all) and their distribution is twice as high in conservative media outlets. Paradoxically, the maneuver that was intended to strengthen in-group cohesion and distance Bosniaks from the out-groups (primarily Serbian and Croatian) actually contributed to the weakening of that cohesion. Owing to their distribution in use, they are likely to separate more conservative Bosniaks from those who are less conservative.

The outcome of the dynamics between the elite maneuvers and speaker feedback is a surface-level lexical profile of the standard language, which is based on three components and their corresponding indicators: fragmentation, internal distance (vertical and horizontal), and external distance (vertical and horizontal).

Fragmentation is a measure of distinguishable subcomponents that a standard language has (e.g., ethnic, geographical variants). The crudest measure would be that the value of 0 means no such subcomponent exists, and the higher the number, the higher the fragmentation (the value of 1 is assigned for a two-way split). For example, among Slavic languages, Serbo-Croatian, which features four ethnic variants: Serbian, Croatian, Bosnian, and Montenegrin, will be assigned the fragmentation value of 3 while Russian or Polish, which are not fragmented, will feature the value of 0. While it is immediately clear that some standard languages are more fragmented than others, it is often problematic to establish what exactly constitutes a variant of a standard language. If one takes

---

[2] For more information about interpreting statistical parameters, see Ross (2010).

an example of English, should one assign the value of 1 (assuming a two-way split between British and American English, or, more precisely Eastern and Western hemisphere English), or the value of 4 (acknowledging American, Canadian, British, Australian, and New Zealand English as separate variants, to mention only those from Kachru's, 1992, inner circle)? A more accurate solution may be to calculate the effective number of components using the aforementioned Herfindahl–Hirschman's Index (HHI).[3] If one calculates the percentage of lexical peculiarities in each variant (the words that are not generally used in other variants), a generally available free software can be used[4] to calculate the HHI, and then the concentration index and the effective number of components based on the widest set of possible variants. Thus, if we (purely hypothetically) base the calculation of the variants of Serbo-Croatian on the aforementioned data on new words (only three variants were generally recognized in the late 1990s, when this research was performed), it turns out that in the sphere of ethnically marked lexicon, 63% is Serbian, 27% Croatian, and 10% Bosnian. The calculation at the aforementioned web page yields an HHI of 0.4798, a normalized HHI of 0.2197, with the concentration of 0.53, which means that the effective number of components for the part of the lexicon that is variant-specific (i.e., the lexicon that is not common to all of them) is 1.89 (i.e., 1/0.53).

Internal Vertical Distance refers to the lexical distance between the formal and colloquial standard (the indicator shows the percentage of the words from the colloquial standard which cannot be used in the formal standard languge form). Thus, if we take the previously presented data from the Serbian monolingual dictionary, it turns out that those entries marked with normative and crypto-normative labels constitute only 4 percent. That percentage is certainly higher in languages like Czech or Slovenian, where the colloquial standard is more distant from the formal standard.

Internal Horizontal Distance pertains to the lexical distance between distinct subcomponents of the standard language. Its indicator comprises the percen-tage of the words that are not common to the subcomponents, i.e., those words that are marked as belonging to one of the other variants of the standard language. Thus, if we (again, purely hypothetically) evaluate the Serbo-Croatian situation based on data from new words, we can calculate that, on average, the distance between the three variants is 6.9% (the total that is ethnically marked) divided by 1.89 (the effective number of components), which is 3.65%. In reality, this number is lower, given that the differences in new words from the time when the differences were underlined is considerably

---

[3] For an accessible explanation of the measure, see Taagapera and Goffman (1981).
[4] www.wessa.net/rwasp_concentration.wasp (accessed on December 14, 2017).

higher than in the lexicon at large. Most informal estimates for the differences in the general lexicon range between 2% and 3% (according to my surveying of ten colleagues in December 2017), which would give an average distance between 1.06 and 1.59 on the value of this indicator.

External Vertical Distance pertains to the lexical distance between the standard language and its urban and rural dialectal base. Its indicator points to the percentage of the words that are used in these forms but not in the standard language. This can only be calculated for the languages that are based on a dialectal, rather than on a literary tradition, or the revival of a previously used language form, etc. If we take the East Herzegovinian dialect as the main base for the Serbian standard and consider the aforementioned dictionary (Karadžić, 1818) as a lexical snapshot of dialects, we can estimate that the external vertical distance in this case is rather low (with less than 10 percent of words or their meanings not commonly used in the standard).

External Horizontal Distance pertains to the distance of the standard language in question toward lexically the most closely related standard language (e.g., Czech to Slovak, Macedonian to Bulgarian). Its indicator is the percentage of words that are different in these two standard languages. Thus, if we take the Czech–Slovak differential dictionary such as Nečas (1989), who lists 11,000 words, we can see that the percentage of differences is relatively modest (if we consider 80,000-entry monolingual dictionaries as the total of words involved in this comparison, external horizontal distance would be some 14 percent). To use another example on a smaller sample, if we use Swadesh's (2017) data discussed in Chapter 4, we can see that the external horizontal distance between Russian and Serbo-Croatian is somewhat higher than the distance between Russian and Polish.

What was obvious in Part IV of this monograph was that the surface lexical layer of cultural identity represents a dynamic area of negotiation between lexical macro maneuvers (implemented by the elites through a series of micro maneuvers) and the attitudes of the general body of speakers. The focus in this layer is again on features that words bear rather than the words in their entirety – something is correct or incorrect, standard or colloquial, acceptable or unacceptable, and so on. Given that an event of lexical planning can happen in any unstabilized lexical area, the lexicon affected by the maneuvers of the surface layer is random. The changes in this layer are fast – a new word can be introduced and accepted or rejected in a matter of weeks or months. Speakers have a real control over shaping this lexical layer of their identity – they can accept or reject the product of lexical planning on the part of the elites. The role of the elites is dominant in this layer, as all maneuvers come from them. Finally, the interventions are direct – the goal of each maneuver is either to change the use of words or to shift value judgments toward them.

Part V

Synthesis

13   Interaction between the Layers

In the previous nine chapters linguistic layers of identity were construed as separate areas of research. This organization of the epistemological construct proposed in the present monograph has distinct advantages given that the techniques deployed in the exploration of each layer differ and that there are significant differences in the focus and structure of the layers, the role of the elites and the speakers, and the intervention type. However, this does not mean that the layers are isolated and that no communication between them exists.

There are many ways in which the three layers of lexical identity are connected. Let us consider the following example. Popović (1955:7), writing about Serbo-Croatian, notes its connections with two groups of languages:

Sa jednima je u genetskoj vezi, tojest s njima ga vezuje zajedničko poreklo ... Sa drugim jezicima nije u genetskoj vezi ... ali ga je u realnu vezu dovela istorijska stvarnost: zajednički život na istom tlu ... ipak se i do danas srpskohrvatski jezik tretira izolovano, kao da od vremena izdvajanja iz opšteslovenske zajednice nije primio nikakve elemente sa strane. Razume se da je ovakav lingvistički romantizam i "rasizam" jednostran i nedijalektički.

(With one group of languages there is a genetic relationship, i.e., it is tied to them through a common origin ... with other languages it is not a genetic relationship ... however historical reality, i.e., life together at the same territory, brought those languages together ... Nevertheless, even to this day Serbo-Croatian is treated in isolation as if no elements from other sources were adopted since its separation from the common Slavic community. Needless to say, this linguistic romanticism and "racism" is one-sided and non-dialectical.)

Popović advocates the idea of the importance of lexical exchange, in addition to the deep layer, and he also expresses his negative attitudes toward conscious maneuvers in the surface layer aimed at the suppression of the importance of the exchange layer.

If we look at some concrete examples, the connection between the two layers will become more obvious. In Russian, there are pairs of word stems where one of them is originally Russian and the other is borrowed from Old Church Slavonic, e.g., Russian word: *голова* 'head, anatomically'; Old Church Slavonic borrowing: *глава* 'head, of a committee, etc.' Russian word:

ровный 'even, i.e., flat'; Old Church Slavonic: *равный* 'even, i.e., equal'. Most commonly in these pairs of roots, the original Russian form is more concrete and the borrowed Old Church Slavonic form more abstract. The process of borrowing (i.e., a process from the exchange layer) has eventually created a distinction in the deep layer, given that many languages will not have lexical distinctions of this kind. Similarly, in Serbo-Croatian, lexical borrowing from Turkish (of the words that eventually can be from various other Near and Middle Eastern sources) has created pairs of words, where one is either from the inherited Slavic stock or borrowed from a Western European language. In these pairs, the Turkish borrowing is stylistically marked as restricted in some way while its counterpart remains neutral, e.g., inherited Slavic *oprostiti* 'to forgive': a borrowing from Turkish *halaliti* 'to forgive, restricted to the use in Islam and colloquially in some regions', a borrowing from German *klozet* 'toilet, neutral': a borrowing from Turkish *ćenifa* 'toilet, archaic or regional colloquial'.

All this is not unlike the pairs in English stemming from the Norman Conquest, where the Anglo-Saxon words typically mean something more concrete, and Old French words something more abstract (or processed, sophisticated, etc., semantically or stylistically) as in Anglo-Saxon *cow, pig, deer, thinking, wish, wild* versus Old French borrowings *beef, pork, venison, pensive, desire, savage*. Here too, a process in the exchange layer has led to language-specific distinctions in the deep layer.

In the present chapter I will outline a unified model of interaction between the three layers. While each layer represents a distinct object of research with its specific features (as previously shown in Chapter 3 and elaborated in Chapters 4–6 for the deep, 7–9 for the exchange, and 10–12 for the surface layer), there still exists the need to explore the interaction between them, given that some phenomena cut across the borders of the layers. Sociocultural and technological changes in the environment in part trigger the movements in the exchange and surface layers, but they are also determined by the fact that the lexical material in the deep layer is insufficient to accommodate the changes in the environment. The need for information from the deep layer is thus a stimulus for the processes of the other two layers. These two layers, on the other hand, are the venue where new lexical units are introduced (by lexical exchange or engineering), which eventually may lead toward rearranging the distinctions and the density of lexical fields in the deep layer. The surface layer, in turn, operates with interventions and attitudes (e.g., of purism or laissez-faireism) on the material from the exchange layer (such as acceptable and not acceptable introductions of new words, delegitimization of existing words) or directly on the material of the deep layer (in case no borrowed lexemes are encompassed by the maneuver, e.g., the one in which the elites postulate incorrect use of an inherited Slavic word). These relations are depicted in Figure 13.1.

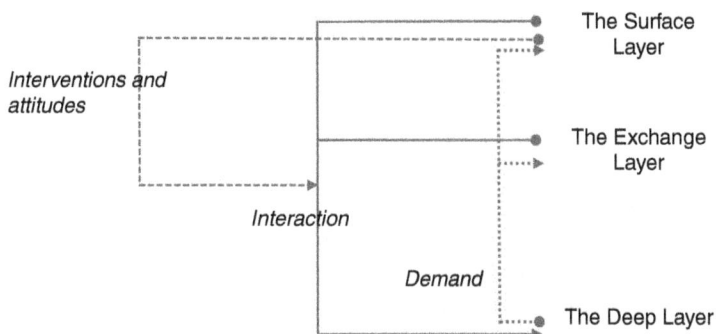

Figure 13.1 Interaction between the three lexical layers of identity

The interaction of the layers was evident in the previously discussed nineteenth- and late twentieth-century Croatian maneuvers in the surface layer (more information can be found in Thomas, 1988 and Langston and Peti-Stantić, 2014). There was a demand for new lexical items that were not available in the deep layer, or for a redistribution of the existing lexical items. Both were triggered by a broader environment and its sociopolitical and technological changes. Maneuvers of lexical planning intended to meet those demands are confronted with the attitudes of the speakers. Some of them have stabilized and become a constituent of the deep layer; in case of others, either an exchange lexical item or status quo have prevailed and an engineered lexicon has not been accepted. As previously emphasized, the surface and the exchange layers operate in conjunction with the deep layer, which in turn eventually includes not only the inherited lexicon that evolves over time but also borrowed and engineered words that have stabilized in the deep layer.

The layers are also connected at the level of speakers. Speakers are culturally defined by all three lexical layers concurrently. They function in the deep layer generally without agency and cognizance of what is determining them culturally. They are generally cognizant, but their agency is extremely limited in the exchange layer, while the surface layer features their full agency and cognizance. What connects the three layers are the mental lexicons of the speakers and their linguistic behavior pertaining to lexical choices and evaluations alike. That is where they coexist and interact. The features of the words, such as borrowed or inherited, standard or non-standard, are linked in the speakers' mental lexicons with the words in the deep layer, which carve out the conceptual sphere in sharing it with other words, that have their own internal semantic structure, that participate in idioms, lexical relations, word formation, and associative networks. Any choice that speakers make in using or not using the words affected by a maneuver in the surface layer is also related to the other two layers. It contributes to a broader or narrower use of the words from the deep layer, and it often concerns the features from the exchange layer (e.g., in the case that the maneuver is a purist one).

To demonstrate this, I will use an example from the 1990s, a real-life laboratory of lexical changes in all Slavic countries (given the transition from communist systems and planned economy to capitalism and free-market economy along with all technological and lifestyle changes that were also happening elsewhere). These changes were particularly far-reaching in Serbo-Croatian, which combined these changes with the revival of nationalism and religious zealotism. I will take the following three Croatian word cohorts that came under the spotlight during the 1990s and that exemplify a range of possible situations in lexical engineering, refereeing, and the dynamics of the relationship between the elites and general speakers: *sučelje:interfejs* 'interface', *privreda:ekonomija:gospodarstvo* 'economy', *pasoš:putovnica* 'passport'.

The word for computer interface was a lexical lacuna in the deep layer, which needed to be filled once computers became widely used by the general population of the speakers. This triggered the lexical borrowing of the English term, which also activated the exchange layer, but there was also a maneuver in the surface layer to use a word created from the existing material (which again involves the deep layer), namely combining: *su-* 'next to (prefix)', *čelo* 'front (of a head)', and *'-e* 'object, device (suffix)'. The lexical planning maneuver in the surface layer involved negative lexical refereeing of the borrowed lexical item and the engineering of the new word. Speakers were confronted with the possibility of accepting the lexical maneuver (which would then block the item in the exchange layer) or rejecting it and using the borrowed lexical item (which would block the surface-layer maneuver). In the end, both lexical items were preserved and the attitudes of the speakers created a type of variation which culturally defined them, as they had a choice of using either of the two terms or both of them. This choice process then varies from speaker to speaker and from situation to situation. It should be clear by now that the situation involved all three layers and their interaction.

The nest *privreda:ekonomija:gospodarstvo* 'economy' was even more complex. The pre-1990s deep-layer situation in all Serbo-Croatian variants encompassed two closely related words: *privreda* 'economy' and *ekonomija* 'economics'. The first word is a nineteenth-century engineered word, which roughly means 'contribution to the value'. The second word is a borrowing from Latin via German and French. In the 1990s there was a maneuver in Croatian to replace the word *privreda* with another engineered word, i.e., *gospodarstvo* (*gospodar* is 'owner' and *-stvo* is the suffix which roughly means 'the field of'). This word was used at some point in nineteenth-century Croatian, but its revival was primarily modeled after Slovenian, which has been using that word since the nineteenth century. The sole purpose of the maneuver was to emphasize the Croatian ethnic identity at the time when the Croatian state was created – the maneuver was not purist; both involved words were ultimately of the inherited stock. The maneuver was generally accepted by the speakers of Croatian and the word *privreda* is not used anymore in this variant of Serbo-Croatian (it is continuously used in its other variants). However, the influence of the exchange layer and the fact that *economy* and *economics* sound similar in English brought about the same process in all variants of Serbo-Croatian. The word *ekonomija* is now used to mean not only 'economics' (which has never changed) but also 'economy'. Eventually, the speakers of Croatian began having a deep-layer distinction for using formal *gospodarstvo* (from the surface layer) and informal *ekonomija* (from the exchange layer). Again, the example features intensive interaction of all three layers and a negotiated outcome where speakers' attitudes operate on the elites' maneuvers.

Finally, *pasoš*, a borrowed word, was used in Croatian for 'passport' before the 1990s, when there was a maneuver to replace it with an engineered word *putovnica* (*put* 'trip, travel' and *–ovnica* 'document (suffix)'). The engineered word was loosely based on Slovenian *potni list* 'travel document'. Its primary purpose was to emphasize the Croatian ethnic identity by using a word different from Serbian. The maneuver was eventually accepted and *pasoš* is used only marginally (it continues to be used in all other variants of Serbo-Croatian). Again, all three layers were involved.

The way in which the exchange layer shapes the deep layer can be seen in the differences of naming certain animals in Slavic languages, in comparison to the same process in English. In Slavic languages, where there was no interference from the exchange layer, the deep layer featured word-formation links between the name for the animal and the name for its edible meat. For example, in Russian there is *свиня:свинина* 'pig:pork', *теля:телятина* 'calf:veal', *олень: оленина* 'deer:venison', that is, names for the meat are suffixally derived from animal names. In English, in contrast, the lexical exchange induced by the Norman Conquest has eliminated these links as in *pig:pork, calf:veal, deer: venison*.

To demonstrate that an interaction of this kind is by no means restricted to the South Slavic or Slavic realm, one can mention a well-known example of the multiword unit *silk road*. The term was actually introduced by a German geographer by the name of Ferdinand von Richthofen in 1877 (Waugh 2007:4) as *Seidentraße* 'silk road', that is, it is something that was engineered in the surface layer. It was then a part of the exchange layer to be adopted in all major languages. Curiously, one of them was Chinese which features 丝绸之路, *Sīchóu zhī Lù* 'route of silk', now a part of the deep layer, with speakers being unaware that this is not an ancient Chinese term.

There are numerous other examples like this that can demonstrate the interaction of the three layers either in the times of intensive lexical changes or in less turbulent times. It is important to understand that the general parameters of the deep or even exchange layer do not change with scores or even hundreds of words like the ones used to exemplify the interaction. The changes happen when a critical mass of words or their features is reached and it is impossible to point to its exact moment, as the change, like any other in historical linguistics, assumes a gradual process that takes prolonged periods of time to complete. General lexical distinctions in the deep layer or a general presence of a borrowed lexicon in the exchange layer (that culturally defines speakers) is still there, even after the abrupt period of changes, given that the changes affect only limited vocabulary ranges (as we could see in the example of the new Serbo-Croatian words in the 1990s that was discussed in Chapter 12).

It is also important to note that the demand from the deep layer is a reaction to triggers from the sociocultural environment (which was also apparent from the analysis in Chapter 12). These triggers range from the need to introduce new words to cover a conceptual sphere as a consequence of technological advancement, to the need to replace existing words to emphasize ethnic identity or enforce a specific form of the standard lexicon and hence linguistic authority.

Having pointed out the areas of interaction between the layers, the fact should be repeatedly stressed that each of the three layers features specific ingredients that profile the speakers' cultural identity in a way that is different from the other two layers. Similarly, the research techniques for the study of the linguistic markers of cultural identity are different in each one of the three layers.

14   Main Findings

The present monograph advances a proposal for a more systematic study of lexical layers of cultural identity. What is proposed here is an epistemological construct which outlines lexical phenomena that profile cultural identity and the techniques that may contribute to a more systematic exploration of these phenomena. The proposal made in this book is merely an epistemological construct, that is, the only claim made about it is that it represents a convenient tool for a more comprehensive and systematic study of lexical markers of cultural identity. It is also a call for a new cultural linguistic program and, as all pioneering proposals, it only outlines a possible research direction without giving definite answers to any questions.

The review of the relevant research in the field shows that approaches such as Russian linguistic culturology, the Natural Semantic Metalanguage (NSM) theory, and cultural linguistics deserve due credit for bringing the attention of the research community to the nexus of language and culture. This was an enormous achievement in light of the fact that the dominant, so-called formal approaches, such as the minimalist program (Chomsky, 1995) or optimality theory (Kager, 1999) completely excluded these phenomena from linguistic analysis, concentrating exclusively on what is common in the languages of the world, thus mostly on syntax and phonology.

However, the "cultural turn" in linguistics leaves unresolved the following problems and consequently does not address potential areas of improvement.

a. Isolationism: cultural practices in language are analyzed as having no connection to cross-cultural psychology and other similar approaches. For example, a well-known parameter of collectivism versus individualism is not of interest to "linguoculturologists."

b. Particularism: there is no connection to other fields of Slavic scholarship, e.g., the study of loanwords, which may have established certain culturally relevant distinctions in the lexicon.

c. Elitism: this approach exaggerates the role of literature, intellectuals, etc. – some cultural features may exist in literature, or in a narrow elite group from a population, and be absent from the mental lexicons of the majority of the population.

d. Atomism: the analysis is often overly fine-grained to be applicable; it goes into very peculiar features of one or several words.

e. Determinism: the authors commonly postulate a possible cause of a feature, leaving no room for random events.

f. Ethnocentrism: the authors seem to be equating an ethnic group with a particular language, like talking about Russian, or any other, national mentality, etc., while in reality every language is used by various ethnic groups with their distinct cultures.

g. Arbitrariness: only words that supposedly prove the claim are chosen, while other cases that do not confirm the claim are disregarded.

In reaction to all the aforementioned problems, I proposed here a model comprising three lexical layers of cultural identity: the deep, the exchange, and the surface layer. The deep layer entails specific words, specific ways in which those words divide the cognitive and affective space of that given culture and the way they are connected with other words. This layer encompasses stable lexical strata where changes are only glacial and where any conscious interventions are only marginal and remote. The speakers are given those specific lexemes, distinctions, and connections, which simply shape their cultural identity without their knowledge or consent. At its core are the most common lexemes, which offer the strongest contribution to the profiling of cultural identity given that the speakers are exposed to them more frequently than to any other lexemes (no matter how culture-specific they may be).

The exchange layer comprises the lexemes resulting from cultural contacts with other people. This layer is also given to the speakers without their consent, but, unlike the deep layer, they generally have an idea about the main sources of lexical influence on their language and they can often recognize the word as being the product of such influence. What shapes a speaker's cultural profile in this layer are the features of the words (rather than the words themselves) borrowed from a certain cultural or contact environment. Some very limited possibilities of intervening in this layer exist (e.g., in the form of purist maneuvers from the surface layer), but generally, none of these interventions change the general landscape of cultural and contact influences. These influences can be stronger or weaker, depending on the concrete subject-matter field, so the distribution of fields (rather than the general core-periphery structure) is important in shaping the speakers' cultural profile.

The surface layer is the area of an unstable lexicon where cultural identity is a result of constant negotiation between linguistic elites and the general body of speakers. Practically any lexical sphere can be affected by normative intervention. The intervention is conscious, direct, and conducted by linguistic elites (such as linguists, writers, journalists, legislators). The intervention is transmitted through public discourse and the school system, to eventually meet certain attitudes by the general body of speakers, leading to their acceptance, partial acceptance, or rejection, which gives the body of speakers ultimate control over the development of this layer. Cultures and their speakers differ in the prominence of linguistic elites and their intervention, in the strength and centrality of the attitudes of the speakers. The lexicon of the standard language is the ultimate product of this negotiation between the elites and the speakers. Speakers' cultural profile is determined by the fragmentation of this lexicon and the distance from similar standard language forms.

The present epistemological construct of the three lexical layers of identity is intended to eliminate the aforementioned shortcomings of mainstream cross-cultural anthropocentric linguistics. First, the three layers require a methodological apparatus from cross-cultural linguistics (mostly in the deep layer), contactology (i.e., the study of linguistic contacts, in the exchange layer), and lexicological sociolinguistics (in the surface layer). Second, the methodological apparatus from all three linguistic approaches should be connected to the dimensions established in cross-cultural psychology and anthropology. In addition to these three innovations, the following principles of analysis were advocated and demonstrated:

a. Comprehensiveness: all members of the category are analyzed rather than just those individual cases that confirm research claims.

b. Sensitivity to stakeholders complexity: the analysis distinguishes between the body of speakers and linguistic elites and sees both these entities as most diversified collectives.

c. Multi-perspectiveness: various linguistic and extra-linguistic perspectives are brought into the analysis.

d. Linguistic autonomism: this recognizes that languages do not necessarily have to overlap with ethnic groups and that linguistic identity concerns speakers of languages rather than members of ethnic groups.

e. Sensitivity to linguistic complexity: this recognizes the complexity of language varieties, such as dialects and ethnic variants.

f. Limited determinism: there is an understanding that some developments are random and the analysis can account for only a part of phenomena.

g. Explanatory succinctness: the simplest possible explanatory tools are sought to encompass the broadest and widest fields of the phenomenon being explained.

As noted in Chapter 3, in its core, the model comprises the deep layer (which consists of relatively stable lexical distinctions and includes core research on language and culture), the exchange layer (which involves slowly evolving material from the lexical transfer between different languages and their cultures and includes linguistic contactology), and the surface layer (comprising an engineered and a refereed lexicon susceptible to rapid changes, involving sociolinguistic research). The characteristics of the three layers are presented in Table 14.1.

Table 14.1 *The characteristics of the three lexical layers of cultural identity*

Layer	Focus	Structure	Changeability	Speakers' control	Elites' presence	Intervention type
Surface	features	random	fast	real	dominant	direct
Exchange	features	thematic	slow	potential	limited	indirect
Deep	words	core-periphery	glacial	negligible	marginal	remote

All these factors within the three layers are distilled into a lexical profile of cultural identity of the speakers of any given language. There is a great deal of overlap in the content of that profile between individual speakers but also significant variation in some of its segments (see Trudgill, 2001 for more details about variation). Part of the variation will be based on factors such as the speakers' age, gender, some on factors such as the territory of their residence and ethnicity, and some part of it is governed by the factors that are too complex and unpredictable to be explained.

The speakers' lexical profile is determined by the words used in a particular culture, but not in most other cultures and their languages. Much more so than certain words (typically names of local customs, foods and drinks, musical instruments and dances, etc. with an occasional abstract concept), however, the speakers' lexical profile is shaped by the distinctions that a particular lexicon makes in the field of most common words (e.g., if the language differentiates between the words for hand and arm, older and younger brother, neck of a person and that of an animal, etc.). They are furthermore defined by the internal semantic structure of their words, e.g., whether the word *bed* extends to mean river bed, bed of flowers, etc., or not. Finally, the way the most common words connect in lexical relations (e.g., how many synonyms the word meaning 'bad' will have), participate in idioms, have association links (e.g., what the word for color 'red' is most commonly associated with) and word-formation networks (e.g., in how many derivatives, compounds, and idioms can one find the word for 'mother') also culturally profile the speakers. Various segments of the lexical cultural profile are in part expressions of broader cultural dimensions (individualism/collectivism, low/high contextualness, polychronism/monochronism, etc.). To use a very obvious example, in high-context cultures, the words for evaluating anything will have a range of contextually driven meanings, sometimes opposite from the first meaning of the word, as in using OK as an unfavorable evaluation of a meal, movie, or event. All of the aforementioned parameters are given to the speakers. They unconsciously act inside their lexical profiles without any real possibility to change anything. Similarly, any direct interventions in this lexical sphere would be destined to fail. The variation between the speakers is relatively modest, at least in the core of the most common words and their meanings. The principal driver of the variation is the linguistic education of the speaker, the fact that some will know more words, their meanings, and the links between them than others (in common parlance this would be the difference between more or less "cultured" or "well-read" speakers).

The next two layers, exchange and surface, operate on the material of the deep layer in that lexical borrowings fill gaps in the deep-layer vocabulary or compete with its existing words and meanings, and surface-level maneuvers almost always include the deep-layer vocabulary in the maneuvers of lexical engineering and refereeing. In numerous instances, they also include the exchange layer. What is most important is that the speakers' cultural profile is determined by the other two layers in a very different way.

What determines the speakers in the exchange layer are the features of the lexemes. First whether the feature is inherited or borrowed, and then what is the source of borrowing (cultural or contact). Another relevant feature is the subject-matter field of borrowing, as some subject-matter fields feature an increased number of borrowings from certain macrolanguage sources. This layer is then thematically organized. The distribution of macrolanguage imports in the general vocabulary and particular subject-matter fields is given to the speakers, but, unlike in the deep lexical layer of cultural identity, they are generally aware of the features that define them culturally. For example, even modestly educated speakers of all Slavic languages will be aware of the classical, Greek and Latin, origins of parts of their vocabulary; while German lexical influence will typically be known even to most uneducated strata of users of the standard language in most Slavic languages. Over a prolonged period of time and collectively, speakers have the potential of making changes in the ratio of the inherited and borrowed lexicon (e.g., by accepting a purist maneuver in the surface layer, which eventually changes the exchange layer). However, the general distribution of sources of borrowing and of their subject-matter fields are the kinds of elements that are not conducive to rapid changes. Most often, purist maneuvers, even if they are successful in enforcing an engineered word, do not expunge the borrowed one from the vocabulary – as a rule, they remain in the standard language, either with lower frequency or a limited field of usage. The changes here are faster than in the deep layer, but they are still very slow. They do not happen before our eyes as they do in the surface layer. While a loanword may enter the vocabulary abruptly and it may equally abruptly be supplanted by another word, it takes decades and most commonly generations of speakers to change general proportions in the lexicon. By the same token, the presence of elites is limited here. They may resort to macro- and micro maneuvers in the surface layer, but they cannot really change the general parameters of the exchange layers that culturally profile its speakers (e.g., dramatically decrease the number of Near Eastern borrowings in Croatian or dramatically increase their number in Bosnian, both of which would amount to linguistic nationalism). That also means that their lexical interventions are only indirect – by direct maneuvers in the surface layers, provided that the attitudes of the general body of speakers toward them are favorable, and with the flow of time, some proportion of the features defining speakers' cultural profile in this layer might change. Even this indirect intervention is difficult to assess. For example, the proportion of Near Eastern words in today's Serbo-Croatian (and its Bosnian variant which claims principal cultural heritage to this lexical sphere) is considerably smaller than a century ago. However, it is difficult to say how much of that change is a result of the conscious interventions of the elites (including a general pro-European orientation, ironically enough, triggered in part by Kemalist reforms in Turkey) and how much of it is a consequence of simple obsolescence of the entities that were named with these words (such as old trades and their tools, meals, customs).

The surface layer, unlike the previous two, is a place of abrupt changes in consequence of negotiation between interventionalist elites and the general body of speakers. These changes can happen practically anywhere in the lexical system. Just as in the exchange layer, what contributes to the cultural profile of speakers are features of the lexemes – this time those that exclude them from the standard lexicon, restrict them to only some genres or speech situations, or exclude them from the lexicon of the standard language. Speakers are keenly aware of the changes in this layer and they take an active stance toward them. The layer is dominated by the elites and their direct interventions, but the speakers enjoy true agency and eventually have the final say on which macro maneuver is going to take hold. What comes about as an ultimate consequence of this negotiation between the elites and the speakers is a particularly shaped lexicon of the standard language. In the surface layer, speakers are culturally defined by their range of possibilities of accepting and rejecting interventionist maneuvers (which may be weaker or stronger, unified or fragmented, etc., depending on the standard language and its culture). Speakers are also defined by the features of their particular standard language lexicon. Thus, a speaker of Czech is defined by how strictly he/she enforces the difference between standard and common Czech and also by the fact that standard Czech is closely related and defined in a way by common Czech. A speaker of the Croatian variant of Serbo-Croatian is defined by his/her possibilities in accepting or rejecting the use of the so-called proper standard Croatian lexemes. These most often include avoiding forms that Croatian has in common with Serbian, in those cases where there is a specific Croatian word. This speaker is also determined by the fact that the Croatian variant is defined by its relationship with other variants of Serbo-Croatian.

What should have become evident from the nine core chapters of this book and the present review of the main findings is that the cultural identity of a speaker of any language is defined by a considerably broader range of factors than key words, cultural scripts and concepts, etc. A speaker is defined by the distinctions within his/her core lexicon (which includes the aforementioned keywords, scripts, and concepts). At the same time the speaker's cultural identity is determined by the cultural influences and neighboring languages that have contributed to the lexicon of their language and by their negotiation of the interventionist elite maneuvers. All this should be included in the speakers' lexical profile of their cultural identity. It should also be clear by now that there is a range of research techniques and readily available lexical datasets that have the potential to make important contributions to our understanding of the lexical layers of cultural identity.

Throughout the present monograph, I have used examples from Slavic languages. Along with demonstrating the points about the factors that are lexically profiling speakers' cultural identity, the goal of these examples was to show that Slavic studies in lexicology and linguistics still make sense. As should have become apparent, especially from the examples in the deep layer, the idea of Slavdom (discussed at length in Chapter 1) still plays a role in the cultural profiling of each particular Slavic language – there are wide ranges of overlapping inherited lexicon, there are closer or more distant patterns of continuation and change between various Slavic languages, there are shared sources of cultural influences, and so on. Perhaps more importantly, in a great body of Slavic dictionaries and lexicological monographs there is a wealth of readily available data that can be explored in elucidating the lexical layers of cultural identity of the speakers of Slavic languages. Their number and variety were considerably richer before the process of dissolving traditional philology into general linguistics on the material of Slavic languages and comparative literature (again, using Slavic writers). Nevertheless, their influx is steady even in this day and age. Perhaps the time is ripe to solve the dilemma of having Slavic departments and organizations across the English-speaking world but no consistent research traditions of Slavic studies in linguistics. What I hope to have shown is that Slavic studies offers almost endless research possibilities in elucidating lexical layers of cultural identity. What I hope to encourage is the idea that Slavic departments and organizations become venues for Slavic linguistic research, rather than Slavic languages serving only as a source of examples for research on general linguistic problems.

15   An Outlook

In this chapter, I will outline the prospects of further research in this field. Examples provided throughout the present monograph are intended to exemplify the range of data to be included in the research of the lexical layers of cultural identity and the techniques of a consistent analysis of that data. They definitely do not build complete cultural-lexical profiles of any languages that were used and not all processes and features are characteristic for all Slavic languages. Neither do they represent an in-depth analysis of any discussed phenomena. I will therefore devote my attention here to research possibilities that can lead toward more definite accounts of languages and phenomena.

One obvious issue to discuss at the very outset are datasets and possible ways of improving them. I have repeatedly discussed research limitations stemming from the differences in datasets, most notably those that are brought about by different strategies and lexicographic solutions that authors of various Slavic dictionaries deploy. To overcome problems of this kind, it would be most useful to develop monolingual and bilingual lexicographic standards, which would lead to normalized data in comparing Slavic languages. It would be incumbent on Slavic studies centers and professional organizations, most notably the International Committee of Slavists (see Committee, 2017), to carry out such work. The benefits of such standards or guidelines would be multifold. They would enable cross-linguistic comparison of Slavic lexical data but, more than that, they would offer a platform for a consistent lexicographic treatment in all Slavic languages. Obviously, guidelines should account for the peculiarities of lexicographic traditions of each individual language. In addition to offering guidelines for lexicographic treatment, the standard should also encompass a standard for data representation (e.g., using the Text Encoding Initiative (TEI) scheme, version 5, see Burnard and Bauman, 2013, or Lexical Markup Framework (LFM); see Francopulo et al., 2007). Thus, for example, the guidelines could specify a consistent manner of stating in loanword dictionaries all languages in the chain of borrowing (e.g., the language of direct borrowing, further languages of origin). These guidelines should also specify appropriate descriptions for the language of direct, first indirect, second indirect, etc. etymology in the chosen data-representation standard.

The next possible contribution to creating more useful datasets could involve solutions that would normalize the existing anisomorphic data. The aforementioned guidelines could be useful to authors of future dictionaries. However, a wealth of data exists in various monolingual and bilingual Slavic dictionaries that needs to be normalized in order to make datasets for Slavic cross-linguistic research operational. The solutions in this field may include search-and-replace patterns that would appropriately tag the elements of the dictionary entry or extract lexical data from monographs. For example, if a dictionary states the language of direct borrowing using an angular bracket and the abbreviation for that language, e.g., *[lat.*, the search-and-replace pattern would look for this sequence and replace it with an appropriate tag, e.g. <etym type=borrowing> <lang n=1>lat.</lang></etym>, etc.

I will now address the possibilities for further research that the proposed epistemological construct offers. Two general research directions offer particularly strong opportunities for the elucidation of lexical layers of cultural identity: lexical-cultural language profiles and in-depth contrastive studies. I will discuss them in turn.

Lexical-cultural language profiles offer the possibility of incorporating material from the rich body of literature of the dominant approaches to language and culture (most notably from linguistic culturology) into a broader and more systematic account of the lexical aspects of cultural identity. These profiles for each language and for their variants would specify general lexical ingredients that culturally determine the speakers of the given language or variant and the areas of variation between the speakers. Some of the features are overwhelmingly present in virtually all speakers, while others feature significant variation. To take an example of deep-layer carving of the conceptual sphere, in Slavic languages the lack of the distinction between *arm* and *hand*, *leg* and *foot*, *finger* and *toe*, etc. will almost universally be one of the profilers of cultural identity. On the other hand, the adjectives that describe different food items that have gone bad will be used with enormous variation – some speakers will use the equivalent of *bad* for all of them, while others will use specific designations such as *stale bread, sour milk, rancid butter*, etc. However, even in the latter case, the speakers will be culturally profiled by having a potential to use more specific terms. Potential is there even for those who have not mastered those adjectives, as they have a theoretical possibility to eventually master them. Similarly, the exchange layer may feature some sources of origin that generally define all speakers of the same language (e.g., Greco-Latin borrowings in all Slavic languages, which define the speakers as those from the European cultural circle), whereas other sources may exhibit strong geographical variation. Thus, Near Eastern loanwords not only profile Serbo-Croatian as similar to Bulgarian and Macedonian and distant from most other Slavic languages, but also mark a territorial identity of the speakers from the regions that had the longest periods of Ottoman Turkish rule (especially Bosnia and Herzegovina, and Southern Serbia). These speakers are likely to know and use more of these words than those in other areas where the same standard language is used. In the surface layer, common to practically all speakers is the need to participate in negotiating standard language lexicon with elites (paying no attention to elites may even be a negotiation strategy). What varies from speaker to speaker are the kinds of attitudes they may have and what their level of compliance with the lexical norms is. In building lexical profiles, one could concentrate on more stable areas with less variation among the speakers, but then also list the areas with more variation which contribute somewhat less to their general cultural profile.

In-depth contrastive studies offer the possibility to focus on specific subject-matter fields in the deep and exchange layer and concrete norming maneuvers in the surface layer. Looking, for example, at fields such as common flora and fauna to examine the ratio of an inherited, a borrowed, and an engineered lexicon can reveal not only the differences stemming from the different environments of each Slavic language, but also differences stemming from cultural influences and geographical contacts. Similarly, if we look at the legal terminology in general use, we may be able to discover language-specific mental images and distinctions as well as those that are widespread in the Slavic realm and beyond it.

Another interesting field of research may be the relative availability of multiple equivalents. To exemplify this, I conducted a brief survey among the members of the Facebook group Naš jezik (devoted to Serbo-Croatian, with over 11,000 members in May of 2018, mostly from Belgrade, Serbia). I asked a question about the three Serbo-Croatian equivalents of the English word 'uncle': *ujak* 'one's mother's brother', *stric* 'one's father's brother', and *tetak* 'one's mother's or father's sister's husband'. The question was formulated as follows. When I hear the word *дядя, Onkel, oncle, tio, tío, uncle*,[1] I think about: a. *ujak*, b. *stric*, c. *tetak*. Words before *uncle* were the same term in Russian, German, French, Portuguese, and Spanish, respectively. The survey was performed on February 18 and 19, 2018, and the respondents preponderantly chose 'one's mother's brother' (*ujak* 117 respondents – 91%, *stric* 9 respondents – 7%, *tetak* 2 respondents – 2%). Conducting research on the availability of lexical items from a broader and consistent dataset may reveal interesting facts. In this particular case, the three words for 'uncle' have the same frequency and they are similar phonologically and morphosyntactically. One possible explanation of this preponderance of responses selecting the word for 'one's mother's brother' may be a hypothesis about a higher prominence of mother (who in

---

[1] I.e. one German, French, Spanish, Portuguese, and English word for 'uncle' that covers all three Serbo-Croatian equivalents was provided.

a traditional family tends to home and children) – hence the choice of something that comes from the maternal side. To confirm it, one would need to select a whole lexical field and see if this factor is equally present in it.

I have already shown in Chapter 11 how the micro maneuver of using normative and cryptonormative labels can be studied in major Slavic monolingual dictionaries. Similar microanalyses can be done for macro maneuvers of enforcing the use of the standard lexicon and their micro maneuvers of stigmatizing lexical errors, giving normative advice. While all these may be present in all Slavic standard languages and their ethnic variants, the manner of their implementation may be very different, contributing thus to the cultural identity of each particular language in question. It seems that two grand ideological concepts play a pivotal role in these macro maneuvers: authority (using the tripartite model proposed by Weber, 1919) and nationalism (using the model initially proposed by Gellner, 1983). In particular, to use the three Weberian types of authority, while the authors of macro maneuvers always try to justify their authority as rational-legal, the facts on the ground may be different. It is hence interesting to see the extent to which these macro maneuvers rely on traditional authority (purist maneuvers seem to follow this pattern) and charismatic authority (especially in the various declarations of language councils, academies of sciences, and media appearances of prominent linguists). It is equally interesting to see, from a diachronic perspective, how much linguistic macro maneuvers have contributed to the formation of nations (using the aforementioned Gellnerian model of nation formation and the Brubakerian model of ethnicity).

An interesting possibility of diachronic research has been opened up by Vendina (2002) in her analysis of Old Church Slavonic as an expression of medieval mentality. Indeed, in each of the three layers the parameters change with the flow of time and an analysis of the lexicon of a distinct historical period may bring about insights into the cultural identity of that particular period in time. A related analysis may concern stability and change in time. Some of the parameters of cultural profiles are most resilient, others change abruptly. An interesting question is what contributes to resilience and what causes changes. Vendina (2014) announced another important possibility of looking into the distribution of lexemes in different areas of Slavic languages. Her analysis is based on dialectal data, but the same can be done with standard languages, concentrating on those lexemes that contribute to the cultural profiling of various speakers of Slavic languages.

One possible research direction lies in the field of corpus research. The examples throughout this book use lexical frequency in various dictionary datasets. This kind of lexical frequency can be called systemic frequency. Words and their forms also feature textual frequency, the frequency with which they are used in the texts of their language. To use a known example, the lexical class of prepositions constitutes a rather modest proportion of the lexicon, but they are very prominent in the corpora of any language. For example, in Russian (according to Ljaševskaja and Šarov, 2009) there are 18 prepositions in the top 100 words and 4 of them are in the top 10 in this particular Russian corpus, which is certainly considerably more than their percentage in the lexicon. One possibility to expand the research proposed in the present monograph is to compare Slavic corpus data. Some of those data have already been included in the present research by using frequency data to come up with consistent lexical datasets in Chapter 4, but existing corpora of various languages enable the expansion of the current research. However, one should insert a word of caution here. Corpus datasets are considerably more problematic than their dictionary counterparts. Dictionaries might not perfectly represent the lexicon, but corpora are notorious in the variation of numerous criteria that can influence research. Take, for example, negative and positive characterizations of people, an example used in Chapter 5. The ratio of negative and positive characterizations will be drastically different if a newspaper corpus contains readers' comments. In that case the number of negative characterizations will generally be higher. If no readers' comments are present, then there is a lower number of negative characterizations, as the journalists are typically more guarded with such characterizations than the authors of the comments. This does not mean that corpus research on the lexical layers of cultural identity is impossible; it only requires sophisticated mechanisms for addressing the possible effects of non-representativeness. These mechanisms are certainly much more demanding than those deployed here for dictionary datasets.

In the concrete contexts of Slavic languages, most of them have relatively reliable corpora, and in some cases (e.g., with the Russian National Corpus, www.ruscorpora.ru) lexically and semantically tagged data and filtering tools enable quite sophisticated queries.

Using subjective frequency in addition to lexical frequency, addressed throughout the present monograph, and corpus frequency, a proposed area of expansion, may be a further area of meaningful data analysis. The speakers' subjective feeling of the frequency of some group of words (e.g., those stemming from a maneuver in the surface layer) may be not only indicative of their attitude but also decisive in their constant negotiation with linguistic elites.

I have already noted in Chapter 12 that attitudes, with their intensity, centrality, affective, cognitive, and behavioral components, represent an intricate cognitive construct and require fine-tuning of the research tools proposed here. This offers a distinct opportunity for interdisciplinary research with psychologists in conducting large-scale sophisticated surveys of all these attitude components and aspects. A further research prospect lies in the application of the models of attitude change to the study of lexical engineering and refereeing maneuvers. In that light, the maneuvers would be seen as effective or ineffective mechanisms of attitude change.

To put it succinctly, the epistemological construct of the three lexical layers of cultural identity proposed in the present book offers the possibility to conduct in-depth analyses and to create general cultural profiles in a systematic and comprehensive manner, and thus to utilize the wealth of data that is available in various dictionaries and monographs.

Throughout the present monograph, I use examples from Slavic languages, which, as noted in the Foreword, offer ample material on lexical changes and various parameters of all three layers. However, this does not mean that the kind of analysis proposed here is restricted to those languages. In this sense, one distinct possibility lies in applying the research techniques demonstrated here (that are meant to be universally deployable) to the material of other languages. Obviously, some modifications will be needed in each group of languages and each contrasted language pair, but the general parameters should be useful in analyzing any standard language.

A further possibility may lie in the study of the cultures of urban and rural dialects or languages that have not been standardized. In such research expansion, the deep and the exchange layer would principally be used. There may also be cases of languages in the process of standardization where only some segments of the surface layer could be explored (for example, the cases of micro-languages where we only have the maneuvers of linguistic elites and the general body of speakers that remain unaware or uninterested in those maneuvers).

What I hope to have achieved here is the initiation of a new, more consistent, manner of exploring lexical layers of cultural identity. The proof of the pudding will be in potential research stemming from this first step and using the proposed methodology, modifying it where necessary, to produce an armamentarium for tackling the elusive links between language, culture, and identity.

References

Adler, Nancy. 1997. *International Dimensions of Organizational Behavior* (3rd ed.). Cincinnati, OH: South-Western College Publishing.

Ajduković, Jovan. 2004a. *Kontaktološki rečnik adaptacije rusizama u osam slovenskih jezika.* Belgrade: Foto Futura.

2004b. *Uvod u leksičku kontaktologiju: Teorija adaptacije rusizama.* Belgrade: Foto Futura.

2012. *Radovi iz lingvističke kontaktologije.* Belgrade: Foto Futura.

Alekseenko, M. A. 2006. *Slavjanskie jazyki v svete kul'tury: Sbornik naučnyh statej.* Moscow: *A Temp.*

Alekseev, Mikhail and Boris Ataev. 1998. *Avarskij jazyk.* Moscow: Institute of Linguistics of the Russian Academy of Sciences.

Alekseev, Mikhail and Enver Šejkhov. 1997. *Lezginskij jazyk.* Moscow: Institute of Linguistics of the Russian Academy of Sciences.

Alekseev, Mikhail and Sabrina Šihalieva. 2003. *Tabasaranskij jazyk.* Moscow: Institute of Linguistics of the Russian Academy of Sciences.

Alvarado, Salustio. 1989. Eslavismos en el lexico espanol. *Boletin de la Real Academia Espanola* 69(248):403–416.

1990. Mas eslavismos para el lexico espanol. *Boletin de la Real Academia Espanola* 70(250):421–427.

Ammon, Ulrich. 1995. *Die deutsche Sprache in Deutschland, Österreich und der Schweiz: das Problem der nationalen Varietäten.* Berlin: De Gruyter.

2004. Standard variety/Standardvarietät. In Ulrich Ammon, Norbert Dittmar, Klaus J. Mattheier, and Peter Trudgill (eds.), *Sociolinguistics: An International Handbook of the Science of Language and Society / Soziolinguistik: Ein internationales Handbuch zur Wissenschaft von Sprache und Gesellschaft* (2nd ed.). Berlin: Walter de Gruyter, vol. I, pp. 273–283.

Anić, Vladimir. 1994. *Rječnik hrvatskoga jezika* (2nd rev. and enlarged ed.). Zagreb: Novi Liber.

Apte, Mridula. 1994. Language in sociocultural context. In R. E. Asher (ed.), *The Encyclopedia of Language and Linguistics.* Oxford: Pergamon Press, vol. IV, pp. 2000–2010.

Arkušin, Grigorij. 2014. *Narodna leksika zahidnogo polissja.* Luck: Lesja Ukrainka Eastern European National University.

Armstrong, Nigel and Ian E. Mackenzie. 2013. *Standardization, Ideology and Linguistics.* Houndmills: Palgrave Macmillan.

Avruch, Kevin. 1998. *Culture and Conflict Resolution.* Washington, DC: United States Institute of Peace Press.

Babenko, L. G. 1989. *Leksičeskie sredstva oboznačenija emocij v russkom jazyke.* Sverdlovsk: Ural University.

Bajec, Anton, Janko Jurančič, Mile Klopčič, Lino Legiša, Stane Suhadolnik, et al. 2000. *Slovar slovenskega knjižnega jezika.* Ljubljana: Slovenska akademija znanosti in umetnosti. http://bos.zrc-sazu.si/sskj.html (main body), www.fran.si/130/sskj-slo var-slovenskega-knjiznega-jezika/datoteke/SSKJ_Uvod.pdf (front matter).

Bartels, Hauke. 2009. Loanwords in Lower Sorbian, a Slavic language of Germany. In Martin Haspelmath & Uri Tadmor (eds.), *Loanwords in the World Languages: A Comparative Handbook.* Berlin: Walter de Gruyter, pp. 304–329.

Bartmiński, Jerzy. 2005. Koncepcja językowego obrazu świata w programie slawis-tycznych badań porównawczych. *Studia z Filologii Polskiej i Słowiańskiej* 40:259–280.

    2013. Obraz mira v pol'skoj narodnoj tradicii. In S. M. Tolstaja. (ed.), *Ethnolinguistica Slavica: K 90-letiю akademika Nikity Il'iča Tolstogo.* Moscow: Indrik, pp. 26–42.

    2014. Basic assumptions of Slavic ethnolinguistics. In Karl Gutschmidt, Sebastian Kempgen, Tilman Berger, and Peter Kosta (eds.), *Die slavischen Sprachen: /The Slavic Languages: An International Handbook of their Structure, their History and their Investigation.* Berlin: De Gruyter Mouton, vol. II, pp. 1165–1174.

Bartmiński, Jerzy and Wojciech Chlebda. 2008. Jak badać językowo-kulturowy obraz świata Słowian i ich sąsiadów? *Etnolingwistyka* 20:11–27.

Bartschat, Brigitte. 2009. Die Beziehung von lexikalischer Bedeutung und innerer Form. In Sebastian Kempgen, Peter Kosta, Tilman Bergen, and Karl Gutschmidt (eds.), *Die slavischen Sprachen/The Slavic Languages: An International Handbook of their Structure, their History and their Investigation.* Berlin: De Gruyter Mouton, vol. I, pp. 883–888.

Bauman, John. 2007. *General Service List.* http://jbauman.com/gsl.html, accessed on July 18, 2017.

Bazilev, V. N. ed. 1999. *Problemy lingvističeskoj kontaktologii: materialy rabočej konferencii, 23 oktjabrja 1999 goda.* Moscow: Dialog.

Beekes, R. S. P. 2011. *Comparative Indo-European Linguistics: An Introduction* (2nd ed.). Amsterdam: John Benjamins.

Béjoint, Henri. 2010. *The Lexicography of English.* Oxford: Oxford University Press.

Bellosztenecs, Joannes. 1740. *Gazophylacium seu latino-illyricorum onomatum aerarium, select. synonymis, phraseologiis, verb. construct, metaphoris, adagiis. et nunc primum peculiariter Illyriorum commodo apertum.* Zagreb: Johannes Baptista Weitz.

Benson, Morton. 1992. *Srpskohrvatsko-engleski rečnik.* Belgrade: Prosveta.

    1993. *Benson's Tagged SerboCroatian–English Dictionary* (electronic document), Philadelphia: University of Pennsylvania Press.

    1998. *Standard English–SerboCroatian, SerboCroatian–English Dictionary: A Dictionary of Bosnian, Croatian, and Serbian Standards.* Cambridge: Cambridge University Press.

Berezovič, E. L. 2014. *Russkaja leksika na obščeslovjanskom fone: semantiko-motivacionnaja rekonstrukcija.* Moscow: Dmitrij Pozharski University.

Bernsand, Nikklas. 2001. Surzhyk and national identity in Ukrainian nationalist lan-guage ideology. *Berliner Osteuropa-Info* 17:38–47.

Bernstein, Basil. 2003 (1971). *Class, Codes and Control: Theoretical Studies Towards a Sociology of Language* (vol. I). London and New York: Routledge.

Bernštejn, S. B. 1961. *Očerk sravnitel'noj grammatiki slavjanskih jazykov* (vol. I). Moscow: Academy of the Sciences of USSR.

1974. *Očerk sravnitel'noj grammatiki slavjanskih jazykov*. Moscow: Nauka.

Berry, John W., Ype H. Poortinga, and Janak Pandey, eds. 1997. *Handbook of Cross-Cultural Psychology* (2nd ed.). Boston, London, Toronto, Sydney, Tokyo, and Singapore: Allyn and Bacon.

Bierich, Alexander. 2011. Kultursemantische Aspekte des slavischen Wortschatzes (am Beispiel des Polnischen, Tschechischen, Russischen, Kroatischen/Serbischen). In Irina Abisogomian (ed.), *Lingvokul'turnoe prostranstvo sovremennoj Evropy čerez prizmu malyh i bol'šіh jazykov: k 70-letiιo professora Aleksandra Dmitrieviča Duličenko*. Tartu: Tartu Ülikooli Kirjastus, pp. 137–150.

Bloomfield, Leonard. 1933. *Language*. New York: Holt, Rinehart and Winston.

Bockholt, Volker. 1990. *Sprachmaterialkonzeptionen und ihre Realisirung in der kroatischen und serbischen Lexikographie*. Essen: Die Blaue Eule.

Bogusławski, Andrzej. 1985. *Ilustrowany słownik rosyjsko-polski polsko-rosyjski* (3rd ed.). Warsaw: Wiedza powszechna.

Bopp, Franz, 1853. *A Comparative Grammar of Sanskrit, Zend, Greek, Latin, Lithuanian, Gothic, German, and Sclavonic Languages*. London: James Madden.

Bošković, Radoslav. 1977. *Osnovi uporedne gramatike slovenskih jezika*. Belgrade: Naučna knjiga.

Bragina, A. A. 1978. *Russkoe slovo v jazykakh mira*. Moscow: Prosveščenie.

Breu, Walter. 2014. Substrate auf slavischem Sprachgebiet (Südslavisch). In Karl Gutschmidt, Sebastian Kempgen, Tilman Berger, and Peter Kosta (eds.), *Die slavischen Sprachen/The Slavic Languages: An International Handbook of their Structure, their History and their Investigation*. Berlin: De Gruyter Mouton. pp. 1175–1180.

Britsyn, Victor M. 1996/1997. Ukraine. In Hans Goebl, Peter H. Nelde, Zdenek Stary, and Wolfgang Wölck (eds.), *Kontaktlinguistik: Ein Internationales Handbuch zeitgenössiger Forschung/Contact Linguistics: An International Handbook of Contemporary Research* (2 vols.). Berlin and New York: Walter De Gruyter, vol. II, pp. 1926–1933.

Brodnjak, Vladimir. 1991. *Razlikovni rječnik srpskog i hrvatskog jezika*. Zagreb: Školske novine.

Browne, Wayles. 1993. Serbo-Croat. In Bernard Comrie and Greville G. Corbett (eds.), *The Slavonic Languages*. London and New York: Routledge, pp. 306–387.

Brozović-Rončević, Dunja, Alemko Gluhak, Vesna Muhvić-Dimanovski, Branko Sočanac, and Lelija Sočanac. 1996. *Rječnik novih riječi*. Zagreb: Minerva.

Brozović, Dalibor. 1969. *Rječnik jezika ili jezik rječnika*. Zagreb: Kultura.

1970. *Standardni jezik: Teorija, usporedbe, geneza, povijest, suvremena zbilja*. Zagreb: Matica hrvatska.

2001. Peculiar sociolinguistic features of the Slavic world. In *International Journal of the Sociology of Language* 147: 5–15.

Brozović, Dalibor and Pavle Ivić. 1988. *Jezik: Srpskohrvatski/hrvatskosrpski, hrvatski ili srpski*. Zagreb: Leksikografski zavod "Miroslav Krleža."

Brubaker, Rogers. 2002. Ethnicity without groups. *Archives of European Sociology* 43(2):163–189.
    2004. *Ethnicity Without Groups*. Cambridge, MA: Harvard University Press.
    2009. Ethnicity, race, and nationalism. *Annual Review of Sociology* 35:21–42.
Brugmann, Karl and Berthold Delbrück. 1886–1900. *Grundriss der vergleichenden Grammatik der indogermanischen Sprachen*. Strassburg: Karl J. Trübner.
Bugarski, Ranko. 2001. Language, nationalism and war in Yugoslavia. *International Journal of the Sociology of Language* 151:69–87.
Bugarski, Ranko and Celia Hawkesworth, eds. 2004. *Language in the Former Yugoslav Lands*. Bloomington: Slavica.
Burke, Peter and Jan Stets. 2009. *Identity Theory*. Oxford: Oxford University Press.
Burnard Lou and Syd Bauman, eds. 2013. *TEI P5: Guidelines for Electronic Text Encoding and Interchange*. Charlottesville, VA: Text Encoding Initiative Consortium.
Capuz, Juan Gómes. 1997. Toward a typological classification of linguistic borrowing (illustrated with Anglicisms in Romance languages). *Revista Alicantina de Estudios Ingleses* 10:81–94.
Cejtlin, R. M. 1996. *Sravnitel'naja leksikologija slavjanskih jazykov X/XI–XIV/XV vv. Problemy i metody*. Moscow: Nauka.
Chomsky, Noam. 1995. *The Minimalist Program*. Cambridge, MA: MIT Press.
Cipra, Franjo and Bratoljub Klaić (with the cooperation of the staff from the Office of the Croatian Language). 1944. *Hrvatski pravopis*. Zagreb: Naklada odjela Hrvatske državne tiskare.
Clarkson, James. 2007. *Indo-European Linguistics: An Introduction*. Cambridge: Cambridge University Press.
Clyne, Michael. 2004. *Dynamics of Language contact*. Cambridge: Cambridge University Press.
Cmejrková, Světla. 2011. Česká jazyková situace a teorie diglosie. In Abisogomjan, Irina (ed.), *Lingvokul'turnoe prostranstvo sovremennoj Evropy čerez prizmu malyh i bol'šihʹ jazykov: k 70-letiю professora Aleksandra Dmitrieviča Duličenko*. Tartu: Tartu Ülikooli Kirjastus, pp. 312–323.
Coetsem, Franz Van. 2000. *A General and Unified Theory of the Transmission Process in Language Contact* (Monographien zur Sprachwissenschaft 19). Heidelberg: Winter.
Collins English Thesaurus. 2017. www.collinsdictionary.com/dictionary/english-the saurus, accessed on August 11, 2017.
Committee 2017. *Komissija po leksikologii i leksikografii pri Meždunarodnom komitete slavistov*. www.ruslang.ru/agens.php?id=lexcomission, accessed on May 23, 2017.
Comrie, Bernard. 2000. Language contact, lexical borrowing, and semantic fields. *Studies in Slavic and General Linguistics* 28:73–86.
Comrie, Bernard and Greville G. Corbett. 1993. *The Slavonic Languages*. London: Routledge.
Comrie, Bernard and Lucía Golluscio, eds. 2015. *Language Contact and Documentation/Contacto lingüístico y documentación*. Berlin and Boston: De Gruyter.
Cruse, D. A. 1986. *Lexical Semantics*. Cambridge: Cambridge University Press.

Crystal, D. 1987. *The Cambridge Encyclopedia of Language*. Cambridge: Cambridge University Press.

Curta, Florin. 2001. *The Making of the Slavs: History and Archeology of the Lower Danube Region, c. 500–700*. Cambridge: Cambridge University Press.

Cvrček, Václav. 2006. Kodifikační praxe. In Hana Gladkova and Václav Cvrček (eds.), *Sociální aspekty spisovných jazyků slovanských*. Prague: Filozofická fakulta UK, Euroslavica, pp. 16–35.

Czerwiński, Maciej. 2005. *Język – Ideologia – Naród: Polityka językowa w Chorwacji a język mediów*. Kraków: Scriptum.

Čaušević, Ekrem. 2016. Miloš Mandić i njegov rječnik turcizama (O prvome rječniku turcizama u povjesti turkologije). In Katica Jurčević, Ozana Ramljak, and Zlatko Hasanbegović (eds.), *Hrvatska i Turska Povijesno-kulturni pregled*. Zagreb: Srednja Europa and Institut društvenih znanosti Ivo Pilar, pp. 85–92.

Čermák, František. 2006. Preskriptivismus: Variabilita versus stabilita, faktory a problémy. In Hana Gladkova and Václav Cvrček (eds.), *Sociální aspekty spisovných jazyků slovanských*. Prague: Filozofická fakulta UK, Euroslavica, pp. 36–45.

Čundeva, Nina. 2017. *Rusizmite vo makedonskiot literaturen jazik*. Skopje: *UKiM*.

Ćirković, Svetlana and Mirjana Mirić. 2017. *Romsko-srpski rečnik knjaževačkog gurbetskog govora*. Knjaževac: Narodna biblioteka Njegoš.

Ćosić, Pavle. 2008. *Rečnik sinonima*. Belgrade: Kornet.

Dahl, Stephan. 2004. Intercultural research: The current state of knowledge. *Middlesex University Discussion Paper No. 26*. January 12, 2004. Available at SSRN: http://ssrn.com/abstract=658202.

Dalewska-Greń, Hanna. 1997. *Języki słowiańskie*. Warsaw: PWN.

Daneš, František. 1979. Postoje a hodnotící kritéria při kodifikaci. In *Aktuální otázky jazykové kultury v socialistické společnosti*. Prague: Academia, pp. 79–91.

2003. The present-day situation of Czech. *International Journal of the Sociology of Language* 162:9–18.

Danilenko, V. P. 1977. *Russkaja terminologija*. Moscow: Russian Language Institute of the Academy of Sciences of the USSR.

Davies, Winifred. 2012. Myths we live and speak by: Ways of imagining and managing language and languages. In Matthias Hüning, Ulrike Vogl, and Olivier Moliner (eds.), *Standard Languages and Multilingualism in European History*. Amsterdam: John Benjamins, pp. 45–69.

Della Bella, Ardelio 1785. *Dizionario italiano–latino–illirico*. Ragusa: Cristoforo Zanne.

Derksen, Rick. 2008. *Etymological Dictionary of the Slavic Inherited Lexicon*. Leiden and Boston: Brill.

Deroy, Louis. 1954. *L'emprunt linguistique*. Paris: Les Belles Lettres.

Devetak, Silvo. 1996/1997. Ethnicity. In Hans Goebl, Peter H. Nelde, Zdenek Stary, and Wolfgang Wölck (eds.), *Kontaktlinguistik: Ein Internationales Handbuch zeitgenössiger Forschung/Contact Linguistics: An International Handbook of Contemporary Research* (2 vols.). Berlin and New York: Walter De Gruyter, vol. I, pp. 203–210.

Dimitrovski, Todor, Blaže Koneski, Blagoja Korubin, and Trajko Stamatoski. 1961–1966. *Rečnik na makedonskiot jazik so srpskohrvatskite tolkuvanja*. Skopje: Institut Krste Misirkov.

Dittmar, Norbert. 1976. *Sociolinguistics: A Critical Survey of Theory and Application*. London: Edward Arnold.

2004. Umgangsprache – nonstandard/Vernacular – nonstandard. In Ulrich Ammon, Norbert Dittmar, Klaus J. Mattheier, and Peter Trudgill (eds.), *Sociolinguistics: An International Handbook of the Science of Language and Society/ Soziolinguistik: Ein internationales Handbuch zur Wissenschaft von Sprache und Gesellschaft* (2nd ed.). Berlin: Walter de Gruyter, vol. I, pp. 250–262.

Dobosiewicz, Maciej. 2002. Przysłowia serbsko-chorwacko i polskie dotyczące relacji kobieta – mężczyzna w ujęciu językoznawczym (MA thesis). Poznań: UAM.

Dragićević, Rajna. 2010a. *Leksikologija srpskog jezika*. Belgrade: Zavod za udžbenike.

2010b. *Verbalne asocijacije kroz srpski jezik i kulturu*. Belgrade: Društvo za srpski jezik i književnost Srbije.

ed. 2016. *Reči pod lupom*. Belgrade: Tanesi.

2018. *Srpska leksika u prošlosti i danas*. Novi Sad: Matica srpska.

Drvodelić, Milan. 1989. *Hrvatsko ili srpsko engleski rječnik*. Zagreb: Školska knjiga.

Duličenko, A. D. 1981. *Slavjanskie literaturnye mikrojazyki: Voprosy formirovanija i razvitija*. Tallin: Valgus.

1995. The West Polesian literary language. In *Language, Minority, Migration: Yearbook 1994/1995 from the Centre for Multiethnic Research*. Uppsala: Centre for Multiethnic Research, pp. 119–131.

2005. *Malye slavjanskie literaturnye jazyki (mikrojazyki)*. Moscow: Academia.

Durkin, Philip. 2014. *Borrowed Words: A History of Loanwords in English*. Oxford and New York: Oxford University Press.

Eagleton, Terry. 2016. *Culture*. New Haven, CT: Yale University Press.

Eagly, Alice H. and Shelly Chaiken. 1998. Attitude structure and function. In Daniel T. Gilbert, Susan Fiske, and Gardner Lindzey (eds.), *The Handbook of Social Psychology* (4th ed.). New York: Oxford Univeristy Press, pp. 269–322.

Edwards, John. 1985. *Language, Society and Identity*. Oxford and New York: Basil Blackwell.

Egorova, T. V. 2014. *Slovar' inostrannyh slov sovremennogo russkogo jazyka*. Moscow: Adelant.

Eluerd, Roland. 2000. *La lexicologie* (Collection "Que sais-je?", no. 3548). Paris: Presses Universitaires de France.

Evsjukova, T. V. and E. Ju. Butenko. 2016. *Lingvokulturologija* (4th ed.). Moscow: Flinta, Nauka.

Fasold, R. 1984. *The Sociolinguistics of Society*. Oxford: Basil Blackwell.

1990. *The Sociolinguistics of Language*. Oxford: Basil Blackwell.

Fazio, Russell H. and Michael A. Olson. 2003. Attitudes: Foundations, functions, and consequences. In M. A. Hogg and J. Cooper (eds.), *The Sage Handbook of Social Psychology*. London: Sage, pp. 139–160.

Felber, Helmut. 1984. *Terminology Manual*. Paris: Unesco.

2001. *Allgemeine Terminologielehre, Wissenslehre und Wissenstechnik: Theoretische Grundlagen und philosophische Betrachtungen*. Vienna: TermNet.

Felber, Helmut and Gerhard Budin. 1989. *Terminologie in Theorie und Praxis*. Tübingen: Gunter Narr Verlag.

Ferguson, Charles A. 1996. *Sociolinguistic Perspectives: Papers on Language in Society, 1959–1994*. Oxford: Oxford University Press.

Ferraro, Gary. 1998. *The Cultural Dimension of International Business* (3rd ed.). Upper Saddle River, NJ: Prentice Hall.

Fielder, Grace. 1996/1997. Bulgaria. In Hans Goebl, Peter H. Nelde, Zdenek Stary, and Wolfgang Wölck (eds.), *Kontaktlinguistik: Ein Internationales Handbuch zeitgenössiger Forschung/Contact Linguistics: An International Handbook of Contemporary Research* (2 vols.). Berlin and New York: Walter De Gruyter, vol. II, pp. 1487–1496.

Filipec, Josef and František Čermák. 1985. *Česká leksikologie*. Prague: Akademia.

Filipović, Rudolf. 1986. *Teorija jezika u kontaktu: uvod u lingvistiku jezičnih dodira*. Zagreb: JAZU.

1989. *Englesko-hrvatskosprski rječnik*. Zagreb: Školska knjiga.

1997. *The Theoretical Background of the Project "The English Element in European Languages." Studia-Romanica-et-Anglica-Zagrabiensia* 42:105–111.

Fishman, Joshua. 1972. *Language and Nationalism: Two Integrative Essays*. Rowley, MA: Newbury House. st

ed. 1999. *Handbook of Language and Ethnic Identity*. Oxford: Oxford Univesity Press.

2010. *New Perspectives on Language and Education: European Vernacular Literacy – A Sociolinguistic and Historical Introduction*. Bristol: Channel View Publications.

Fisiak, Jacek, Arleta Adamska-Sałaciak, Mariusz Idzikowski, Ewelina Jagła, Michał Jankowski, et al. 2011. *Słownik współczesny angielsko-polski, polsko-angielski* (2nd ed.). Harlow: Longman.

Flier, Michael S. 1998. Surzhyk: The rules of engagement. In Zvi Gitelman, Lubomyr Hajda, John-Paul Himka, and Roman Solchanyk (eds.),*Cultures and Nations of Central and Eastern Europe: Essays in honor of Roman Szporluk* (Harvard Series in Ukrainian Studies, vol. 22). Cambridge, MA: Ukrainian Research Institute, Harvard University.

Fomina, M. I. 1978. *Sovremennyj russkij jazyk: Leksikologija*. Moscow: Vysšaja škola.

Fouse, Gary. 2000. *The Languages of the Former Soviet Republics: Their History and Development*. Lanham, MD: University Press of America.

Francopulo, Gil, Monte George, Nicoletta Calzolari, Monica Monachini, Nuria Bel, et al. (2007). *Lexical Markup Framework: ISO standard for semantic information in NLP Lexicons*. Tübingen: GLDV (Gesellschaft für linguistische Datenverarbeitung).

Friedman, Victor A. 1993. Macedonian. In Bernard Comrie and Greville G. Corbett (eds.), *The Slavonic Languages*. London and New York: Routledge, pp. 249–305.

1996/1997. Macedonia. In Hans Goebl, Peter H. Nelde, Zdenek Stary, and Wolfgang Wölck (eds.), *Kontaktlinguistik: Ein Internationales Handbuch zeitgenössiger Forschung/Contact Linguistics: An International Handbook of Contemporary Research* (2 vols.). Berlin and New York: Walter De Gruyter, pp. 1442–1451.

1999. *Linguistic Emblems and Emblematic Languages: On Language as Flag in the Balkans* (Kenneth E. Naylor memorial lecture series in South Slavic linguistics). Columbus: Ohio State University.

Garry, Robert. 2006. Collective identity formation and linguistic identities in the Austro-Italian-Slovene border region. In Dieter Stern and Christian Voss (eds.), *Marginal Linguistic Identities*. Wiesbaden: Harrasovitz Verlag, pp. 103–118.

Geeraerts, Dirk, Stefan Grondelaers, and Peter Bakema. 1994. *The Structure of Lexical Variation: Meaning, Naming and Context*. Berlin and Boston: De Gruyter.

Geeraerts, Dirk, Gitte Kristiansen, and Yves Peirsman. 2010. *Cognitive Linguistics Research: Advances in Cognitive Sociolinguistics*. Berlin: Walter de Gruyter.

Gellner, Ernest. 1983. *Nations and Nationalism*. Ithaca, NY: Cornell University Press.

Goddard, Cliff. 2002. The search for the shared semantic core of all languages. In Cliff Goddard and Anna Wierzbicka (eds.), *Meaning and Universal Grammar: Theory and Empirical Findings*. Amsterdam: John Benjamins, vol. I, pp. 5–40.

2008. *Cross-Linguistic Semantics*. Amsterdam: John Benjamins.

2011. Ethnopragmatics: A new paradigm. In *Ethnopragmatics: Understanding Discourse in Cultural Context*. Berlin: Walter de Gruyter, pp. 1–30.

2012. Semantic primes, semantic molecules, semantic templates: Key concepts in the NSM approach to lexical typology. *Linguistics* 50(3):711–743.

Goddard, Cliff and Anna Wierzbicka. 2002. Opening statement: Meaning and universals. In Cliff Goddard and Anna Wierzbicka (eds.), *Meaning and Universal Grammar: Theory and Empirical Findings*. Amsterdam: John Benjamins, vol. I, pp. 1–3.

Goebl, Hans, Peter H. Nelde, Zdenek Stary, and Wolfgang Wölck, eds. 1996/1997. *Kontaktlinguistik: Ein Internationales Handbuch zeitgenössiger Forschung/ Contact Linguistics: An International Handbook of Contemporary Research* (2 vols.). Berlin and New York: Walter De Gruyter.

Gołąb, Zbigniew. 1991. *The Origins of the Slavs: A Linguist's View*. Columbus, OH: Slavica.

Golubović, Biljana. 2007. *Germanismen im Serbischen und Kroatischen*. Munich: Otto Sagner.

Gortan-Premk, Darinka, Vera Vasic, and Rajna Dragićević. 2003. *Semantičko-derivacioni rečnik*, vol. I. Novi Sad: Filozofski fakultet, Odsek za srpski jezik i lingvistiku.

Greenberg, Joseph. 1957. Genetic relationship among languages. In Joseph H. Greenberg (ed.), *Essays in Linguistics*. Chicago: University of Chicago, pp. 35–45.

Greenberg, Robert. 2004. *Language and Identity in the Balkans Serbo-Croatian and its Disintegration*, Oxford: Oxford University Press.

Greenberg, Robert and Motoki Nomachi, eds. 2012. *Slavia Islamica: Language, Religion and Identity*. Sapporo: Slavic and Eurasian Center.

Grenoble, Lenore A. 2010. Contact and the development of the Slavic languages. In Raymond Hickey (ed.), *The Handbook of Language Contact*. Oxford: Wiley-Blackwell. DOI:10.1002/9781444318159.ch28.

Grujić, Branislav. 1959. *Rečnik englesko-srpskohrvatski i srpskohrvatsko-engleski sa kratkom gramatikom engleskog jezika*. Belgrade: Stožer.

Gustavsson, Sven. 1996/1997. Byelorussia. In Hans Goebl, Peter H. Nelde, Zdenek Stary, and Wolfgang Wölck (eds.), *Kontaktlinguistik: Ein Internationales Handbuch zeitgenössiger Forschung/Contact Linguistics: An International Handbook of Contemporary Research* (2 vols.). Berlin and New York: Walter De Gruyter, vol. II, pp. 1919–1926.

1998. Sociolinguistic typology of Slavic minority languages. *Slovo* (Uppsala), No. 46:75–89.

Gutschmidt, Karl, Sebastian Kempgen, Tilman Berger, and Peter Kosta, eds. *Die slavischen Sprachen: /The Slavic Languages: An International Handbook of their Structure, their History and their Investigation*. Berlin: De Gruyter Mouton.

Guy, Gregory R. 1990. The sociolinguistic types of language change. *Diachronica* 7(1): 47–67.

Haarman, Harald. 1996/1997. Identitat. In Hans Goebl, Peter H. Nelde, Zdenek Stary, and Wolfgang Wölck (eds.), *Kontaktlinguistik: Ein Internationales Handbuch zeitgenössiger Forschung/Contact Linguistics: An International Handbook of Contemporary Research* (2 vols.). Berlin and New York: Walter De Gruyter, vol. I, pp. 218–233.

Habdelić, Juraj 1670. *Dictionarium Croatico-Latinum: Dictionar, ili Reči slovenske z vekšega vkup zebrane, v red postavljene i diačkemi zlahkotene*. Graz: Widmanstadiuss.

Hadrovics Lászlo. 1985. *Ungarische Elemente im Serbokroatischen*. Budapest: Akademiai kiádo.

Halilović, Senahid, Ismail Palić, and Amela Šehović. 2010. *Rječnik bosanskog jezika*. Sarajevo: Filozofski fakultet.

Hall, Edward T. 1959. *The Silent Language*. Garden City, NY: Doubleday and Co. 1966. *The Hidden Dimension*, Garden City, NY: Doubleday and Co.

Hamm, Sanda, Jadranka Mlikota, Borko Baraban, and Alen Orlić. 2014. *Hrvatski jezični savjeti*. Zagreb: Školska knjiga.

Hanks, Patrick. 2013. *Lexical Analysis: Norms and Exploitations*. Cambridge, MA: MIT Press.

Hartmann, R. R. K and G. James. 2001. *Dictionary of Lexicography*. London and New York: Routledge.

Haspelmath, Martin. 2006. Against markedness and what to replace it with. *Journal of Linguistics* 42(1):25–70. 2009. Lexical borrowing: concepts and issues. In Martin Haspelmath and Uri Tadmor, (eds.), *Loanwords in the World Languages: A Comparative Handbook*. Berlin: Walter de Gruyter, pp. 35–54.

Haugen, Einar. 1950. The analysis of linguistic borrowing. *Language* 26(2):211–231.

Hausmann, Franz Joseph. 1989. Die Markierung im allgemeinen einsprachigen Wörterbuch: eine Übersicht. In F.-J. Hausmann, O. Reichmann, H. Wiegand, and L. Zgusta (eds.), *Dictionaries: An International Encyclopedia of Lexicography*. Berlin and New York: Walter de Gruyter, vol. I, pp. 649–657.

Havránek, Bohuslav. 1980. *Vývoj českého spisovného jazyka*. Prague: Státní pedagogické nakladatelství.

Hentschel, Gerd. 2014. Belarusian and Russian in the mixed speech of Belarus. In Juliane Besters-Dilger, Cynthia Dermarkars, Stefan Pfänder, and Achim Rabus (eds.), *Congruence in Contact-Induced Language Change: Language Families, Typological Resemblance, and Perceived Similarity*. Berlin and Boston: De Gruyter, pp. 93–121.

Herne, Gunnar. 1954. *Die Slavischen Farbenbenennungen: Eine semasiologisch-etymologische Untersuchung*. Uppsala: Almqvist & Wiksells Boktryckerei AB.

Hickey', Raymond, ed. 2012. *Handbook of Language Contact*. Somerset: Wiley.

Hidekel', S. S. and M. R. Kaul'. 2006. *Russko-anglijskij ob'jasnitel'nyj slovar' russko-anglijskih sootvetstvij*. Moscow: ACT Astrel' Tranzitkniga.

Hill, Peter. 1988. Lexical revolutions as an expression of nationalism in the Balkans. In Peter Hill and Volkmar Lehmann, *Standard Language in the Slavic World: Papers on Sociolinguistics by Hamburg Slavists*. Munich: Verlag Otto Sagner, pp. 147–159.

2010. Language and national identity. In Armin Bachman, Christliebe El Mogharbel, and Katja Himstedt (eds.), *Form und Struktur in der Sprache: Festschrift für Elmar Ternes*. Tübingen: Narr Francke Attempto Verlag GmbH, pp. 105–112.

2014a. Slavonic languages in emigre communities. In Karl Gutschmidt, Sebastian Kempgen, Tilman Berger, and Peter Kosta (eds.), *Die slavischen Sprachen/The Slavic Languages: An International Handbook of their Structure, their History and their Investigation*. Berlin: De Gruyter Mouton, vol. II, pp. 2116–2135.

2014b. Ausgewählte lexikalisch-semantische Gruppen. In Karl Gutschmidt, Sebastian Kempgen, Tilman Berger, and Peter Kosta (eds.), *Die slavischen Sprachen/The Slavic Languages: An International Handbook of their Structure, their History and their Investigation*. Berlin: De Gruyter Mouton, vol. II, pp. 1740–1766.

Hinrichs, Uwe. 2013. *Multi Kulti Deutsch: Wie Migration die deutsche Sprache verändert*. Munich: Beck.

2014. Soziolekte (serbisch/kroatisch/bosnisch). In Karl Gutschmidt, Sebastian Kempgen, Tilman Berger, and Peter Kosta (eds.), *Die slavischen Sprachen/The Slavic Languages: An International Handbook of their Structure, their History and their Investigation*. Berlin: De Gruyter Mouton, vol. II, pp. 2171–2185.

Hock, Hans Henrich. 1986. *Principles of Historical Linguistics*. Berlin, New York, and Amsterdam: Mouton de Gruyter.

Hofstede, Geert. 2001. *Culture's Consequences: Comparing Values, Behaviors, Institutions, and Organizations across Nations* (2nd ed.). London: Sage.

Hofstede, G. and G. J. Hofstede. 1994. *Cultures and Organizations: Software of the Mind*. London: HarperCollins.

Horálek, Karel. 1955. *Úvod do studia slovanských jazyků*. Prague: Akademia.

Huemer. Michael. 2013. *The Problem of Political Authority: An Examination of the Right to Coerce and the Duty to Obey*. New York: Palgrave Macmillan.

Humboldt, Wilhelm von. 1841. *Gesammelte Werke: Erster Band*. Berlin: G. Reimer.

1959. *Bildung und Sprache; eine Auswahl aus seinen Schriften*, prepared by Clemens Menze. Paderborn: Schöningh.

Institut Slavjanovedenia RAN. 2014. *Balto-slavjanskie issledovanija*. Moscow and St. Petersburg: Nestor-Istorija.

Isaković, Alija. 1992. *Rječnik karakteristične leksike u bosanskome jeziku*. Sarajevo: Bambi.

1995. *Rječnik bosanskog jezika*. Sarajevo: Bosanska knjiga.

Ivanov, V. V. and V. N. Toporov. 1958. *K postanovke voprosa o drevnejših otnošenijah baltijskih i slavjanskih jazykov*. Moscow: Academy of Sciences of the USSR.

Ivić, Pavle. 1987. O Vukovom Rječniku iz 1818. Godine. In Vuk Stefanović Karadžić, *Srpski rječnik*. Belgrade: Prosveta – Nolit.

Ivir, Vladimir and Damir Kalogjera, eds. 1991. *Languages in Contact and Contrast*. Berlin: Walter de Gruyter.

Ivšić, Stjepan. 1979. *Poredbena slavenska gramatika*. Zagreb: Školska knjiga.

Jackson, Howard. 2000. *Words, Meaning and Vocabulary: An Introduction to Modern English Lexicology.* London and New York: Cassell.

Jahić, Dževad. *1999. Školski rječnik bosanskog jezika.* Sarajevo: Ljiljan

Jahoda, Gustav. 2012. Critical reflections on some recent definitions of "culture." *Culture and Psychology* 18(3):289–303.

Jakobson, R. 1960. Concluding statement: Linguistics and poetics. In T. Sebeok (ed.), *Style in Language.* New York: Wiley, pp. 350–377.

[1959] 1966. On linguistic aspects of translation. In Reuben A. Brower (ed.), *On Translation.* New York: Oxford University Press, pp. 232–239.

Jankowiak, Lucyna Agnieszka. 1997. *Prasłowańske dziedzictwo leksylane we współczesnej polszczyźnie ogólnej.* Warsaw: Slawistyczny ośrodek wydawniczy.

Jedlička, Alois. 1978. *Spisovný jazyk v současné komunikaci.* Prague: Universita Karlova.

Jenkins, Richard 2014. *Social Identity.* London: Routledge.

Jenks, Chris. 1993. *Culture.* London: Taylor and Francis.

Jernudd, Bjorn H. 1996/1997. Language planning. In Hans Goebl, Peter H. Nelde, Zdenek Stary, and Wolfgang Wölck (eds.), *Kontaktlinguistik: Ein Internationales Handbuch zeitgenössiger Forschung/Contact Linguistics: An International Handbook of Contemporary Research* (2 vols.). Berlin and New York: Walter De Gruyter, vol. I, pp. 833–842.

Johnson, Samuel. 1755. *Dictionary of the English Language.* London: J & P. Knapton.

Jonke, Ljudevit and Mihailo Stevanović, eds. 1967–1976. *Rečnik srpskohrvatskoga književnog jezika.* Novi Sad and Zagreb: Matica srpska/Matica hrvatska (vols. I and II).

Jovanović, Ranko and Laza Atanacković. 1980. *Sistematski rečnik srpskohrvatskoga jezika.* Novi Sad: Matica srpska.

Jurančić, Janko. 1982. Konfrontacija slovenačkoga i srpksohrvatskog rečničkog fonda u leksikografiji. In Drago Ćupić and Darinka Gortan-Premk (eds.), *Leksikologija i Leksikografija.* Belgrade and Novi Sad:SANU/Filozofski fakultet, pp. 83–90.

Kachru, Braj. 1992. World Englishes: Approaches, issues and resources. *Language Teaching* 25:1–14.

Kadić, Safet. 2014. *Bosanski jezik između lingvocida i lingvosuicida.* Sarajevo: Planjax komerc.

Kager, René. 1999. *Optimality Theory.* Cambridge: Cambridge University Press.

Kalinin, A. V. 1971. *Leksika russkogo jazyka.* Moscow: Moscow University Press.

Kamper-Warejko, Joanna. 2007. *Studia nad słownictwem dawnym i współczesnym języków słowiańskich.* Toruń: Wydawnictwo Uniwersytetu Mikołaja Kopernika.

Kamusella, Tomasz, Motoki Nomachi, and Catherine Gibson, eds. 2016. *The Palgrave Handbook of Slavic Languages, Identities and Borders.* Basingstoke: Palgrave Macmillan.

Karadžić, Vuk Stefanović 1818. *Srpski rječnik.* Vienna: Armenian Monastery.

1852. *Srpski rječnik.* Vienna: Armenian Monastery.

Karaulov, Ju. N. 2010. *Russkij jazyk i jazykovaja ličnost'.* Moscow: LKI.

Karaulov, Ju. N., G. A. Čerkasova, N.V. Ufimceva, Ju. A. Sorokin, and E. F. Tarasov 2002. *Russkij associativnyj slovar'.* Moscow: Astrel' – ASVOL.

Karlinskij, A. E. 1990. *Osnovy teorii vzaimodejstvija jazykov.* Alma-Ata: Gulum.

Katičić, R. 2001. Croatian linguistic loyalty. *International Journal of the Sociology of Language* 147:17–29.

Kazojć, Jerzy 2009. *Otwarty słownik frekwencyjny leksemów*. https://pl.wiktionary.org/ wiki/Indeks:Polski_-_Najpopularniejsze_słowa_1–1000_wersja_Jerzego_Kazojcia, accessed on August 9, 2017.

Keesing, Roger M. 1974. Theories of culture. *Annual Review of Anthropology* 3:73–97.

Kempgen, Sebastian, Peter Kosta, Tilman Berger, and Karl Gutschmidt, eds. 2007. *Die slavischen Sprachen: Ein internationales Handbuch zu ihrer Struktur, ihrer Geschichte und ihrer Erforschung*, vol. I. Berlin and New York: Mouton de Gruyter.

eds. 2014. *Die slavischen Sprachen: Ein internationales Handbuch zu ihrer Struktur, ihrer Geschichte und ihrer Erforschung*, vol. II. Berlin and New York: Mouton de Gruyter.

Khodova, K. I. 1960. *Jazykovoe rodstvo slavjanskih narodov (na materiale slovarja)*. Moscow: GUP Ministerstva prosveščenija RSFR.

Kilgarriff, Adam. 2013. *Terminology Finding, Parallel Corpora and Bilingual Word Sketches in the Sketch Engine*. www.mt-archive.info/10/Aslib-2013-Kilgarriff.pdf, accessed on May 22, 2018.

Kinezsa, István. 1955. *A magyar nyelv szláv jövevényszavai*. Budapest: Akadémiai kiado.

Klaić, Bratoljub. 1951. *Rječnik stranih riječi, izraza i kratica*. Zagreb: Zora.

Klajn, Ivan. 1992. *Rečnik novih reči*. Novi Sad: Matica srpska.

1996. Leksika. In Milorad Radovanović (ed.), *Srpski jezik na kraju veka*. Belgrade: Institut za srpski jezik SANU – Službeni glasnik, pp. 37–87.

1998. O jednom "lahko" napisanom udžbeniku. *Jezik danas* 7:17–19.

2001. Neologisms in present-day Serbian. *International Journal of the Sociology of Language* 151:89–110.

2017. *Rečnik jezičkih nedoumica* (13th ed.). Novi Sad: Prometej.

Klajn, Ivan and Milan Šipka. 2006. *Veliki rečnik stranih reči i izraza*, Novi Sad: Prometej.

Kondrašov, N. A. 1986. *Slavjanskie jazyki*. Moscow: Prosveščenie.

Koopmann-Holm, B. and J. L. Tsai. 2014. Focusing on the negative: Cultural differences in expressions of sympathy. *Journal of Personality and Social Psychology* 107(6):1092–1115.

Kordić, Snježana. 2010. *Jezik i nacionalizam*. Zagreb: Durieux.

2017. Personal web page http://snjezana-kordic.from.hr, containing the author's published papers on Serbo-Croatian, accessed on August 25, 2017.

Kornilov, O. D. 2003. *Jazykovye kartiny mira kak proizvodnye nacional'nyh mentalitetov* (2nd ed.). Moscow: ČeRo.

2014. *Jazykovye katrtiny mira kak proizvodnye nacional'nyh mentalitetov* (4th ed.). Moscow: Knižnyj dom Universitet.

Korolev, N. 2017. *Anglo-russkij slovar'*. slovarus.info/eng_k.php, accessed on August 10, 2017.

Kosta, Peter. 1986. *Probleme der Švejk-Übersetzungen in den west- und südslavischen Sprachen. Linguistische Studien zur Translation literarischer Texte*. Munich: Sager.

Kovačec, August. 1996/1997. Bosnie-Herzegovine. In Hans Goebl, Peter H. Nelde, Zdenek Stary, and Wolfgang Wölck (eds.), *Kontaktlinguistik: Ein Internationales Handbuch zeitgenössiger Forschung/Contact Linguistics: An International*

Handbook of Contemporary Research (2 vols.). Berlin and New York: Walter De Gruyter, vol. II, pp. 1434–1442.

Kövecses, Zoltán. 2003. Language, figurative thought, and cross-cultural comparison. *Metaphor & Symbol* 18(4):311–320.

2004. Introduction: Cultural variation in metaphor. *European Journal of English Studies* 8(3):263–274.

2005. *Metaphor in Culture: Universality and Variation.* Cambridge: Cambridge University Press.

2010. Culture and language. *Studia Slavica* 55(2):339–345.

Kramer, Christina. 1996/1997. Bulgarian-Macedonian. In Hans Goebl, Peter H. Nelde, Zdenek Stary, and Wolfgang Wölck (eds.), *Kontaktlinguistik: Ein Internationales Handbuch zeitgenössiger Forschung/Contact Linguistics: An International Handbook of Contemporary Research* (2 vols.). Berlin and New York: Walter De Gruyter, vol. II, pp. 1498–1506.

Krečmer, Ana 2015. O pitanjima slovenskog jeziičkko-kulturnog identiteta pravoslavni Sloveni van pravoslavne Slavije. *Južnoslovenski filolog* 71(3–4):9–27. DOI 10.2298/JFI1504009K.

Kroskrity, Paul V. 2010. Language ideologies: Evolving perspectives. In Jaspers, Jürgen, Jan-Ola Östman, and Jef Verschueren (eds.) *Society and Language Use* (Handbook of Pragmatics Highlights 7). Amsterdam: John Benjamin, pp. 192–211.

Kuznetsova, E. V. 1982. *Leksikologija russkogo jazyka.* Moscow: Vysšaja škola.

Kymlicka, Will. 1995. *Multicultural Citizenship.* Oxford: Oxford University Press.

Labrie, Normand. 1996/1997a. Politique linguistique. In Hans Goebl, Peter H. Nelde, Zdenek Stary, and Wolfgang Wölck (eds.), *Kontaktlinguistik: Ein Internationales Handbuch zeitgenössiger Forschung/Contact Linguistics: An International Handbook of Contemporary Research* (2 vols.). Berlin and New York: Walter De Gruyter, vol. I, pp. 826–833.

1996/1997b. Territorialite. In Hans Goebl, Peter H. Nelde, Zdenek Stary, and Wolfgang Wölck (eds.), *Kontaktlinguistik: Ein Internationales Handbuch zeitgenössiger Forschung/Contact Linguistics: An International Handbook of Contemporary Research* (2 vols.). Berlin and New York: Walter De Gruyter, vol. I, pp. 210–218.

Lakoff, George 1987. *Women, Fire, and Dangerous Things,* Chicago: University of Chicago Press.

Lakoff, George and Mark Johnson 1980. *Metaphors We Live By.* Chicago: University of Chicago Press.

1999. *Philosophy in the Flesh: The Embodied Mind and its Challenge to Western Thought.* New York: Basic Books.

Lallukka, G. 1985. Sopostavlenie slavjanskih zaimstvovanii v vengerskom i finskom jazykah. *Studia Slavica Finlandensia* 2:81–109.

Langacker, Ronald W. 1987. *Foundations of Cognitive Grammar: Theoretical Prerequisites.* Stanford, CA: Stanford University Press.

1991. *Concept, Image, and Symbol: The Cognitive Basis of Grammar.* The Hague: Mouton de Gruyter.

Langston, Keith and Anita Peti-Stantić. 2014. *Language Planning and National Identity in Croatia.* Houndmills and New York: Palgrave Macmillan.

Larionova, A. Ju. 2014. *Frazeologičeskij slovar' sovremennogo russkogo jazyka.* Moscow: Adelant.

László, Bulcsú. 1993. Pabirci redničkoga i obavjèstničkoga pojmovlja oko razumnih sustava. In *Obrada jezika i prikaz znanja.* Zagreb: Zavod za informacijske studije, pp. 11–73.

Lehmann, Alise and Françoise Martin-Berthet. 1998. *Introduction à la lexicologie: Sémantique et morphologie.* Paris: Dunod.

Lehmann, Volkmar. 1988a. An essay on crosslinguistic phenomena in the development of Slavic standard languages. In Peter Hill and Volkmar Lehmann, *Standard Language in the Slavic World: Papers on Sociolinguistics by Hamburg Linguists.* Munich: Verlag Otto Sagner, pp. 126–146.

1988b. Introduction: Slavic standard languages and the relationship between language contiua and language systems. In Peter Hill and Volkmar Lehmann, *Standard Language in the Slavic World: Papers on Sociolinguistics by Hamburg Linguists.* Munich: Verlag Otto Sagner, pp. 9–23.

Lehr-Spławiński, Tadeusz. 1946. *O pochodzeniu i praojczyźnie Słowian.* Poznań: Wydawnictwo Instytutu Zachodniego.

1951. *Język polski: pochodzenie, powstanie, rozwój.* Warsaw: Arcta.

1957. Zapożyczenia łacińskie w języku prasłowiańskim. In *Studia i szkice wybrane z językoznawstwa słowiańskiego,* vol. I, pp. 196–200.

Lekov, Ivan. 1955. *Edinstvo i nacionalno svoeobrazie na slavjanskite ezici v tehnija osnoven rečnikov fond.* Sofia: BAN.

Lewaszkiewicz, Tadeusz. 2011. Tendencje integracyjne/unifikacyjne i dezintegracyjne w historii języków słowiańskich. In Irina Abisogomjan (ed.), *Lingvokul'turnoe prostranstvo sovremennoj Evropy čerez prizmu malyh i bol'šihjazykov: k 70-letiio professora Aleksandra Dmitrieviča Duličenko.* Tartu: Tartu Ülikooli Kirjastus, pp. 124–137.

Lilič, G. A. 1973. K probleme ustanovlenija mežslavjanskogo leksičeskogo i semantičeskogo vlijanija. *Vestnik Leningradskogo universiteta* (Serija "Istorija, jazyk", no. 14):111–116.

Lindert, Bronisława. 1989. Nazwy zabudowań mieszkalnych w językach Słowiańskich. In Stefan Warchoł (ed.), *Interferencje językowe na różnych obszarach słowiańszczyzny.* Lublin: UMCS, pp. 177–182.

Lipka, Leonhard. 1992. *An Outline of English Lexicology* (1st ed.). Tübingen: Max Niemeyer.

2002. *Outline of English lexicology* (3rd ed.). Tübingen: G. Narr.

Liskovec, I. V. 2002. Trasjanka: proishoždenie, suščnost', funkcionirovanie. In *Antropologija: Fol'kloristika – Lingvistika. Sbornik statej,* 2. St. Petersburg: European University, pp. 329–343.

Ljaševskaja O. N. and S. A. Šarov, 2009. *Častotnyj slovar' sovremennogo russkogo jazyka (na materialah Nacional'nogo korpusa russkogo jazyka).* Moscow: Azbukovnik.

Logar, Tine. 1983/1984. Slovenski dialekti – temeljni vir za rekonstrukcijo razvoja slovenskega jezika. *Jezik in slovstvo* 29:285–288.

Logar, Tine and Jakob Rigler. 2016. *Karta slovenskih narečij z večjim naselji* (Tine Logar and Jakob Rigler, 1983), amended by the Dialectological Section of the ISJFR ZRC SAZU. www.fran.si/204/sla-slovenski-lingvisticni-atlas/datoteke/SL A_Karta-narecij.pdf, accessed on September 17, 2017.

Lubaś, Władysław. 2014. Sprach(en)politik in Ländern mit slavischer Mehrheitssprache. In Karl Gutschmidt, Sebastian Kempgen, Tilman Berger, and Peter Kosta (eds.), *Die slavischen Sprachen/The Slavic Languages: An International Handbook of their Structure, their History and their Investigation*. Berlin: De Gruyter Mouton, vol. II, pp. 1985–1997.

Lučić, Radovan. ed. 2002. *Lexical Norm and National Language: Lexicography and Language Policy in South Slavic Languages after 1989* (Die Welt der Slaven Sammelband 14). Munich: Otto Sagner.

Lunt, Horace G. 1984. Some sociolinguistic aspects of Macedonian and Bulgarian. In Benjamin A. Stolz, I. R. Titnik, and Lubomir Doležel (eds.), *Language and Literary Theory: In Honor of Ladislav Matejka*. Ann Arbor: University of Michigan Department of Slavic Languages and Literatures, pp. 83–132.

Lustig, Myron. W. and Jolene Koester. 1999. *Intercultural Competence: Interpersonal Communication across Cultures* (3rd ed.). New York: Longman.

Maglajlić, Munib. 2002. *Za bosanski jezik.* http://vkbi.open.net.ba/Aktuelnosti/021114 _files/PoveljaBJezik.htm, accessed on December 17, 2017.

Markova, E. M. 2016. Semantičeskaja evolucija praslovjanskoj leksiki (na materiale imën suščestvitel'nyh). Moscow: Moscow State University Press.

Markowski, Andrzej. 2004/2005. Językoznawstwo normatywne dziś i jutro: zadania, szanse, zagrożenia. *Postscriptum* 48–49:126–139.

2005. *Kultura języka polskiego*. Warsaw: Wydawnictwo naukowe PWN.

Marti, Roland. 2014. Rechtlicher und faktischer Status slavischer Standardsprachen und Sprachenkonflikte. In Karl Gutschmidt, Sebastian Kempgen, Tilman Berger, and Peter Kosta (eds.), *Die slavischen Sprachen/The Slavic Languages: An International Handbook of their Structure, their History and their Investigation*. Berlin: De Gruyter Mouton, vol. II, pp. 1972–1984.

Mathiot, Madeleine and Dorothy Rissel. 1996/1997. Lexicon and word formation. In Hans Goebl, Peter H. Nelde, Zdenek Stary, and Wolfgang Wölck (eds.), *Kontaktlinguistik: Ein Internationales Handbuch zeitgenössiger Forschung/ Contact Linguistics: An International Handbook of Contemporary Research* (2 vols.). Berlin and New York: Walter De Gruyter, vol. I, pp. 124–130.

Matras, Yaron. 2009. *Language Contact*. Cambridge: Cambridge University Press.

Matsumoto, David. 1996. *Culture and Psychology*. Pacific Grove, CA: Brooks/Cole.

Matthiessen, C. M. I. M, Marvin Lam, and Kazuhiro Teruya. 2010. *Key Terms in Systemic Functional Linguistics*. London: Continuum International Publishing.

Mayo, Peter. 1993. Belorussian. In Bernard Comrie and Greville G. Corbett (eds.), *The Slavonic Languages*. London and New York: Routledge, pp. 887–946.

McEnery, T. and A. Wilson. 2001. *Corpus Linguistics*. Edinburgh: Edinburgh University Press.

Meillet, Antoine. 1903. *Introduction à l'étude comparative des langues indo-européennes*. Paris: Libraire Hachette et Cie.

Mencken, H. L. 1921. *The American Langauge*. New York: Alfred Knopf. www.bar leby.com/185, accessed on May 5, 2018.

Mešanović-Meša, Emina. 2012. Rječnici bosanskog jezika. In Josip Baotić, Senahid Halilović, Jagoda Jurić-Kappel, Marina Katnić-Baakaršić, and Svein Mønnesland (eds.), *Bosanskohercegovački slavistički kongres I*, Sarajevo: Slavistički komitet, pp. 35–45.

Micaglia, Jacobus. 1649–1651. *Thesaurus linguae illyricae sive Dictionarium Illyricum in quo verba Illyrica Italice et Latine redduntur. Blago jezika slovinskoga ili slovnik u komu izgovarju se rječi slovinske latinski i diački*. Lauratium: Serafini.

Mihaljević, Milan. 2002–2014. *Slavenska poredbena gramatika* (vols. I and II). Zagreb: Školska knjiga.

Miklosich, Franz. 1875. *Vergleichende Grammatik der Slavischen Sprachen*. Vienna: Wilhelm Braumüller.

Milroy, James and Lesley Milroy. 2012. *Authority in Language: Investigating Standard English* (4th ed.). Oxford: Routledge.

Miodunka, Władysław. 1989. *Podstawy leksykologii i leksykografii*. Warsaw: PWN.

Mitrinović, Vera. 2012. *Południe – Północ: Serbsko-polskie paralele językowe*. Poznań: Wydawnictwo Naukowe Uniwersytetu im. Adama Mickiewicza.

MKS. 1965. *Voprosnik Obščeslavjanskogo lingvističeskogo atlasa*. Moscow: Nauka.

MLA. 2017. *MLA International Bibliography*, electronic database. http://info.lib.asu.edu/NetAns2/gate.exe?f=doc&p_d=dbdb&state=8q4bq6.2.1, accessed on November 9, 2017.

Mokienko, Valerij. 2009a. Phraseologie/Phraseology. In Karl Gutschmidt, Sebastian Kempgen, Tilman Berger, and Peter Kosta (eds.), *Die slavischen Sprachen/The Slavic Languages: An International Handbook of their Structure, their History and their Investigation*. Berlin: De Gruyter Mouton, vol. I, pp. 792–801.

2009b. *Phraseologische Einheiten*. In Karl Gutschmidt, Sebastian Kempgen, Tilman Berger, and Peter Kosta (eds.), *Die slavischen Sprachen/The Slavic Languages: An International Handbook of their Structure, their History and their Investigation*. Berlin: De Gruyter Mouton, vol. I, pp. 802–808.

Mokienko, Valerij M. and Harry Walter. 2014. Soziolekte in der Slavia (Überblick). In Karl Gutschmidt, Sebastian Kempgen, Tilman Berger, and Peter Kosta (eds.), *Die slavischen Sprachen/The Slavic Languages: An International Handbook of their Structure, their History and their Investigation*. Berlin: De Gruyter Mouton, vol. II, pp. 2145–2170.

Moore, Colleen, A. 1980. Major definitions of the concept of culture: A review of the Literature. *Information Analysis* 70 (January). https://files.eric.ed.gov/fulltext/ED229292.pdf.

Morkovkin, V. V. and Morkovkina, V. A. 1997. *Russkie agnonimy slova kotorye my ne znaem*. Moscow: Institut russkogo jazyka im. A. S. Puškina.

Moskovljević, Miloš 1966. *Rečnik savremenog srpskohrvatskog jezika s jezičkim savetnikom*. Belgrade: Tehnička knjiga, Nolit.

Mršević-Radović, Dragana. 2008. *Frazeologija i nacionalna kultura*. Belgrade: Društvo za srpski jezik i književnost Srbije.

Müller, Daniel and Monika Wingender. 2013. *Typen slavischer Standardsprachen Theoretische, methodische und empirische Zugänge*. Wiesbaden: Harrassowitz Verlag.

Myers-Scotton, Carol. 2002. *Contact Linguistics: Bilingual Encounters and Grammatical Outcomes*. Oxford and New York: Oxford University Press.

Nahtigal, Rajko. 1952. *Slovanski jeziki*. Ljubljana: Državna založba Slovenije.

Nečak Lük, Albina. 1996/1997. Slovenia. In Hans Goebl, Peter H. Nelde, Zdenek Stary, and Wolfgang Wölck (eds.), *Kontaktlinguistik: Ein Internationales Handbuch zeitgenössiger Forschung/Contact Linguistics: An International Handbook of Contemporary Research* (2 vols.). Berlin and New York: Walter De Gruyter, vol. II, pp. 1416–1424.

Nečas, Jaroslav. 1989. *Slovensko-český a česko-slovenský slovník rozdílných výrazů.* Prague: Státní pedagogické nakladatelství.

Nekvapil, Jiri. 1996/1997. Tschechien. In Hans Goebl, Peter H. Nelde, Zdenek Stary, and Wolfgang Wölck (eds.), *Kontaktlinguistik: Ein Internationales Handbuch zeitgenössiger Forschung/Contact Linguistics: An International Handbook of Contemporary Research* (2 vols.). Berlin and New York: Walter De Gruyter, vol. II, pp. 1641–1650.

Neweklowsky, Gerhard. 1996/1997. Jugoslawien. In Hans Goebl, Peter H. Nelde, Zdenek Stary, and Wolfgang Wölck (eds.), *Kontaktlinguistik: Ein Internationales Handbuch zeitgenössiger Forschung/Contact Linguistics: An International Handbook of Contemporary Research* (2 vols.). Berlin and New York: Walter De Gruyter, vol. II, pp. 1407–1416.

ed. 2003. *Bosanski – hrvatski – srpski /Bosnisch – Kroatisch – Serbish Aktuelna pitanja jezika Bošnjaka, Hrvata, Srba i Crnogoraca* (Wiener Slawistischer Almanach, Sonderband 57). Vienna: Gesellschaft zur Förderung slawistischer Studien (Wien).

Niklas-Salminen, Aïno. 1997. *La lexicologie.* Paris: Armand Colin.

Nisbett, Richard E. 2003. *The Geography of Thought.* New York, London, Toronto, and Sydney: The Free Press.

Oczko, Anna. 2014. *Rumuńska słowianszczyzna.* Kraków: Collegium Columbinum.

OED. 1989. *Oxford English Dictionary Online* (www.oed.com). Oxford: Oxford University Press.

Okano, Kaname. 2015. Leksiko-semantičeskie osobennosti glagolov peremeščenija v serbskom i russkom jazykah. In Ljudmila Popović and Motoki Nomachi (eds.), *The Serbian Language as Viewed by the East and the West: Synchrony, Diachrony, and Typology.* Sapporo: Slavic and Eurasian Research Center, pp. 203–218.

Okuka, Miloš. 1998. *Eine Sprache – viele Erben: Sprachpolitik als Nationalisierungsinstrument in Exjugoslawien.* Klagenfurt: Wieser Verlag.

Olivesi, Claude. 1996/1997. Nationalismes. In Hans Goebl, Peter H. Nelde, Zdenek Stary, and Wolfgang Wölck (eds.), *Kontaktlinguistik: Ein Internationales Handbuch zeitgenössiger Forschung/Contact Linguistics: An International Handbook of Contemporary Research* (2 vols.). Berlin and New York: Walter De Gruyter, vol. I, pp. 200–203.

Ondrejovič, Slavomír. 1996/1997. Slowakei. In Hans Goebl, Peter H. Nelde, Zdenek Stary, and Wolfgang Wölck (eds.), *Kontaktlinguistik: Ein Internationales Handbuch zeitgenössiger Forschung/Contact Linguistics: An International Handbook of Contemporary Research* (2 vols.). Berlin and New York: Walter De Gruyter, vol. II, pp. 1669–1678.

2011. Jazyková norma z pohľadu slovenskej sociolingvistiky. In Irina Abisogomjan (ed.), *Lingvokuľturnoe prostranstvo sovremennoj Evropy čerez prizmu malyh i boľših jazykov: k 70-letiju professora Aleksandra Dmitrieviča Duličenko.* Tartu: Tartu Ülikooli Kirjastus, pp. 334–342.

Ondruš, Pavel. 1972. *Slovenská leksikológia: II Náuka o slovnej zásobe.* Bratislava: Slovenské pedagogické nakladateľstvo.

Onysko Alexander and Esme Winter-Froemel. 2011. Necessary loans – luxury loans? Exploring the pragmatic dimension of borrowing. *Journal of Pragmatics* 43 (6):1550–1567. http://dx.doi.org/10.1016/j.pragma.2010.12.004.

Ordeshook, Peter. 1992 *A Political Theory Primer*. London: Routledge.

Otašević, Đorđe. 2001. Electronic list of 2000 new words kindly made available by the author.

2012. *Frazeološki rečnik srpskog jezika*. Novi Sad: Prometej.

Ožegov, S. I. and N. Ju. Švedova. 1992. *Tolkovyj slovar' russkogo jazyka*. Moscow: Az'.

Palmer, Garry. 1996. *Toward a Theory of Cultural Linguistics*. Austin: University of Texas Press.

Panzer, Baldur, ed. 2000. *Die sprachliche Situation in der Slavia zehn Jahre nach der Wende*. Frankfurt am Main: Peter Lang.

Papp, Ferenc. 1973. A few general characteristics of words of Slavic origin in the Hungarian language. In *VII Międzynarodowy Kongres Slawistów w Warszawie 1973: Streszczenia referatów i komunikatów*. Warsaw: PAN, pp. 407–408.

Paulasto, Heli, Lea Meriläinen, Helka Riionheimo, and Maria Kok, eds. 2014. *Language Contacts at the Crossroads of Disciplines*. Newcastle-upon-Tyne: Cambridge Scholars Publishing.

Pecyna, Aneta. 1998. Leksyka obsceniczna w języku polskim i serbsko-chorwackim (MA thesis). Poznań: UAM.

Picchio, Riccardo. 1984. Guidelines for a comparative study of the language question among the Slavs. In Riccardo Picchio and Harvey Goldblalt (eds.), *Aspects of the Slavic Language Question*. New Haven, CT: Yale Concilium on International and Area Studies, pp. 1–42.

Picchio, Riccardo and Harvey Goldblalt, eds. 1984. *Aspects of the Slavic Language Question*. New Haven, CT: Yale Concilium on International and Area Studies.

Picoche, Jacqueline. 1977. *Précis de lexicologie française*. Paris: Nathan-Université.

Piper, Predrag. 2003. Asocijativni rečnici slovenskih jezika i etnokulturni stereotipi. *Slavistika* 7:22–32.

Plotnikova, A. A. 2000. *Slovari i narodnaja kul'tura: Očerki slavjanskoj leksikografii*. Moscow: Institut slavjanovedenija RAN.

Pohl, Heinz-Dieter. 1990. Slovenske (in slovanske) izposojenke v nemškem jeziku Koroške. *Slavistična revija* 38(2):101–104.

Polanski, Kazimierz. 1993. Polabian. In Bernard Comrie and Greville G. Corbett (eds.), *The Slavonic Languages*. London and New York: Routledge, pp. 795–825.

Polguère, Alain. 2002. *Notions de base en lexicologie*. Montreal: OLST.

Poplack, Shana and Nathalie Dion. 2012. Myths and facts about loanword development. *Language Variation and Change* 24:279–315.

Poplack, Shana and David Sankoff. 1984. Borrowing: The synchrony of integration. *Linguistics* 22:99–135.

Poplack, Shana, David Sankoff, and Christopher Miller. 1988. The social correlates and linguistic processes of lexical borrowing and assimilation. *Linguistics* 26:47–104.

Popović, Ivan. 1955. *Istorija srpskohrvatskog jezika*. Novi Sad: Matica srpska.

Popović, Ljudmila i Motoki Nomahci. 2015. *The Serbian Language as Viewed by the East and the West: Synchrony, Diachrony, and Typology*. Sapporo: Hokkaido University SRC.

Popović, Miodrag. 1964. *Vuk Stef. Karadžić*. Belgrade: Nolit.

1981. *Jota.* Tršić and Belgrade: Vukov sabor/Vukova zadužbina – Rad.

Popowska-Taborska, Hanna, ed. 1997. *Leksyka słowiańska na warsztacie językoznawcy.* Warsaw: Słowiański ośrodek wydawniczy.

1998. *Szkice z kaszubszczyzny.* Gdańsk: GTN.

2014. *Wczesne dzieje Słowian w świetle ich języka* (3rd ed.). Warsaw: Instytut Slawistyki PAN.

Popowska-Taborska, Hanna and Wiesław Boryś. 1996. *Leksyka kaszubska na tle słowiańskim.* Warsaw: Słowiański ośrodek wydawniczy.

Preston, Peter W. 1997. *Political/Cultural Identity: Citizens and Nations in a Global Era.* London: Sage Publications.

Priestly, Tom. 1983. Slovene and German in contact: Some lexical analyses. *Canadian Slavonic Papers* 25(1):128–146.

1993. Slovene. In Bernard Comrie and Greville G. Corbett (eds.), *The Slavonic Languages.* London and New York: Routledge, pp. 388–453.

Pronk-Tiethoff, Saskia. 2013. *Germanic Loanwords in Proto-Slavic.* Amsterdam: Editions Rodopi. ProQuest Ebook Central, accessed on September 28, 2017.

Prutkov, K. P. 1854. *Plody razdum'ja: Mysli i aforizmy.* http://lib.ru/LITRA/PRUTKOW/plody.txt, accessed on December 2, 2018.

Pupovac, Milorad. 1996/1997. Croatia. In Hans Goebl, Peter H. Nelde, Zdenek Stary, and Wolfgang Wölck (eds.), *Kontaktlinguistik: Ein Internationales Handbuch zeitgenössiger Forschung/Contact Linguistics: An International Handbook of Contemporary Research* (2 vols.). Berlin and New York: Walter De Gruyter, vol. II, pp. 1424–1434.

Quirk, Randolph, Sidney Greenbaum, Geoffrey Leech, and Jan Svartvik. 1985. *A Comprehensive Grammar of the English Language.* London: Longman.

Radbil', T. B. 2013. *Osnovy izučenija jazykovogo mentaliteta* (3rd ed.). Moscow: Flinta, Nauka.

Radić, Prvoslav. 2015. On the Oriental lexicon in the Serbian language. In Ljudmila Popović and Motoki Nomahci (eds.), *The Serbian Language as Viewed by the East and the West: Synchrony, Diachrony, and Typology.* Sapporo: Hokkaido University SRC, pp. 133–149.

Revzina, O. G. 1969. *Struktura slovoobrazovatel'nyh polej v slavjanskih jazykah.* Moscow: University of Moscow Press.

Rey, Alain. *La lexicologie* (Lectures 3e tirage). Paris: Klincksieck, 1980.

Riley, Philip. 2007. *Language, Culture and Identity: An Ethnolinguistic Perspective.* London: Continuum.

Rimaschrewskaja, E. L. 1999. *Modernes Deutsch-Russisches Russisch-Deutsches Wörterbuch* (3rd ed.). Moscow: Firma NIK P.

Ristić, Svetomir and Jovan Kangrga. 1936. *Enciklopedijski nemačko-srpskohrvatski rečnik sa srpskofonetičnom oznakom izgovora književnoga nemačkoga.* Belgrade: Ćuković.

Roget, Peter Mark. 1916. *Thesaurus of English Words and Phrases.* London: Longmans, Green, and Co.

Rokoszowa, Jolanta. 1996/1997. Poland. In Hans Goebl, Peter H. Nelde, Zdenek Stary, and Wolfgang Wölck (eds.), *Kontaktlinguistik: Ein Internationales Handbuch zeitgenössiger Forschung/Contact Linguistics: An International Handbook of Contemporary Research* (2 vols.). Berlin and New York: Walter De Gruyter, vol. II, pp. 1583–1594.

Romaine, Suzanne. 2000. *Language in Society: An Introduction to Sociolinguistics* (2nd ed.). Oxford: Oxford University Press.

Romanova, N .P. 1985. *Slovoobrazovanie i jazykovye svjazi*. Kiev: Naukova dumka.

Ross, Sheldon. 2010. *Introductory Statistics*. Amsterdam: Academic Press/Elsevier.

Rothstein, Robert A. 1993. Polish. In Bernard Comrie and Greville G. Corbett (eds.), *The Slavonic Languages*. London and New York: Routledge, pp. 686–758.

Rozencvejg, V. Ju. 1972a. Osnovnye voprosy teorii jazykovyh kontaktov. *Novoe v lingvistike* 6 (special issue: *Jazykovye kontakty*):5–24.

1972b. *Jazykovye kontakty: Lingvističeskaja problematika*. Leningrad: Nauka.

Rozwadowski, Jan Michał. 1961. Stosunki leksykalne między językami słowiańskimi a irańskimi. *Wybór pism* 2:114–125.

Rupnik, J. 1996. Reawakening of European nationalisms. *Social Research* 63 (2):41–75.

Samardžija, Marko. 2015. *Srpsko–hrvatski objasnidbeni rječnik*. Zagreb: Matica hrvatska.

Sapir, Eduard. 1921. *Language: An Introduction to the Study of Speech*, New York: Harcourt, Brace. www.bartleby.com/186, accessed on May 5, 2018.

Saussure, Ferdinand de. [1916] 1972. *Cours de linguistique Générale: Edition critique*, ed. & comm. Tullio de Mauro. Paris: Payot.

Savezni zavod za statistiku. 1993. *Popis stanovništva, domaćinstava i stanova 1991 godine: Nacionalna pripadnost, podaci za opštine i naselja* knj.1. Belgrade: Savezni zavod za statitstiku (National Bureau of Statistics).

Savić, Svenka. 2009. Uputsvo za standardizaciju rodno osetljivog jezika. In *Integritet naučne misli, Njegoševi dani 1*, Nikšić: Filozofski fakultet, pp. 301–320.

Saville-Troike, Muriel. 1997. The ethnographic analysis of communicative events. In N. Coupland and A. Jaworski (eds.), *Sociolinguistics: A Reader and Coursebook*. Basingstoke: Macmillan, pp. 126–144.

Scatton, Ernest A. 1993. Bulgarian. In Bernard Comrie and Greville G. Corbett (eds.), *The Slavonic Languages*. London and New York: Routledge, pp. 188–248.

Schein, Edgar. 1984. Coming to a new awareness of organizational culture. *Sloan Management Review* 252:3–16.

1990. Organizational culture. *American Psychologist* 452:109–119.

Schenker, Alexander M. 1993. Proto-Slavonic. In Bernard Comrie and Greville G. Corbett (eds.), *The Slavonic Languages*. London and New York: Routledge, pp. 60–124.

1995. *The Dawn of Slavic*. New Haven and London: Yale University Press.

Schleicher, August 1861. *Compendium der vergleichenden Grammatik der Indogermanischen Sprachen*. Weimar: Böhlau.

Schulte, Kim. 2009. Loanwords in Romanian. In Martin Haspelmath and Uri Tadmor (eds.), *Loanwords in the World Languages: A Comparative Handbook*. Berlin: Walter de Gruyter, pp. 230–259.

Schwartz, S. H. 1992. Universals in the content and structure of values: Theoretical advances and empirical tests in 20 countries. In M. Zanna (ed.), *Advances in Experimental Social Psychology*. San Diego: Academic Press, 1–65.

1994. Beyond individualism/collectivism: New dimensions of values. In U. Kim, H. C. Triandis, C. Kagitcibasi, S. C. Choi, and G. Yoon (eds.), *Individualism and Collectivism: Theory Application and Methods*. Newbury Park, CA: Sage, 85–119.

Schwartz, Seth J., Marilyn J. Montgomery, and Ervin Briones. 2006. The role of identity in acculturation among immigrant people: Theoretical propositions, empirical questions, and applied recommendations. *Human Development* 49:1–30.

Schwarze, Christoph i Dieter Wunderlich. 1985. *Handbuch der Lexikologie.* Königstein: Athenäum.

Selimović, Meša. 1967. *Za i protiv Vuka.* Belgrade: BIGZ.

Seliščev, A. M. 2010 [1914]. *Vedenie v sravnitel'nuю grammatiku slavjanskih jazykov.* Moscow: KomKniga.

Sharifian, Farzad 2011. *Cultural Conceptualisations and Language.* Philadelphia: John Benjamins.

2017. *Cultural Linguistics.* Philadelphia: John Benjamins.

Shevelev, George. 1965. *A Prehistory of Slavic: The Historical Phonology of Common Slavic.* New York: Columbia University Press.

1993. Ukrainian. In Bernard Comrie and Greville G. Corbett (eds.), *The Slavonic Languages.* London and New York: Routledge, pp. 947–998.

Short, David. 1993a. Czech. In Bernard Comrie and Greville G. Corbett (eds.), *The Slavonic Languages.* London and New York: Routledge, pp. 455–532.

1993b. Slovak. In Bernard Comrie and Greville G. Corbett (eds.), *The Slavonic Languages.* London and New York: Routledge, pp. 533–592.

Sierociuk, Jerzy. 1993. O możliwości badania zmian zachodzących w systemie leksykalnym języka wsi uwag kilka. In Joanna Kamper-Warejko (ed.), *Studia nad słownictwem dawnym i współczesnym języków słowiańskich.* Toruń: Wydawnictwo Uniwersytetu Mikołaja Kopernika, pp. 285–290.

Simonović, Marko. 2015. Lexicon immigration service: Prolegomena to a theory of loanword integration. Doctoral thesis. www.lotpublications.nl/Documents/393_ fulltext.pdf, accessed on January 25, 2018.

Singleton, F. 1989. *A Short History of the Yugoslav Peoples.* Cambridge: Cambridge University Press.

Skvorcov, L. I. 1980. *Teoretičeskie osnovy kul'tury reči.* Moscow: Nauka.

Smakman, Dick. 2012. The definition of the standard language: A survey in seven countries. *International Journal of the Sociology of Language.* No. 218 (November):25–58.

Smith, Peter B. and Michael H. Bond. 1998. *Social Psychology across Cultures.* London: Prentice Hall Europe.

Sočanac, Lelija. 2002. Talijanizmi u hrvatskom jeziku. *Suvremena lingvistika* 53/54 (1–2): 127–142.

Spencer-Oatey, Helen. 2008. *Culturally Speaking: Culture, Communication and Politeness Theory* (2nd ed.). London: Continuum.

2012. What is culture? A compilation of quotations. *GlobalPAD Core Concepts.* Available at GlobalPAD Open House, http://go.warwick.ac.uk/globalpadintercultural, (accessed on June 27, 2017.)

Stachowski, Stanisław. 2014. *Słownik historyczno-etymologiczny turcyzmów w języku polskim.* Kraków: Księgarnia akademicka.

Stanišić, Vanja. 1995. *Srpsko-albanski jezički odnosi.* Belgrade: Balkanološki institut SANU

Stanković, Bogoljub. ur. 1998. *Srpsko-ruski rečnik* (2nd ed.). Novi Sad and Moscow: Budućnost/ Matica Srpska and Russkij jazik.

Steen, Gerard. 2007. *Finding Metaphor in Grammar and Usage*. Amsterdam: John Benjamins.

Stefanović, Marija, Predrag Piper, and Rajna Dragićević. 2005. *Asocijativni rečnik srpskog jezika*. Belgrade: Belgradeska knjiga.

Stern, Dieter and Christian Voss, eds. 2006. *Marginal Linguistic Identities*. Wiesbaden: Harrasovitz Verlag.

Stieber, Zdzisław. 1979. *Zarys gramatyki porównawczej języków słowiańskich*. Warsaw: PWN.

Stone, Gerald. 1993a. Cassubian. In Bernard Comrie and Greville G. Corbett (eds.), *The Slavonic Languages*. London and New York: Routledge, pp. 759–794.

1993b. Sorbian. In Bernard Comrie and Greville G. Corbett (eds.), *The Slavonic Languages*. London and New York: Routledge, pp. 593–685.

Strel'čuk, E. N. 2012. Kul'tura reči: analiz terminov i ponjatij. *Vestnik RUDN, serija Russkij i inostrannye jazyki i metodika ih prepodavanija* 1:12–17.

Suprun, A. E. 1983. *Leksičeskaja tipologija slavjanskih jazykov*. Minsk: Izdatel'stvo BGU im. V. I. Lenina.

Sussex, Ronald and Paul Cubberley. 2006. *The Slavic Languages*. Cambridge: Cambridge University Press.

Svensén, Bo. 2009. A *Handbook of Lexicography: The Theory and Practice of Dictionary-Making*. Cambridge: Cambridge University Press.

Swadesh, Maurice. 2017. *Slavic Swadesh Lists*. https://en.wiktionary.org/wiki/Appendix: Slavic_Swadesh_lists, accessed on August 11, 2017.

Šagirov, A. K. 1989. *Zaimstvovannaja leksika abhazo-adygskih jazykov*. Moscow: Nauka.

Ščerba, L. V. 1957. Sovremennyj literaturnyj russkij jazyk. In *Izabrannye raboty po russkomu jazyku*. Moscow: Nauka, pp. 110–129.

Škaljić, Abdulah. 1966. *Turcizmi u srspkohrvatskom jeziku*. Sarajevo: Svjetlost.

Šipka, Danko. 1987. Vukov leksikografski postupak /na primjeru odnosa prema vulgarizmima i homonimiji. In *Zbornik radova o Vuku Karadžiću*. Sarajevo: Institut za jezik i književnost, pp. 117–122.

1991. *Della Bella* kao začetnik moderne koncepcije rječničkog članka u našoj leksikografiji. *Filologija* 19:31–36.

2000. *A Bibliography of Serbo-Croatian Dictionaries: Serbian, Croatian, and Bosnian Muslim*. Springfield, VA: Dunwoody Press.

2001. *A Database of 44879 Bosnian/Croatian/Serbian Neologisms*, electronic document.

2002a. *A Dictionary of New Bosnian, Croatian, and Serbian Words*. Springfield, VA: Dunwoody Press.

2002b. Poljski i srpski korisnički računarski diskurs: kontrastivna analiza. *Zbornik MS za slavistiku* 61:168–174.

2004. Slavic lexical borrowings in English: Patterns of lexical and cultural transfer. *Studia Slavica Hungarica* 49(3–4):353–364.

2005. *Osnovi leksikologije i srodnih disciplina*. Novi Sad: Matica srpska.

2007a. Osnovna leksička lista. www.staff.amu.edu.pl/~sipkadan/pp/shpo1500.txt, accessed on July 18, 2007.

2007b. *Prilozi za građu leksikološke i metaleksikografske bibliografije*. Belgrade: Alma.

2015. *Lexical Conflict: Theory and Practice.* Cambridge: Cambridge University Press.

2016. Sociolinguistic factors in South Slavic lexicographic traditions: Domingues Rodrigues. In Mᵃ Victoria Domínguez-Rodríguez, Alicia Rodríguez-Álvarez, Gregorio Rodríguez Herrera, and Verónica C. Trujillo-González (eds.), *Words across History: Advances in Historical Lexicography and Lexicology.* Universidad de Las Palmas de Gran Canaria: Servicio de Publicaciones y Difusión Científica, pp. 413–424.

2017a. Leksički slojevi slovenskog kulturnog identiteta. In Rajna Dragićević (ed.), *Putevima reči.* Belgrade: Čigoja, pp. 131–143.

2017b. Semantic change in Slavic inherited lexicon: An initial analysis. *Wiener Slawisticher Almanach* 79:1–24.

Šipka, Milan. 2001. *Standardni jezik i nacionalni odnosi u Bosni i Hercegovini 1850–2000 – Dokumenti,* Sarajevo: Institut za jezik.

2011. *Pravopisni rečnik srpskog jezika.* Novi Sad: Prometej.

Šmelev, D. A. 2005. Leksičeskij sostav russkogo jazyka kak otraženie "russkoj duši." In A. A. Zaliznjak, I. B. Levontina, and A. D. Šmelev, *Ključevye idei russkoj jazykovoj kartiny mira.* Moscow: Jazyki slavjanskoj kul'tury, pp. 25–32.

Šmelev, D. N. 1977. *Sovremennyj russkij jazyk. Leksika.* Moscow: Prosveščenie.

Taagepera, Rein and Bernard Grofman. 1981. Effective size and number of components. *Sociological Research and Methods* 10:63–81.

Takahashi, Hideaki. 2004. Language norms/Sprachnorm. In Ulrich Ammon, Norbert Dittmar, Klaus J. Mattheier, and Peter Trudgill (eds.), *Sociolinguistics: An International Handbook of the Science of Language and Society / Soziolinguistik: Ein internationales Handbuch zur Wissenschaft von Sprache und Gesellschaft* (2nd ed.). Berlin: Walter de Gruyter, vol. I, pp. 172–179.

Temmerman, Rita. 2000. *Towards New Ways of Terminology Description: The Sociocognitive Approach,* Amsterdam: John Benjamins.

Thomas, George 1985. Problems in the study of migratory loanwords in the Slavic languages. *Canadian Slavonic Papers* 27(3): 307–325.

1988. *The Impact of the Illyrian Movement on the Croatian Lexicon.* Munich: Verlag Otto Sagner.

1991. *Linguistic Purism.* London and New York: Longman.

Thomas, Paul-Louis. 1998. Fonction communicative et fonction symbolique de la langue sur l'exemple du serbo-croate: bosniaque, croate, serbe. *Revue des études slaves* 70(1): 27–37.

Thomason, Sarah G. 2001. *Language Contact: An introduction,* Washington, DC: Georgetown University Press.

Tihonov, A. N. 2003. *Slovoobrazovatel'nyj slovar' russkogo jazyka,* vols. 1 and 2. Moscow: Astrel' – ASVOL.

Timberlake, Alan. 1993. Russian. In Bernard Comrie and Greville G. Corbett (eds.), *The Slavonic Languages.* London and New York: Routledge, pp. 827–886.

Timofeev, Boris. 1961. *Pravil'no li my govorim?* Leningrad: Lenizdat.

Tolstaja, S. M., ed. 2013. *Ethnolinguistica Slavica: K 90-letiю akademika Nikity Il'iča Tolstogo.* Moscow: Indrik.

Tolstoj, N. I. 1988. *Istorija i struktura slavjanskih literaturnyh jazykov*. Moscow: Nauka.

1997–1999. *Izabrannye trudy*, vols. 1–3. Moscow: Jazyki russkoj kul'tury.

Trabant, Jürgen. 2006. *Europäisches Sprachdenken von Platon bis Wittgenstein*. Munich: Beck.

2012. *Weltansichten: Wilhelm von Humboldts Sprachprojekt*. Munich: Beck.

Treder, Jerzy. 1996/1997. Polish-Kashubian. In Hans Goebl, Peter H. Nelde, Zdenek Stary, and Wolfgang Wölck (eds.), *Kontaktlinguistik: Ein Internationales Handbuch zeitgenössiger Forschung/Contact Linguistics: An International Handbook of Contemporary Research* (2 vols.). Berlin and New York: Walter De Gruyter, vol. II, pp. 1600–1606.

Triandis, Harry C. 1972. *The Analysis of Subjective Culture*. New York: Wiley.

1994a. Culture and social behavior. In Walter J. Lonner and Roy Malpass (eds.), *Psychology and Culture*. Boston: Allyn & Bacon, pp. 169–173.

1994b. *Culture and Social Behavior*. New York: McGraw Hill.

1995. *Individualism and Collectivism*, Boulder, CO: Westview Press.

Triandis, Harry C. and Eunkook M. Suh 2002. Cultural Influences on Personality. *Annual Revew of Psychology* 53:133–60.

Trier, Jost. 1931. *Der deutsche Wortschatz im Sinnbezirk des Verstandes; die Geschichte eines Sprachlichen Feldes*. Heidelbert: C. Winter.

Trompenaars, Fons and Charles Hampden-Turner. 1997. *Riding the Waves of Culture: Understanding Cultural Diversity in Business* (2nd ed.). London: Nicholas Brealey.

Trubačev, O. N. 1999. *Indoarica v Severnom Pričernomor'e*. Moscow: Nauka.

Trudgill, Peter. 2001. *Sociolinguistic Variation and Change*. Edinburgh: Edinburgh University Press.

Uskufi, Muhamed Hevaji 1631. *Makbuli-'Arif*. Manuscript. Alija Nametak has published an annotated edition in *Građa za povijest književnosti hrvatske*, vol. 29, 1968, pp. 231–280.

Uspenskij, L.V. 1976. *Kul'tura reči*. Moscow: Znanie. http://filfucker.ru/pervoistoch niki/l-v-uspenskiy-kultura-rechi, accessed on May 5, 2017.

Vaillant, André 1950–1977. *Grammaire comparée des langues slaves*. Lyon and Paris: IAC, Paris: Klincksieck.

Vajzović, Hanka. 1999. *Orijentalizmi u književnom djelu: lingvistička analiza*. Sarajevo: Institut za jezik.

Van den Berg, H., Antony S. R. Manstead, Joop van der Pligt, and Daniël H. J. Wigboldus. 2006. The impact of affective and cognitive focus on attitude formation. *Journal of Experimental Social Psychology* 42:373–379.

Van Hout, Roeland and Pieter Muysken. 1994. Modeling Lexical Borrowability. *Language Variation and Change* 6(1):39–62.

Velat, D. 1987. *Popis stanovništva, domaćinstava, stanova u 1981. godini: uporedni pregled broja stanovnika i domaćinstava, 1948, 1953, 1961, 1971 i 1981 i stanova 1971 i 1981: rezultati po opštinama*. Belgrade: Savezni zavod za statistiku.

Veleva, Slavica. 2006. *Tendencii vo zboroobrazuvanjeto vo makedonskiot jazik*. Skopje: author published.

Vendina, T. I. 2002. *Srednevekovyj čelovek v zerkale staroslavjanskogo jazyka.* Moscow: Indrik.

1998. *Russkaja jazykovaja kartina mira skvoz' prizmu slovoobrazovanija: Makrokosm.* Moscow: Indrik.

2014. *Tipologija leksičeskih arealov Slavii.* Moscow and St. Petersburg: Institute of Slavic Studies of the Russian Academy of Sciences/Nestor-Istorija.

Verantius, Faustus. 1595. *Dictionarium quinque nobilissimarum Europae linguarum, Latinae, Italicae, Germanicae, Dalmatiae et Ungaricae cum vocabulis Dalmaticis quae Ungari sibi usurparunt.* Venice: Moretto.

Verkuyl, Henk J., Maarten Janssen, and Frank Jansen. 2003. The codification of usage by labels. In Piet van Sterkenburg (ed.), *A Practical Guide to Lexicography.* Amsterdam: Benjamins, pp. 297–311.

Vesku, Viktor. 1973. Prilog proučavanju rumunskih pozajmica u srpskohrvatskom jeziku. *Književni jezik* 2(1–2):41–44.

Vincenz, Andrzej de and Gerd Hentschel. 2010. *Wörterbuch der deutschen Lehnwörter in der polnischen Schrift- und Standardsprache* (Studia Slavica Oldenburgensia. Band 20). Oldenburg: BIS-Verlag (online).

Vinogradov, V. V. 1967. *Problemy literaturnyh jazykov i zakonomernostej ih obrazovanija i razvitija.* Moscow: Nauka.

Vinokur, G. O. [1929] 2006. *Kul'tura jazyka.* Moscow: Labirint.

Vlajić-Popović, Jasna. 2015. Serbian and Greek: A long history of lexical borrowing in Popović, Ljudmila and Motoki Nomahci. In *The Serbian Language as Viewed by the East and the West: Synchrony, Diachrony, and Typology.* Sapporo: Hokkaido University SRC, pp. 151–172.

Vojvodić, Stanko. 2002. *Rečnik slavizama u rumunskom jeziku.* Kikinda: Narodna biblioteka "Jovan Popović."

Voltiggi (Voltić), Josip. 1803. *Ricsoslovnik illiricskskoga, italianskoga i nimacskoga jezika, s jednom pridpostavljenom grammatikom ili primenstvom: Illyrisch-italienisch und deutscehs Wörtrebuch und Grammatik.* Vienna: Kurtzbeck.

Vrabie, Emil. 1992. Slavic influence on Romanian: A case of exaggeration. *General Linguistics* 32(2–3): 105–110.

Vujanić, Milica, Darinka Gortan-Premk, Milorad Dešić, Rajna Dragićević, Miroslav Nikolić, et al. 2011. *Rečnik srpskoga jezika.* Novi Sad: Matica srpska.

Walczak, Bogdan. 1997. Słownictwo obcego pochodzenia na warsztacie badacza: problem granic ("głębokości") opisu genetycznego. In Hanna Popowska-Taborska (ed.), *Leksyka słowiańska na warsztacie językoznawcy.* Warsaw: Słowiański ośrodek wydawniczy, pp. 269–280.

Warchoł, Stefan, ed., 1989. *Interferencje językowe na różnych obszarach słowiańszczyzny.* Lublin: UMCS.

Waugh, Daniel. 2007. Richthofen's "silk roads": Toward the archaeology of a concept. *The Silk Road* 5(1):4.

Wearing, Michael. 2011. *Social Identity.* Hauppauge: Nova Science Publishers, Inc.

Weber, Max. 1992, 1919. *Politik als Beruf.* Ditzingen: Reclam.

Weinreich, Max. 1945. The YIVO and the problems of our time. Speech at the Annual YIVO Conference on January 5, 1945.

Weinreich, Uriel. 1953. *Languages in Contact: Findings and Problems*. New York: Linguistic Circle of New York.

Weisgerber, Leo. 1962. *Die sprachliche Gestaltung der Welt* (3rd ed.). Düsseldorf: Schwann.

Wessa, Patrick. 2016. Concentration and Inequality (v1.0.1) in Free Statistics Software (v1.2.1), Office for Research Development and Education, www.wessa.net/rwasp_concentration.wasp/, accessed on December 17, 2017.

Whorf, Benjamin Lee. 1940. Science and linguistics. *Technol. Rev.* No. 6 (April) 42: 229–231, 247–248. http://web.mit.edu/allanmc/OldFiles/www/whorf.scienceand linguistics.pdf, accessed on June 20, 2017.

1956. *Language, Thought, and Reality: Selected Writings*. Ed. and with an introd. by John B. Carroll. Foreword by Stuart Chase. Cambridge, MA: MIT Press.

Wierzbicka, Anna. 1972. *Semantic Primitives*. Frankfurt: Athenäum.

1988. *The Semantics of Grammar*. Amsterdam: John Benjamins.

1992. *Semantics, Culture, and Cognition: Universal Human Concepts in Culture-Specific Configurations*. Oxford: Oxford University Press.

1997. *Understanding Cultures Through their Key Words: English, Russian, Polish, German, and Japanese*. Oxford: Oxford University Press.

2002. Russian Cultural Scripts: The Theory of Cultural Scripts and Its Applications. *Ethos* 30(4):401–432.

Winford, Donald 2003. *An Introduction to Contact Linguistics*. London: Blackwell.

2005. Contact-induced changes: Classification and processes. *Diachronica* 22 (2):373–427.

Wingender, Monika. 2014. Typen slavischer Standardsprachen. In Karl Gutschmidt, Sebastian Kempgen, Tilman Berger, and Peter Kosta (eds.), *Die slavischen Sprachen/The Slavic Languages: An International Handbook of their Structure, their History and their Investigation*. Berlin: De Gruyter Mouton, vol. II, pp. 1958–1971.

Worchel, Stephen, J. Franciso Morales, Dario Paez, and Jean-Claude Deschamps, eds. 1998. *Social Identity: International Perspectives*. London: Sage Publications.

Wundt, Wilhelm. 1911. *Völkerpsychologie*. Leipzig: W. Engelmann.

Yong, Heming Peng Jing, 2007. *Bilingual Lexicography from a Communicative Perspective*. Amsterdam: John Benjamins.

Zahvataeva, K. S. 2010. *Jazykovye kontakty: bazovye ponjatija i ih stratifikacija*. Izvestija Rossijskogo gosudarstvennogo pedagogičeskogo universiteta im. Gercena, no. 126, pp. 165–170.

Zaliznjak, A. A., I. B. Levontina, and A. D. Šmelev. 2005. *Ključevye idei russkoj jazykovoj kartiny mira*. Moscow: Jazyki slavjanskoj kul'tury.

2012. *Konstanty i peremennye russkoj jazykovoj kartiny mira*. Moscow: Jazyki slavjanskih kul'tur.

Zenner, Eline and Gitte Kristiansen. 2013. Introduction: Onomasiological, metho-dological and phraseological perspectives on lexical borrowing. In Eline Zenner and Gitte Kristiansen (eds.), *New Perspectives on Lexical*

Borrowing: Onomasiological, Methodological and Phraseological Innovations. Boston: De Gruyter, pp. 1–18. Accessed on September 28, 2017. ProQuest Ebook Central.

Zgusta, Ladislav (in cooperation with V. Černý, Z. Heřmanová-Novotná, D. Heroldová and others). 1971. *Manual of Lexicography*. The Hague: Mouton.

Žluktenko, Ju. O. 1989. *Jazykovye situacii i vzaimodejstvie jazykov*. Kiev: Naukova dumka.

Index

Kazakh, 149
Kazoić, Jerzy, 72
Keesing, Roger M., 4
Kempgen, Sebastian, 40, 41
Khodova, K. I., 42
Kilgarriff, Adam, 103
Kinezsa, István, 157
Klajić, Bratoljub, 179
Klajn, Ivan, 134, 147, 151, 157, 168, 202
Kluckhohn, Clyde, 3
Komi, 149
Kondrašov, N. A., 41
Koneski, Blaže, 13
Koopmann-Holm, Birgit, 97
Kopitar, Jernej, 194, 195
Kordić, Snježana, xii, 35, 142, 164, 165,
    166, 179
Kornilov, O. D, 18, 19, 20
Korolev, N., 72
Koshino, Go, xvi
Kosta, Peter, 44
Kovačec, August, 34
Kövecses, Zoltán, 27
Kramer, Christina, 34
Krečmer, Anna, 10
Kroeber, Alfred, 3
Kumanoya, Yoko, xvi
Kuznecova, E. V., 7
Kymlicka, Will, 4

Labrie, Normand, xi, 34
laissez-faireism, 212
Lakoff, George, 27
Langacker, Ronald, 8, 27, 53, 106
Langston, Keith, 200, 201, 213
language generality idex, 57
language labeling bias, 55, 56, 132, 133
language prominence index, 57, 147, 149
Larionova, A. Ju., 94
Latin, 7, 32, 44, 55, 56, 66, 73, 135, 136, 137,
    151, 174, 178, 214, 221, 225
    late, 151
Lehman, Alise, 7, 45, 165
Lehr-Spławiński, Tadeusz, 40, 44
Lekov, Ivan, 41, 42
Lew, Robert, xvi
lexeme, xv, 7, 8
lexeme, multiword, 9
lexeme-level contrasting
    synchronic, 104
lexeme-level contrastive profiling, 50, 51, 67
lexeme-level cross-lingusitic contrastive
    analysis, 123
lexeme-level profile, 51
lexical anisomorphism, 79, 84, 86

lexical borrowing, 31, 32, 132, 213
    motivation, 34
lexical changes, 171
lexical divergence tracking, 53, 104, 120,
    123, 127
lexical engineering, 163, 213
lexical exchange, 34
lexical fields, 83, 93, 123, 132
lexical fragmentation, 61
lexical frequency, 227, 228
lexical identity, 83
lexical imbalance, 96
lexical inheritance, 125, 126, 127, 128
lexical interventions, 199, 218, 219, 222
lexical layers
    changeability, 49
    elites' presence, 49
    focus, 49
    intervention types, 49
    speakers' control, 49
    structure, 49
lexical maneuver acceptance indicator, 60, 198
lexical normative categories, 163
lexical norms, 39
lexical planning, 163, 164, 166, 167, 208, 213
lexical planning macro maneuvers, 171, 172
lexical planning maneuvers, 163
lexical planning micro maneuvers, 171, 172
lexical prescriptivism, 168
lexical profile of cultural identity, 223
lexical prominence, 97
lexical refereeing, 163, 164
lexical relations, 51, 82, 93, 101, 123, 220
lexical replacement, 125, 126, 127, 128
lexical transfer, 31, 33
    direction, 58, 131
lexical transfer index, 58, 155
lexical unit, 8
lexical variation, 36
    contextual, 37
    formal, 37
    onomasiological, 37
    semasiological, 37
lexical volume indicator, 169
lexical-cultural language profiles, 225
lexicographic micro maneuvers, 180
lexicographic sociolinguistics, 48
lexicographic strategies, 173, 195
    avoidance, 195
    enforcement, 195
    masking, 195
    submission, 195
lexicography, 45
lexicological sociolinguistics, 219
lexicology, 167